Wil
Winds

Adventures in the Highest Andes

Mark Vogel on Sajama

Ed Darack

Alpenbooks • DP/P

Also by Ed Darack:

6194: *Denali Solo*

Wind • Water • Sun: *A Solo Kayak Journey
Along Baja California's Desert Coastline*

To:

Bill Burmester
Dorothy W. Ross
Ellen Liebowitz
Jill Henes
Scott Titterington

Berlin Camp, Aconcagua

Wild Winds
Adventures in the Highest Andes

Alpenbooks • DP/P
Europe: Cordee
www.Darack.com

Copyright © 2001 by Ed Darack
All Rights Reserved
Edited by Dorothy W. Ross

Printed and bound in Canada by Hignell Book Printing

www.HighestAndes.com

Sajama Village, Bolivia

ISBN 1-884980-81-3

10 9 8 7 6 5 4 3 2 1

Wild Winds was created by Ed Darack in Davis, California
Text, Photography, and Cartography by Ed Darack
Foreword by Alex Van Steen
Typography, Book Design, Art Direction, and Layout by Ed Darack
Text set in Bembo and Trajan

CONTENTS

Clearing storm, west face of Aconcagua

LIVE!!! I'm alive! Ed Darack rekindles the fire beneath my armchair! *Wild Winds* delivers an incredible continent to our senses. Here is *the* adventurer's tale of South America as we travel the backcountry of Argentina, Chile, Bolivia, and Peru in quest of the Western Hemisphere's highest summits.

The mountains of South America have fascinated climbers for more than a century, and for good reasons. The gift to perfectly convey those reasons is undeniably the talent of Ed Darack. The traveler's insatiable wanderlust, the climber's intense passion, and the photographer's uncanny ability to lay witness to beauty are all eloquently united in *Wild Winds*. These stories are superbly, masterfully drawn.

Wild Winds, with climbs of Aconcagua, Cerro Pissis, Ojos del Salado, Llullaillaco, and Sajama, seines together a young man's adventures into one narrative anthology, bound with the thread of elegant maps and stunning photographs. These mountains, from the popular Sentinel of Stone, Aconcagua, to the secretive, elusive Cerro Pissis, are unveiled before us in a very inviting, yet profoundly practical manner. The regions and routes are catalogued in a manner which serves as both an engaging tale and a functional guide. Those wishing to travel to these high peaks will find that practical guide articulate and specific, and those wishing to share the adventures from the comfort of their homes will find the tale an equally enthralling snare.

I first traveled to Argentina's Aconcagua as a climbing guide over a decade ago, and have since returned to the continent some twenty-five times, traveling and climbing in many of its countries. It is more than just the striking mountains that fascinate, drawing me back several times each year. Certainly, it is the people I encounter, alive with a character uniquely South American. There is also the undeniable, endurable chain of life that binds those people to their stunningly beautiful lands. Thrillingly enough, the underlying atmosphere tinted with the subtle risks of life, travel and climbing clearly exists. It is travel adventure unrestrained; it is climbing at its primordial; it is photography in paradise. It is what Ed Darack hands us on a plate—stories and descriptions so profoundly real, and yet remarkably surreal, that words flow as water through the hands of our imagination, and we are left thirsty for another glass.

—Alex Van Steen
Eatonville, Washington, USA

Ojos del Salado

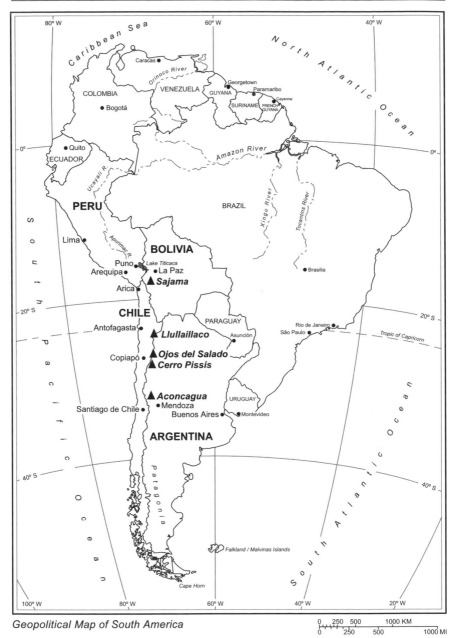

Geopolitical Map of South America

Map shows mountains chronicled in *Wild Winds*. Mountain locations are close approximations. Surrounding countries, major cities, and significant physical features included for reference.

Scale: 1:53,846,154
Azimuthal Equal-Area Projection
Map by Ed Darack

High on a ridge of an unnamed peak, deep in the interior of the central Andes, I crouched behind a small boulder to escape the pummels of a howling wind. My heart pounded like a jackhammer; my ears stung with cold; my lungs gulped at thin air. I shot a glance at Brian Kelly, my climbing partner, to see how he was faring; he grinned with satisfaction. I smiled back, emboldened by the moment. My breathlessness, the wild weather, the immense view before us, and the solitude made me want to roam the highest reaches of the Andes forever. I was living the mountain experience of my dreams.

Muleteers in Horcones Valley, Aconcagua

I gazed down on the turquoise waters of Laguna Santa Rosa, out across a small valley at an exploded volcanic cone, and up a series of rusty slopes to a summit grazed by the ethereal strands of a swirling storm. Clouds ferociously gnawed the upper ramparts of the mountain above us. Mirages shook the air over massive swaths of sun-baked alkali on the valley floor far below. We stood at about 15,000 feet, and though small storms raged all around us, the air felt dry—so incredibly dry—and seemed electrified by the elemental tempest. We were on an acclimatization hike, preparing to climb Cerro Pissis, whose broad

Synthetic aperture radar composite of South America. Base imagery courtesy of USGS. Map is neither scaled nor proportioned.

flanks we could see clearly through the pure air.

Brian and I began our descent after an hour of hunkering down. We zigzagged into a wind-sheltered valley owned by a lone vicuña, who kept his distance but never lost sight of us. Back in the small hut that sits near the shores of Laguna Santa Rosa, we rested, ate, and toasted to having arrived in the heart of the high Andes. We relished the thought that we would soon be on the slopes of one of the mammoths of this great range.

The Andes stretch from coastal Venezuela to Tierra del Fuego in a 5,000 mile wall of volcanoes, ice, precipices, gorges, high lagunas…too much to list in an introduction. A range of superlatives, legends, scale, and beauty, the natural and human history of the Andes fills volumes. Spanning seven modern-day countries—Venezuela, Columbia, Ecuador, Peru, Bolivia, Chile, and Argentina—the range forms the backbone of South America. The character of individual Andean peaks varies from the vertical walls of southern Patagonia, to the jungle-carpeted peaks of northern Columbia, to the symmetric cones of Ecuador, to the world's highest volcanoes that lie hidden within the lonely Puna de Atacama.

Sheep herders above Puno, Peru

My interest in the Andes has been multifaceted. I've always been drawn to the highest of the high—to test myself, maybe to prove something to myself, and to travel the planet's rarefied limits, looking down on what we normally look up to. Simply climbing, however, was never reason enough for me to scale the peaks of this range. Photographically pursuing the aesthetics of the high Andes, as I ascended them, made my ventures truly complete.

Wild Winds chronicles my attempts of five mountains in the Andes: Sajama, the tallest mountain in Bolivia; Ojos del Salado, the highest point in Chile; Aconcagua, the crest of this range and the entire Western Hemisphere; Cerro Pissis, one of the least-visited peaks in South America; and Llullaillaco, a lonely, exquisitely beautiful volcano that is home to the highest archaeological site in the world.

Flamingos, Laguna Santa Rosa

I'll always remember my first trip to the Andes, when my good friend Mark Vogel and I traveled to Bolivia and attempted Sajama. The journey was short, but the airy views, the tempestuous winds, the stunning sunsets, and the vicissitudes of the attempt etched within me an indelible zeal to experience the very highest of this range, and over the course of the next five years, I did.

Looking back on these adventures, I remember much more than just placing one foot in front of the other and straining against gravity and the pain of lactic acid in my legs. On each ascent I fought loneliness, doubt, pessimism—all those obstacles that always seem to emerge during the pursuit of worthy goals. I made great friends, saw and photographed events in nature I never could have imagined, I pushed myself harder than ever before, and most importantly, I learned.

This book is about adventure—in the most pure forms that I could imagine. I set out to climb and photograph the highest peaks of the Andes, but after each expedition I always came back with much more than what I originally sought— and most importantly, I was always surprised—sometimes shocked—by what I'd gleaned. When I reflect on these journeys I recall laughing so hard I could have puked, being so scared I wanted to hide forever under a rock, being so excited by what lay before my eyes that I worried I was going to burst an artery, and being so at peace that I didn't think about anything at all. I wrote *Wild Winds* to bring the stories, the beauty, and the drama of these salient peaks alive for others, and to relate just how it feels to push into the sublime heights of this magnificent part of the world.

High road to Llullaillaco

BOOK I
SAJAMA

Approaching Sajama

CHAPTER ONE

FALLING UP

Midnight street scene, Lima

I couldn't believe that a bus trip could feel so much like a roller coaster ride—and not just any roller coaster, but The Cyclone at Coney Island. The old, rusty body creaked—it swayed—it lunged up and down; the beast twisted and groaned like The Cyclone's girders. The experience would have been unnerving—downright frightening at times—but the tickly sensation in my gut made me giddy as a little kid. The driver, of course, kept the pedal as close to the floor as physics would allow. We were stuffed in the back, sardined into seats that seemed ready to fly off with the next jolt on the rutted and pocked dirt road. But I couldn't complain—at least we had seats. The aisles were jammed with brightly colored bags of food and clothing, and their sleeping owners. The jostling was kind of fun, but the altitude and my exhaustion were starting to wear on me. I'd had virtually no sleep in two days, and was now vaulting to over 12,000 feet with little food in my increasingly nauseated stomach.

The air outside was clear and cold. I pressed my hand against the window and felt my warmth sucked into the night. It was exciting, the cold spiked me awake for a quick moment, reminding me that I was finally heading into one of the mountain ranges of my dreams. I looked down to see Mark sleeping, his head swayed as his neck and body absorbed the jolts of the ride. He seemed content. I cradled my overstuffed camera bag between my head and my knees, closed my eyes, and tried to imagine what the landscape outside would look like during the day.

The driver stopped the bus a few hours later; everybody filed silently out. I nudged Mark awake and we staggered behind the main crowd into the night. We were at a rest stop. A five-foot-high, dimly-lit cinder block house served as the cafeteria, around which people stretched their legs, smoked, and ate. "Let's get some food, Mark. Maybe that'll help us acclimatize," I said, then squat-walked into the restaurant and ordered some soup. A small chunk of goat meat and huge kernels of corn hung suspended in steaming hot water. I was hesitant at first, wondering how my stomach would hold up, but it was delicious, custom-made for just that moment, just that place. My headache and nausea were allayed under the soothing weight of the warm, fatty broth. Mark and I were the only non-Peruvians on the bus; the other passengers looked at us, smiling and gesturing in approval at the comforting power of the meal. The sky above was a brilliant swath of iridescence; stars pricked an uncountable number of holes in the otherwise jet-black canopy of the Andean night. To the east the curtain of blue stipples ended abruptly at the wall of earth we were headed toward—the Altiplano. The air was so clear that even the Milky Way didn't seem so milky. I thought that I could isolate the smallest star from the stellar colloid if I squinted hard enough.

Our bus was bound for Puno, a town on the shores of Lake Titicaca, at an elevation of over 12,000 feet. We were in the middle of an epic run from

Street scene in Arequipa

northern California to an ultimate destination un-known—we didn't care *where*, just so long as it was *above* 6,000 meters. We hopped a handful of con-necting flights through Central America en route to Lima, Peru, then scrambled amidst the hot, hu-mid air of that densely-populated city to catch a 22 hour bus ride to Arequipa, from whence we began the bouncy ride into the sky—in ultimate Peruvian economy class.

We'd chosen Puno as our destination for no bet-ter reason than the town appeared on our map to be in the heart of the Andes. "We should stop there for a few days, Mark," I said, waiting for my partner to agree.

"Yeah," Mark replied with an 'of course' inflection. "Then I think we should go to Sajama." It was the first time either of us had mentioned any solid moun-taineering goal. Up to that point we'd simply announced grandiose vagaries like "we're going to climb all the big ones down there in a month," or "once we climb one, we'll be acclimatized—then we can just run up all the oth-ers...." Now, however, we had the seed of a plan, as briefly stated as it was.

"Just where *is* Sajama?" I asked after tapping my foot for a few pensive mo-ments.

"Bolivia...highest mountain in Bolivia. Read about it in a book. Way out there...don't even know how we'll get there, but it looks good."

"Highest mountain in Bolivia... yeah, that does sound good. Sajama...never heard of it before, though. You sure it's the highest?"

"Yeah, it's the highest. Come on, let's go; they're loading the bus." We climbed back onto the old rig and braced for the last of the journey, unsure of just how long it would be before we'd reach our destination.

We arrived in Puno too many hours later. I woke groggily, not knowing how long I'd been asleep. The words *'Bolivia'* and *'highest mountain'* echoed in my mind, almost as loudly as the words *'thumping headache'* and *'get out of the bus and into a bed.'* "Where are we?... Are we in Puno yet?" I asked, still a bit disoriented.

"Yeah, I think...*I hope*. Yeah, we're here," Mark replied. By then I felt like I needed to wrap duct tape around my torso to keep my kidneys from bursting. I hobbled to my feet only to be pummeled by the altitude. My brain jackhammered against my skull, my stomach clinched, my lower throat con-vulsed to the point of gagging. We stumbled off the bus into the throes of a horde of tourist-prospectors.

"¡Cuzco! ¡Cuzco! ¡Machu Picchu! ¡Machu Picchu!" They surrounded us, not just asking for, but demanding our business. Puno lies on the main line to and from one of the world's great tourist meccas, Cuzco—gateway to Machu Picchu, an easily accessible, world-famous archaeological site—a top-of-the-list destination for any self-respecting globe loper. Although interested in going there some day, Mark and I were far too intent on climbing into the icy heights of the Andes to give a Machu Picchu excursion much thought. "¡Cuzco! ¡Machu Picchu!" the rowdy group cinched around us even tighter. Then the empty bus started convulsing and the noose of 'guides' loosened.

"Watch out!" Mark yelled as the driver and his assistant threw bags down from the roof. My large mule bag came sailing into space and a crowd of taxi drivers went for it like centers after a jump ball. The victorious one had the bag strapped down to his roof just in time to snatch Mark's backpack from its trajectory. I don't know Spanish; Mark can speak just a scintilla more than I, so Mark did the talking. A hostel or a cheap hotel—that was all we wanted, just a place to sleep. We jumped into the suspensionless blue taxicab and weaved down a rough cobblestone street.

"Where are we going?" I asked Mark, who was trying to fan away the blue exhaust smoke that was pouring into the car.

"Some place called 'Hostel Europa.' This guy says its good, cheap, and quiet." I couldn't tell if it was morning or early afternoon—a gray roof of pallid clouds hung low over the town, cloaking the sun's position. The weather seemed suspended in a meteorological limbo where the sky wanted to unleash a torrent, but was somehow reined in from loosing even a drop. I began regaining my sense of time as we jounced into town. *Mid-morning, according to the activity in the streets,* I thought. The intense colors of women's clothing swirled about; markets chock full of more subtly hued fruits and vegetables lined the narrow streets. The kaleidoscope of reds, greens, and blues streaking to and fro totally overwhelmed the asceticism imposed by the hovering gray clouds.

Puno street market

"Oh boy...nice, warm bed, here I come," I muttered to myself as we pulled up to Hostel Europa—a tan building with a modest hand-painted sign dangling from its second story. We paid for two nights—less than ten dollars total—and dragged our bags up a narrow stairwell to the room. That small bit of exercise, of course, was enough to wake me.

"Best not to get our days and nights reversed," Mark reminded me.

"Yeah, maybe we should go out and explore the town."

I stared through our room's tiny window at Puno and the surrounding landscape. The blanket of clouds clung low, revealing only a small slice of green mountains above the streets and buildings of the town. Over the past few years I'd spent a lot of dreamy hours imagining what the Andes would be like. I'd always focused on the very highest, wildest peaks, never giving much thought to towns, roads, buses, and taxis on the Altiplano.

El Misti, a volcano near Arequipa

"Come on, let's go see Lake Titicaca," I said to Mark, "maybe we can go for a swim at 12,000 feet. That'll really wake us up."

"Yeah, and let's get some food, too." Just as we were walking out the door I felt the first rumblings of my gut—not nausea, but something that had invaded my innards and was trying to boot everything else out.

"Maybe I'd better wait around for a while, Mark," I said as I urgently searched for the bathroom.

It was late afternoon before I was finally in shape to venture onto the streets. Mark had already gone on two short forays into town, all the while wondering when 'it' would strike him. "Feel better?" he asked me when we met in a market not far from the hostel.

"Well, there's nothing left in my stomach…so I guess it's safe to stroll around, right?"

"Good logic. Hey, there's a daily bus to La Paz, Bolivia, the best place to get everything together for Sajama."

"What about transport from La Paz to the mountain?"

"Don't know. We'll have to find out once we get there, but La Paz is pretty much the center of everything in Bolivia; we need to go there."

"Do you know the route to the mountain from there? Do you even know where the mountain is?"

"No. I think it's over near the border with Chile, pretty far out of the way of anything. It should be on one of your maps, though."

"Hey look, the sun's coming out. Have you seen the lake yet?" I asked.

"No, let's go. I heard something about giant fish or giant turtles out there or something like that. I want to go check it out." We downed two large Arequepeña beers and headed off in search of a view. It didn't take long before we were relaxing by the lake, watching huge thunderheads spill curtains of rain onto Titicaca's turquoise waters.

"Tomorrow I'm going to break out my camera equipment and find a good spot to shoot that lake from," I said, excited by the expanding view before us. "Look how those clouds are boiling over...I think the scale of these peaks is going to blow us away."

"You and your beloved camera," Mark said, smiling and shaking his head at my voluntary servitude to lenses, tripods, and film. "Hey, come on, let's get back into the main part of town, so we can get some food."

The activity in the streets of Puno had doubled while we were at the lake: more food, more people, more music, more colors. I ambled through the streets in a mild stupor. I felt as if I were walking through a dream; immersed in unaccustomed sounds and sights. I was beyond exhaustion; now I was down-right beat. We found the quietest table in a busy restaurant and ordered plate after plate of food as we elaborated on our plans. "Let's just take it one peak at a time," Mark said, wolfing down a big hunk of chicken, "we'll go to La Paz, hang out, get food, find a climbing club and get information, then head out." I shrugged in approval—there really wasn't anything more to say. Mark had summarized our logistics perfectly. We just had to act on the plan.

By noon the next day I was on a road high above town with my camera. Just a short bus ride and some hiking had brought me to a wide-open vista of Lake Titicaca. The weather over the lake was even more rambunctious than it had been the day before; a small army of billowing thunderclouds marched toward Puno. Beams of sunlight danced across agrarian patchworks. Warm sunshine

Sheets of rain over Lake Titicaca

and shifting breezes balanced each other to create the perfect temperature. I could feel the altitude, but I didn't have a headache, and while I still had a stomach bug, the nausea had subsided. I spent a good two hours traipsing up and down hillsides, finding different camera angles, while pondering the trip

Lake Titicaca

ahead. I was finally in the Andes, the range I'd wanted to visit for so long. I could feel my excitement building as I imagined summiting one of the range's great peaks. I packed my cameras and wandered down to the road. A cacophonous crackle heralded the arrival of an old motorcycle. The driver stopped and gestured for me to jump on the back of his seat. I did, and within ten high-speed minutes of bouncing through ruts while holding fast to my camera, I was back in town with Mark, searching for a bus to La Paz.

We found the main bus station easily enough, and there we met the first tourists we'd seen since Lima. They were two Americans, a quiet man who looked to be near 40, and a woman in her early 20s. "Well, it's the off-season, that's why you haven't seen any other Americans," the woman began.

"Hmmm. Well, that makes sense." Neither Mark nor I had given it much thought.

"That's actually the way we like it. We don't like meeting other Americans when we travel," she finished off with a snip. Mark and I stared at the ground to keep from laughing, "You see," she continued, "we're not tourists, we're *travelers*."

"Oh..." Mark replied.

"We really get into a culture when we travel, you see—look at our genuine Peruvian clothes!" she proudly tugged on her brightly colored Peruvian sweater.

"Hey look, I think we're next in line." I said, seeing a good opportunity to escape. We bought two tickets for La Paz for the next day and bolted. Mark and I roamed through Puno for the remainder of the day before indulging in another feast of fried chicken, fish, and soup.

"This is going to be a great trip," Mark said, inebriated by optimism, "I can tell right now. Sajama...we'll be there in just a few days...."

"I know, I can't wait—just to see what the mountain looks like."

The next day we stepped out of the warm sunshine of early morning onto a bus that was short on comfort, but long on character. It squeaked and chattered so much I swore it was trying to talk to us. I sat just behind the driver, and Mark took the seat in back of me. There wasn't much conversation between us as the bus snaked through the Altiplano, granting new vistas at each turn. We stared mutely at sights we'd never before imagined, from the mundane to the magnificent: small stone houses, looming mountains, and colors...incredible blues and greens, in every direction.

The bus stopped near the town of Copacabana, where Peruvian officials stamped our passports with exit visas. We entered Bolivia just a few minutes later. Waiting in the immigration line, I absorbed views of the white wall of mountains of the Cordillera Real. Beginning with Nevado Ancohuma, the highest mountain I'd ever seen, the range struck a tremendous line southeast toward La Paz. Staring at high mountains is still a little shocking to me; I never

Roadless, but not raftless

expect the picture to be so clear-cut, so bold. The contrast between the darkness of the sky and the blast of light coming off the ice-capped summits of the Cordillera Real confused my irises.

"Hey look at that!" Mark kicked the back of my seat, shaking his finger at the road ahead. Cars and buses stood bumper-to-bumper where the highway met the shoreline of a small arm of Lake Titicaca. I looked for a bridge, but found none. I wondered how we would get across. I laughed when I discovered the answer: vehicles of all shapes and sizes cross the water on the decks of small barges. Very low, very wobbly barges. Our driver queued up the bus then hustled us onto a passenger boat. We watched anxiously as the bus swayed port to starboard, port to starboard on the rickety little barge for nearly a half mile.

Once the bus with our gear was safely repatriated with land, we plied the southeastern shore of Lake Titicaca for a short distance then struck onto what seemed like the last steps below the roof of the world. The road disappeared into the parallax of scale and distance on the huge block of uplifted earth—the Altiplano of my imagination. Wind-scoured, stitched by low walls of cobbles, and grazed by an occasional herd of untended sheep, the gentle plains were buttressed on the east by the cordillera, but fell off to emptiness on the west. The strength of the wind was easy to gauge by watching the driver wrestle the steering wheel. The sun, now well into its late afternoon descent, pulled the third dimension out of the smallest details of distant mountains. I could make out the subtleties of cornices, snow flutes, seracs, and crevasses in the shadow-casting light.

Nevado Illimani, the best known of Bolivia's peaks (and often mistakenly thought to be that country's highest mountain), seemed to rise like a harvest moon as we closed on our destination. The upper portion of Illimani is a huge jumble of glaciers, peaklets, ice falls, and rock outcrops. It is the orographic embodiment of majesty; more than just a landmark, it is a visual anchor. The peak shared a huge slice of the darkening sky with the thundercloud creeping up its broad southwestern shoulder. We crested a gentle knoll, and just as it seemed we would careen into an abyss of nothingness between Illimani and the high ground the road traverses, the urban maw of La Paz appeared. We stared into a giant bowl, plastered edge-to-edge with every form of architecture imaginable, from beefy skyscrapers to wambly shacks piled one on top of the other—the higher the poorer. At the very lip of the bowl, pathetic tin and mud huts clung tenuously to loose dirt and other shacks. The scene was frighteningly desperate, as if a change in the winds could set off an avalanche of adobe, corrugated tin, clothes lines—and people. "Don't sneeze," I joked to Mark as I cringed at the thought of such a destitute existence. Bolivia is the poorest country in South America, and one of the poorest in the world, but until that moment its poverty had been nothing more to either of us than another statistic we'd run our fingers over in a fact book. Now we were in the midst of it, surrounded by it, and as the bus descended the steep grade into the center of the city, submerged in it.

We arrived at a small bus station deep in the heart of La Paz just as darkness fell over the city. I was forced into alert mode, vigilantly guarding all of our gear as Mark searched for a hotel. People pulsed through the narrow streets, many with looks of grave seriousness chiseled on their faces. I hadn't expected La Paz to be much different from Puno, but it was. Within moments of our arrival I sensed that the city had a much harsher edge to it. I hurriedly dragged our bags into a small restaurant near the bus terminal. A man approached me out of nowhere. "Excuse me, sir, but your friend is calling for you!" Just the fact that he spoke English disoriented me—and how did he know I was traveling with a friend?

"Huh?" I turned towards the man with a puzzled look that transcended all languages.

"He is out there—in trouble! He needs you! Go NOW!" I lunged for the street, and paused briefly to look back as I passed through the door. The guy was lifting all of our gear onto his little frame.

"Hey!" I quickly reversed direction. The thief saw me coming back, dropped our precious climbing and photography gear, and laughed as he retreated backwards through a door I hadn't noticed. Panting and looking around heatedly, I piled all of our things into the corner and caught my breath, then tried to relax by ordering some french fries. When it came time to pay, however, I realized that I had only American dollars and Peruvian Soles—no Bolivian money. I paid the attendant with a one dollar bill, receiving exact change in Bolivianos. The attendant, a young girl, smiled at me, as if to say that La Paz might be a bit friendlier than my first impression. I breathed a bit easier and sunk into my seat.

I finished my fries just as Mark walked into the restaurant with four Uruguayan tourists in tow. "These guys say they know of a safe, cheap hotel."

"Good, let's get a taxi, get moved in," I said.

"Nope, no taxi, it's just down the block. We're walking." I threw my mule bag over my shoulders and my camera backpack across my chest, then waddled awkwardly through the door.

"You sure these guys know where they're going?" I asked.

"Got any better ideas?"

We convoyed against a stream of people for a block and a half until a sign reading 'Alojamiento Boston' came into view on the side of an olive drab, 6 story building. One of the Uruguayans pounded on a metal door and yelled something in Spanish. A tiny peephole squeaked open; the eye of an attendant peered out. A few seconds later we shuffled up a steep flight of stairs to the office—just a small break in the stairwell filled with a tiny desk and a drawer full of keys.

"We didn't change any money," Mark said to me quickly.

"I think they take dollars; over at that restaurant they took a dollar. I don't know how lucky we'll be with the exchange rate here, though," I said. They took our dollars, but not quite at the exchange rate the restaurant offered—instead of costing $3.00 per night for a double occupancy room, it amounted to $3.50—not enough to get upset about. We dragged our things to our room on the fourth floor and flopped down on rickety beds. Not only did the room have a great view of the city, but we had roof access. I couldn't complain. We laid around for a few hours, mulled over our maps, and decided to get out of La Paz as soon as possible. We burned with excitement for Sajama.

CHAPTER TWO

CITY IN THE CLOUDS

La Paz, Bolivia

"Look, there's a road that goes from La Paz to Arica, Chile, and it goes right by Sajama," I pointed to a slender, twisting line on our map. "It's the only road that goes anywhere near it. There's got to be a bus that makes that run every day—*at least* once every day." I was sure that there would be a steady flow of traffic between these two major cities. Wrong.

"There's only one bus per *week*, and it left yesterday," Mark announced. "And there's just that one bus, no other company makes the run…nothing." We stood in a crowded bus terminal, staring at one another in disbelief.

"What about hitching?" I asked in a flash of desperation.

"No way, I already asked around. The only traffic on most of those roads is bus traffic. We could sit on the side of the road somewhere and hope for a mining truck, but that's about it, hope. At least if we're in La Paz, we can be sure that we can eat and have a safe place to sleep." Mark was right—we knew nothing about the country, especially the boondocks. We bought the first two tickets for the next bus to Arica, a week in advance.

Forced downtime: we wished that we'd never have to face the prospect of just waiting, but we finally accepted it. Just not for six straight days. "I can't believe this…a week of our trip held up…one less week of climbing!" we lamented during that first day. I felt imprisoned by consequence and our own ignorance as I stared at the city. Not that there wasn't enough to keep us busy in La Paz, and not that the weather wasn't beautiful and the food delicious, and cheap. But at the end of each day we wouldn't be opiated by exhaustion and gushes of endorphins. As great as the food was, we wouldn't cherish it like we would in a survival situation. The nights were cold, just not cold enough to make us kiss our sleeping bags. We were high, but there were places just outside our grasp high enough to make our heads spin—just by pulling socks onto our feet.

To complicate matters further, each of us had a passel of loose ends back home—loose ends that we didn't even want to *consider* pondering; unresolved problems that demanded we do anything but abscond to the netherlands of the Altiplano. Stay and fight, or leave and get doped by altitude, fear, and amazement. Sitting in a hotel room just didn't cut it—even a hotel room in the highest city in the world. "I think we picked the absolute worst time in both of our lives to try this," I said to Mark while watching the afternoon light creep across the room.

"Don't worry about it," he replied with a completely unconvincing tone, "we'll get everything worked out back home…when we get back…I guess."

"Yeah right…" I dragged. I was thinking about my list of growing responsibilities—responsibilities dropped, that is. My first book, *6194 Denali Solo*, had just been published and I bailed exactly when I should have been promoting it. I walked off and left a pile of unanswered messages and faxes regarding my burgeoning stock photography and publishing business. Not to mention that

Sajama Location Map

Map details overland route from Lima, Peru, to La Paz, Bolivia. Major towns, including Arequipa and Puno are included, as are significant natural landmarks, such as Sajama, for reference.

Scale: 1:25,641,026
Azimuthal Equal-Area Projection
Map by Ed Darack

I was in charge of organizing an expedition to Nanga Parbat that was slated to embark in less than three months after our planned return from South America. That expedition was all but doomed, in part because I abandoned my organizational responsibilities to jet off to the Andes.

Thoughts of my tenuously balanced personal life soon percolated into my stew of malaise. I'd been dating a woman until well beyond the 'propose marriage or part ways' limit imposed by her and her parents. I was struggling to deal with all sorts of surprises in my business, and I felt increasingly burdened to plan for a "responsible" future—whatever that meant. My apartment was so mired in clutter that I couldn't find the source of an absolutely loathsome stench in the kitchen. Brian Kelly, one of my closest friends, almost choked with laughter as he pried Mark and me from our search to take us to the airport. At least I *think* the odor came from the kitchen. I didn't care; we had a plane to catch, so I shut the door on my life and jumped headlong into the world of adventure. Now, however, in our La Paz hiatus, realities were beating that door to the ground, and I was losing sleep from it.

"Well, we can't quit now. Can you imagine going back home having done nothing—you not having any photographs to show for the trip?" Mark asked. The notion of quitting seemed absolutely insane, but with so much time on our hands to think about why we shouldn't be there, nagging doubts dogged our thoughts.

"With everything I have to deal with when I get back…I'm not sure I want to *go* back," I said.

"Let's just roam La Paz, pass the time; you can take pictures…besides, we can call this acclimatization, right?" said Mark sarcastically.

"Right, whatever you say," I replied, realizing that we really were acclimatizing—our hotel sat at well over 11,000 feet above sea level.

While anxiety and restlessness characterized the first day of our La Paz layover, we rarely saw the inside of our room during the days that followed. We hiked up and down the hills of the city, poking around shops, restaurants, markets, and bars. La Paz captivated me; isolated high on the Altiplano, the city is one of juxtaposition. Opulent skyscrapers, adorned with the slogans of huge multinationals, lie surrounded by the shanties girdling the city. Rural émigrés—donned in the most traditional of Quechuan clothing—brush past businessmen in pressed suits. Mark and I could eat at a trendy, squeaky-clean pizza café, then walk down the street, turn a corner, and be gorging ourselves on a dish endemic to the Altiplano, relaxing in wobbly chairs, watching a cook prepare food just feet from our table. I was fascinated by the city's location: so high, walled in by enormous peaks, regularly grazed by afternoon thunderheads. The air in La Paz is incredibly clear. I'd never been able to see such detail of a city from any real distance before. The air's lucidity was most noticeable at night. La Paz's disorderly array of lights mirrored the crystal-clear hemisphere of stars above.

Although we spent a fair amount of time together, Mark and I embarked on many solo ventures. Whereas Mark quickly learned the main routes of the city, I spent hours backtracking and seeking my bearings; but all those lost hours led me to a great perch for photographing Illimani and the whole of La Paz.

My aerie jutted from the western edge of the city, at the very rim of the 'bowl.' I visited the spot three times, twice alone, and once with Mark to enjoy the million dollar view in the midst of dire poverty. The locals stared at me, the tall foreigner with a shiny tripod and a bag full of cameras. Throngs of people surrounded me; sweaty men welding steel and colorful women peddling empanadas and sodas. Dust hung low over rutted dirt streets. Drying clothes dangled between rickety houses. The place seemed timeless, it bore no distinguishing edge of style—nothing other than the mien of naked utility on a breathless, densely populated corner of the Andes.

I spent hours at my high vista during my last day in La Paz. I never learned the name of that section of the city; I later wondered if it even had a name. I scanned distant peaks through the viewfinder of my Nikon. Zoom in, zoom out, compose: include some of the city with distant mountains, then isolate the peaks for dramatic effect. *Just hope the light keeps getting better.* It did. The gems of that section of the Altiplano—Huayna Potosi in particular—gave me one last encore of brilliance. I wondered how frigid the air could get high on those slopes; how cold my fingertips would feel; how hard I'd have to swing my arms around to revive my finger's circulation—and how pained they'd be when the blood returned. Those glowing slopes led me to ponder Sajama's appearance—would Sajama have similar features? More ice? Jumbled rock outcrops? Would Sajama be archetypical of the peaks of the Andes? Or unique? What differences would I find between the Andes and the Alaska Range? The Brooks Range? The St. Elias? The Rockies? Would Mark and I reach the summit? Could I fend off my anxiety from all those worries back home? Would the attempt be worth the effort—even a little? I knew—or hoped—that I could spend day after day behind my camera's viewfinder, high above everything, comfortably nestled in a sheltered alcove, running through film. The sun

Huayna Potosi

fell below the horizon and a cavalcade of icy gusts crashed upon the area, clanking tin roofs and tossing dust into the sky. *Time to go*, I thought. I gathered my camera gear and flagged a taxi. The driver stared inquisitively at me, forgoing asking me if I could speak Spanish. I simply pointed down, and we descended into the cirque of nighttime La Paz.

"This is the foundation…the recon," Mark said as we organized our gear. "We're down here to find out everything we can, so that when we come back we know what we're coming back to—how to return, and when to return," with that one statement, Mark revealed the true purpose of our journey.

Festival, La Paz

"Yeah, and we'll come back more than a few times," I added. We packed our bags, including a week's worth of food that we'd carefully chosen from markets around La Paz, then neatly stacked them in the corner of our room. The bus was scheduled to leave early the next morning. We devoured one last dinner at our favorite local restaurant, drank a few beers at a nearby bar, then tried to sleep for a few hours.

"I asked the driver if he could drop us off at Sajama Village; he said that he can't get us in to the town itself, but he'll let us off at the border crossing. We can catch a ride from there into town." *A little vague, but good*, I thought. Mark talked a bit more with the driver before we hauled our bags onto the roof of the old Blue Bird bus. "We have just seven days. We'll have to be back at the border crossing one week from today for the next bus. If we don't catch that bus then we'll have to wait around for another week." Mark relayed the last of the driver's information to me.

"So, do we come back here, or continue to Chile?" I asked, pondering our post-Sajama options.

"I dunno." Mark shrugged his shoulders.

"Let's go to Chile," I continued.

"Yeah. Sounds good. We'll go to the beach…"

The bus doors squealed shut and we rumbled out of the terminal. I closed my eyes and rested my head against my camera pack.

I woke hours later to an expanse of tan earth supporting a baby blue sky. High and wide open, so pure, so basic in its aesthetic, this was the Altiplano I had dreamed of. The bus bumped slowly over a dirt road that was barely scratched onto the perdurable landscape. I woke with sweat beading on my forehead. I slid my window down; stiff, cold air smacked my face.

I pondered the difficulty of describing wind. How does *windy* appear? The Altiplano lies at such a high, unprotected, altitude. The Altiplano and wind seemed so intimately related to me as I studied the region from the bus. For the first time, I really knew how 'windy' appeared, and it was so much more static than I could have ever conceptualized. The plant life was squat and tenacious. The few human structures were built of rocks and cobbles—and sat low. I saw just a handful of people, and I rarely glimpsed anything but their burly, brightly-colored clothing as we rode past.

Lines of cumulus arrived by early afternoon. The clouds seemed alive with motion—building, roiling, then imploding. A sign of inclemency to come, possibly within just a few hours. *Would we pass through a thunderstorm way up here? I asked myself. What would the storm drop—rain? Snow? Hail? Would lightning strike? How often do thunderstorms roll through this region?* I burned with questions about these mountains. I pondered an aspect of one peak, then puzzled over another summit, in a high altitude stream of consciousness.

"Wake up!" Mark shoved me lightly, pulling me out of a dream. I wiped my eyes open to see people shuffling out of the bus. We'd arrived at the Tambo Quemado border crossing, the end of our bus ride. I grabbed my camera and hopped out—into a maelstrom. A powerful gale scoured the landscape. Banners of airborn sand grated anything in their paths. A thick deck of clouds swirled violently.

"Come on, the driver's getting our stuff!" Mark yelled. While the other passengers queued up to get their passports stamped, Mark and I waited under the bus for the driver to hand our gear down to us. But the bags were too heavy for him to lift, so he rolled them off the edge of the roof. "Okay, I'm going to make sure that our ticket stubs will get us the rest of the way to Arica when he comes through next week." Mark said as he picked dirt from his eyes. I nodded, then searched for transport to the village of Sajama. The Bolivian government was constructing a paved highway between La Paz and the border; large transport trucks sat bumper-to-bumper for a quarter of a mile. One of these, I ventured, would be our ride to Sajama Village.

"¿Sajama?" I asked a waiting driver.

"Sí," he responded, then motioned for me to jump onto the bed of the truck, where a few workers were strapping down a large diesel engine. I snagged Mark from his conversation with the bus driver and we jumped onto the oil-soaked wooden truck bed. One of the workers motioned to the driver to start rolling, and with a grind of the gearbox followed by a stout lurch, we began the second leg of the day's journey.

Our ride to Lagunas

The buildings, people, and vehicles of the border crossing shrank quickly as we sped away. I spun around, making sure that at least one hand clutched a rope or a chain that was secured firmly to the flatbed. I looked dead ahead to a tremendous ice-capped volcanic cone, truncated near its apex by turbulent clouds. "¿Nevado Sajama?" I shouted to one of the workers.

"Sí," he answered. Sajama stands alone, surrounded by miles of rolling plains. The muted light shed by the overcast sky made the scene appear frighteningly sinister. The mountain loomed over its environs. Just being on the Altiplano gave me an overwhelming sense of openness and broad scale—seeing a single peak rise so dominantly over this landscape was nearly dizzying. Then I realized that those rolling plains at Sajama's base stood higher than most of the high peaks in my home state of California—a truly dizzying thought.

Other mountains of the Cordillera Occidental came into view as the truck continued east. Two snowcapped volcanoes that appeared to be near-twins crowned a line of peaks that define the western periphery of the plains. Straddling the border between Bolivia and Chile, the duo lies just a few miles north of the border station. Although not as commanding as Sajama, what they lack in prominence they make up with exquisite geometry.

Lagunas, a small settlement about five miles south of Sajama Village, was our next stop. The driver pulled over and motioned for us to jump off, then told us that we could find a ride to Sajama Village in the town square. Although Lagunas sits lower in elevation than the border crossing, the wind continued to run hard. Now, however, the angry sky was relaxing a bit, allowing gushes of sunlight to pour onto Sajama's upper slopes. "¿Sajama?" Mark asked a passing villager. He pointed to an adobe hut where a small group of men stacking llama pelts had gathered. We portaged our gear to the hut and smiled at the villagers. We received nods in return, but not much more. I sensed that the locals were friendly—even warm—but calloused by the rigors of living in such a harsh environment.

After an hour of waiting, a rusty truck that lacked fenders and a windshield chugged around a corner. Another flatbed, this one sported a rickety plywood corral which held a small herd of llamas. I'd never seen a llama up close before, but I had a feeling that Mark and I

Pelts, Lagunas Village

Sajama; distant view from southwest

would get to know these animals intimately in the coming miles. The driver hurled our bags into the back of the corral, sending the half dozen animals on a mini-stampede. The passenger compartment was filled to capacity—with the driver's wife and children. We had only one place to ride—we climbed into the corral; our buck-toothed friends wasted no time introducing themselves by hurling spit all over us.

"Nice llama…nice llama…" I said, promptly receiving another glob of chewed cud on my chest. The local Bolivian passengers—who obviously knew much better—clung to the outer railing of the corral. The llamas never accepted our presence.

Despite our corral mates, the ride couldn't have been more beautiful. The dark ceiling of overcast crumbled, revealing a deeply-pigmented cobalt dome above Sajama's preternatural flanks. I scanned every bit of detail of the peak's

In Lagunas Village

complex medley of ice, rock, and snow. The top eighth of the mountain appeared a flawless paraboloid; not even a crevasse marred its exquisite topology. Lower on its slopes, the volcano revealed its igneous subtleties—layers of pyroclastic stratigraphy, dark ridges, and long sills of hardened lava. The sun closed on the horizon as we rumbled along the single-lane track. Distant streaks of cirrus burned roseate with the day's close, providing a brilliant backdrop to Sajama's glowing summit. *Near light against far light.* The cirrus evaporated as well, leaving Sajama—robust with golden light—standing alone against the darkening void of high altitude sky.

The truck came to a halt just in time for me to expose the scene to film. Mark reminded me to look in the opposite direction after about ten minutes of shooting. A storm dissolved over the twin summits I'd noticed earlier—called "The Payachatas" by locals, the view of these backlit mountains and surrounding clouds capped one of the most beautiful hours I'd ever spent in the mountains. By the time the evening's light had faded, I'd run through six rolls of film—over 200 images.

A wave of cold air crashed upon us as the last of the day's twilight faded. We humped our gear to a small restaurant and ordered dinner. The soup warmed us quickly, but our shortness of breath kept us from really enjoying the food. I slouched in my seat and closed my eyes, welcoming quietude after so many hours of bouncing along dirt roads. We spoke briefly with the matron of the restaurant and her two sons, Pablo and Eduardo, both of whom were proud members of the Bolivian army. "We do as God wills," they stated—explaining that their superiors had direct access to God.   Mark asked them about climbing Sajama: who could provide us with route information, how to find porters, and

Welcoming   committee

where to procure extra supplies. Pablo told us to return the next morning, when he and his brother would provide everything we needed. We finished our dinners, drank a few beers with our new friends, then pitched camp on the outskirts of town, directly underneath Sajama's starlit western slopes.

Summit snowcap of Sajama; view is from the west

CHAPTER THREE

TO BASE CAMP
AND BEYOND

Mark Vogel departing Sajama Village for base camp

An hour before dawn on our first morning under Sajama, I lay wide awake, staring vacuously at the murky-yellow inner wall of my tent. Over a year had passed since I'd last spent time in my Bibler. I reached overhead and scraped frost from the shiny poles that stretched the tent's skin taut, remembering times past when I'd lain in that same position, scraping the same poles, staring the same unfocused stare. I counted the number of days I'd spent inside the tent, resting and waiting for storms to pass. I snapped out of my reverie when I realized that the colors of dawn would soon be arriving. Reminiscing could wait for another time. I grabbed my camera and jumped outside.

The Payachatas commanded my attention as soon as I unzipped my tent. Still deep in the earth's pre-dawn shadow, their high, creamy-white summits would soon be reflecting the first crimson diffractions of the rising sun's light. I peered through my viewfinder to compose what I thought would be the perfect shot—for when the light would be just right. But the light *was* just right at that exact moment. I stepped back from the tripod to see absolutely even illumination—accentuating nothing. The high, cold, clean air made the world's greatest softbox. I concentrated only on the forms of the mountains. Nothing highlighted, nothing glowing, nothing boldly illuminated.

Payachatas

"What are you doing?" Mark asked about a half hour later, as the morning's light slid down the Payachatas.

"Trying to get warmth back into my fingertips," I answered in a pained voice as I 'propellered' my arms in circles— I'd clasped my tripod for too many seconds in the frigid air, a painful mistake.

"Hey, look at that," Mark said as he pointed to a tiny concrete bunker. We walked the hundred odd yards to its front door. We found the structure abandoned and dilapidated. The front door had been smashed; dirt and rubble covered the floor. A cardboard box imprinted with US Military MRE serial numbers hung in place of a broken window.

"The US Army's been here...way out here. Hmmmm," I said.

"Probably a remnant of the 'War on Drugs.' I think this place is a communications outpost—or was. Let's leave it alone," Mark said as he examined the wire of a broken antenna.

"Yeah...good idea. I don't want to get thrown in jail for tresspassing," I said.

The sun finally crested Sajama's southern flanks and washed our camp and the western aspect of the peak with its warming rays, first melting and then evaporating frost from our clothes and equipment. "Hey, what's that line over there?" I asked, pointing to a path beaten into a small hummock at the base of the volcano. The trail ran straight up the slope; no switchbacks, no contouring.

Radio hut

"Maybe a lookout?" Mark said. "Let's get into town." The line held my attention for a few seconds before I tuned back to my morning tasks. "The clock's ticking. We have to be back here in six days," Mark said as he studied the upper portions of Sajama. We quietly packed our bags and huffed into the village. Mark met with Pablo and Eduardo for climbing information while I gathered some last-minute supplies at the town's store. The dirt-floored mercantile carried a couple of dozen items, but I focused on just three: crackers, chocolate, and Argentine meat spread. I bought as much as I thought it would be polite to take; I didn't want to deprive the villagers.

"We're here at the wrong time," Mark stated bluntly when we met an hour later in the village square. "Best to make an attempt between June and August." We'd arrived in early February, the worst time for climbing in the area. "It storms up there every afternoon this time of year; the snow is always unstable…our chances of summitting are slim to none. But let's go anyway! Pablo and Eduardo described the standard route; it's pretty straight-forward. They'll porter our gear to base camp for ten bucks. We're the only team here. We'll have the entire mountain to ourselves." Mark's last statement was the hook—who cared if we didn't make it to the summit? If the views during our climb proved to be anything approaching what I'd witnessed in the past 12 hours, the attempt would be more than worth the effort.

Less than an hour later the bulk of our equipment had been strapped onto two rickety bicycles. *Bikes!* I thought, *I've never heard of porters using bikes!* Mark and I shouldered our backpacks and hiked north along a dirt road, watching the brothers shrink as they pedaled into the distance.

We caught up with the bike-porters a few miles later, resting on the crumbling remains of an old mud-brick building. After allowing a few minutes to recharge ourselves, Pablo and Eduardo motioned for us to follow them up a trail that struck off the main road.

Although storms ravage Sajama's upper slopes almost every day in February, rainfall in the lower elevations is unpredictable. We were, after all, technically in a desert, considered by some to be the very northern aspect of the driest desert in the world, the Atacama. Regardless of classification, the region is dry—dry enough so that water was our main concern. The spot we were heading toward had been chosen as a base camp for just one reason: it's the location of a natural spring, a welcome rarity in the area. The camp also lies directly below the north-west ridge of the mountain, our chosen line of ascent.

We coursed through small, low ridges, lightly vegetated with hardy scrub plants and wind-forged trees until we reached a trickling stream and a wide-open view of the west face of Sajama. Pablo and Eduardo stashed their bicycles and shouldered our bags, aiming directly for the base of the peak, with us in tow. The sky grew thick with clouds; cool breezes swirled down the valley. Another influx of overcast—my favorite condition for hiking, where the elements feel balanced and the strain of exertion is overcome by the rush of vitality; for a short while I felt as if I was floating uphill.

The high altitude and steepening terrain had me gasping for air in short order. At about 14,000 feet, we needed to ascend another thousand to reach base camp. I choreographed my breathing and walking to keep up with the brothers' pace. I managed to keep astride of the lactic acid burning in my legs for a while, but at the top of a long, strenuous rise, gravity and thin air got the best of me. I collapsed.

Green. A small streak of green. I discovered a tiny oasis of verdant life a few minutes after I resumed my measured pace. Small streams braided in and out of one another, providing quenching water for a low carpet of grassy plants. Attention to breathing and walking kept me from focusing on

Pablo, Mark, and Eduardo

any one aspect of the tiny meadow, but flashes of color grabbed my eye. I dropped my backpack on a rock and stared at fragile, white, yellow, and blue flowers. They took hold wherever their diminutive forms could survive. A closer look revealed mushrooms hidden in the mossy shadows of rocks. The grassy mantle was comprised of not one, but a variety of tiers of life. Mark was taken by the scene as well. We alternated between focusing on the delicate and ephemeral, and raising our heads to gawk at the massive and timeless. The west face of Sajama was the most complex, most anfractuous, the most terrifying, most beautiful mountain I'd ever seen. Pablo and Eduardo, anxious to finish their job and get back home, urged us to keep moving. Sajama grew ever larger as we plodded the last steps to our day's goal.

Nature couldn't have placed the freshwater spring that marked our base camp in a better spot. It seemed to be the very focal point of all there was to see of that part of the mountain. We dropped our packs and pointed excitedly to different aspects of Sajama. The overcast gave way to a mackerel sky, motoring along like a conveyer belt. Shadows and sunbeams flickered across the landscape. Chill breezes trickled down with the sky's motion. Cool, dry air slurped the sweat off my forehead. I took off my shirt and let the air massage my skin.

Flowers at 15,000 feet

The tiny spring seemed so pure I worried that I'd sully it by treading near its waters. But I couldn't hold myself back. While the brothers described the route, Mark and I took turns guzzling down icy water. There is no water between base camp and high camp—and the only water at high camp is in the form of snow and ice. Pablo and Eduardo finished off their description and added some Altiplano lore: "Where there is snow, there is gold. Keep your eyes open." They wished us luck, over and over; obviously they thought that we'd really need it at that time of year.

Within an hour we had our tents pitched and I had my camera at the ready for what I hoped would be a sunset light show on Sajama's vertical west face. Our camp was more than 15,000 feet above sea level, the highest altitude yet on the trip. We felt it; our pulses were wound up, our breathing was labored, but worst of all, our heads were pounding. Eat and drink—the best cure for altitude sickness other than descent…*eat and drink—get sugar to the brain.* Problem was, neither of us had much of an appetite.

"Looks like we'll be able to climb right up that ridge to the summit," Mark said quietly while leaning against his backpack. "Just one camp between here and the summit—right up there near that fin of rock." Mark waved his finger toward a rocky dorsal extrusion that sat midway up the long northwest ridge.

"It may be closer than we think, or maybe a whole lot farther. I guess we'll find out soon enough," I said.

"Tomorrow?" Mark prodded.

"I don't know, maybe we should take a rest day, hike around here, see how we feel." I didn't want to hold Mark back, but at the same time I thought we could enjoy lapping up the sights during a full day of rest at base camp.

"Yeah, let's see how we feel in the morning—early morning, that is."

The wild sunset chrominance was everything I'd wished for and more. Just before the sun kissed the horizon, clouds to the west of us dissolved, and somehow that made the reds, pinks, purples—every hue imaginable at sunset—wildly more robust. I'd never seen colors that intense before. At one point the colors seemed almost too saturated. If I'd been examining a photograph instead of reality, I would have guessed that something had gone awry with the development process—wonderfully awry. I was almost paralyzed with adrenaline and excitement as I slapped lenses on my camera and spun through roll after roll of film. Mark laughed at my antics as I jumped around in excitement for the second night in a row. But Mark was captivated by the solar light show as well—he couldn't laugh too hard.

Triangles within triangles—forming yet more triangles. Trigonal in its whole; each diagonal line of snow or rock on the peak's west face met others to create more of this pattern. Sajama displays other forms and patterns as well: organ pipes of crumbly volcanic rock; blocky, stratified stairs into the sky; and dark, towering formations resembling medieval castles silhouetted against the sky.

Mute cascades of fractured ice blocks sat frozen near the apex of the peak's rock face—as if suspended midframe while avalanching off the summit snowdome. Other streaks of snow and ice clung to whatever surface wasn't overhanging. We stared straight into the guts of the extinct volcano—the awesome west face being the result of mega-scale weathering, cleaving, and erosion—a chop right down the center of the beast. Similar to examining the rings of a fallen tree, Mark and I could look back in time and identify subsequent eruptions by discerning distinct andesitic beds.

We didn't leave the next day. Instead we acclimatized, ran around—as much as we could 'run' at that altitude—and ate. By late afternoon we had organized everything we would need for our push to high camp and beyond, if we could get that far. The storms high on the mountain came and went, as predicted. Quick, intense bursts, never lasting too long, but certainly weighty enough to keep us pinned down and praying for a while should we get stuck in one.

The Altiplano treated us to another remarkable sunset that evening, although not as intense as the previous night's. We bedded down early, but I woke a few hours after dusk aware of an eerie brightness. At first I thought the illumination was that of dawn, but the light appeared too far on the greenish-blue side.

Sajama; the northwest ridge rises to the summit from the left

I unzipped my tent and was awestruck by the southern sky—the nocturnal southern sky, free from the polluting lights of cities, towns, or even the moon. Individual stars didn't twinkle—the air was so free from scatter and distortion at that altitude that starlight reached my eyes unmolested. I'd taken a brief glance at the sky during the bus ride to Puno, but now I had a real opportunity to study the stars and constellations without distraction. Seeing the night sky as I hadn't ever before disoriented me. I laughed to myself—*of course I'd never seen it like this before, this is my first time in the Southern Hemisphere.* Two fuzzy masses—balls of nebulous light—intrigued me most. *The Magellanic clouds…*I thought after a few minutes. *I'm finally witnessing the Magellanic clouds.* I'd learned about these dense mini-galaxies in a college astronomy class, but I'd almost forgotten about them.

I climbed out of my tent for a better view of the night sky. In one respect the nighttime dome seemed much larger to me than it had ever before—no doubt a result of the sheer number of stars. On the other hand, the sky seemed contracted; the clarity and luminance of all those points of light far surpassed anything I'd ever seen—as if they were ten times closer than I'd ever observed them. For the first time I actually considered the third dimension in my view of the nighttime sky. The stars shone so brightly that I could easily make out features on Sajama's west face. I reluctantly crawled back into my sleeping bag, knowing Mark would have me up and out early.

We woke just before dawn the next morning. Sunlight struck us just as we climbed out of our tents, urging us to get moving. We packed the barest of climbing and camping essentials, storing our remaining gear in my mule bag.

"Should we hide it—just in case?" I asked Mark.

"I suppose. I'm sure nothing's going to happen to it, but better be safe. If someone comes along and thinks it's free for the taking…you know…." I hiked the bag up a ridge south of base camp where I found a small group of low, element-sculpted trees. I anchored the bag behind one of the trees with some large rocks, then returned to base camp. After returning to California I learned that those trees are called Kenua, and that the small group of Kenua on Sajama is considered to be the highest forest in the world. And I didn't even take a picture.

Mark had his water bottles filled and his pack shouldered by the time I got back. "Want me to wait for you?" he asked as I strapped my camera gear onto my backpack, "I can't believe you're going up there with all of that camera equipment—the tripod, the cameras, all that film."

"Nope, don't wait, see you up there," I said, wondering how my 'super pack' would balance. Mark trotted across a gently arcuate fan of yellow-orange alluvium, eventually disappearing behind a small rise. With the final strap of my camera bag lashed down, I rolled the entire assembly onto a rock, adjusted my trekking poles to the optimal length, took a deep breath, and heaved the monster onto my back. Two one-liter bottles of water dangled from my waist belt. I stared at the water, then at the stretch of barren volcanic landscape ahead of me. "I hope that water holds out," I muttered before crunching my first steps along the coarse surface. The sun's harsh light scoured the mountain through the cloudless morning sky. Heat waves shimmered just off the ground. The stillness of the hour rang eerily in my mind. I stopped after about a hundred yards; my head felt warm. I grabbed my hair—*hot*, it was actually hot to the touch. I guzzled some water then stared at the bottle in disbelief—*first bottle half gone already, just a few steps out of base camp!* I turned toward the spring, thinking about returning to drench myself. *No way, keep going, just get up to high camp, no backtracking!*

My pack flopped with each step; I blew more energy maintaining my balance than on making progress. My trekking poles saved me. I couldn't have gotten much past that first hundred-yard sprint without them. I forced myself to trek with precision—*don't grip the poles too hard, don't keep my arms too tight, don't flex any muscles that don't absolutely have to be flexed!*

The slope ramped to the foot of the northwest ridge almost imperceptibly. At the base of the ridge, I hunched over, relieving the strain from my hips and lower vertebrae. I looked up to see Mark high above me, taking a line up the western flank of the ridge close to the main bulk of Sajama. Mark had struck a direct, steep route. I stood up and let the precariously balanced load slop back into place on my back. Right foot up—grip down on right pole—throw left foot up while throttling the left pole—on and on. I coughed and gagged on

the high, dry air. Five steps—rest for a few seconds—take five more. The ridge had appeared as such a clean line from base camp. Its true nature lay hidden until I stood on it's back: boulders everywhere, scree and loose talus. I slipped and lost my balance too many times.

Sajama, star trails

I'd climbed only a third of the way to the large rock fin when I lifted my second bottle to my mouth and gulped nothing but air—I'd run out of water. My temples thumped painfully in consonance with the beat of my heart. My mouth was dry and gritty with volcanic dust. I stretched my lower lip in a grimace and felt a sharp crack—it split right in the middle. I tried to swallow—to fake myself into thinking I was quenching my body—if only for a second or two. That didn't work—and the temperature just kept rising. Another paradox of the high mountains: excessive heat is often a greater problem than bitter cold. With each breath and each droplet of sweat I lost precious water to the dry Altiplano.

I stood at over 16,000 feet, gasping for water and oxygen. Looking up I saw a baby cloud spinning wildly over the mountain, thousands of feet above me. Adrenaline coursed down my spine and into my arms and legs, tingling every nerve along the way at the realization that I was so high in such a strangely beautiful place. *Only one thing to do*, I thought: *run…up!* I took controlled, concentrated lunges. I even used the flopping of my packs to my advantage, gauging how the shift in weight would move me, then adjusting mid-lunge to gain as much ground as possible. I hammered up the ridge—sparks actually flew from the carbide tips of my poles jabbing into rocks. I navigated by the strain in my quadriceps; so long as they hurt, I knew that I was going up, and that was the only direction I cared about.

By the time I slowed from my sprint, I had nearly reached Mark's altitude. He appeared to be only one hundred yards higher than me. The fin of rock that marked our high camp looked to be just another short burst of energy farther. But now the slope was steeper and more jumbled than ever, and my mouth was so dry that I nearly gagged when I tried to swallow.

I dropped my packs for the first time since base camp and stretched out on a flat rock. My neck fell limp and I got an upside-down view of Mark as he crested the ridge, right under the base of The Fin. High camp wasn't as close as I'd thought; Mark looked small. I desperately needed water. Then I remembered something a friend had given me before I'd left Davis: a small handheld game that used a finger pump to push rings throughout a plastic container to try to land them on pegs. And that plastic container was filled with water! My jacket had more unused pockets than useful ones—I had zipped the game into some hidden compartment during the plane ride out of California. I yanked open every zipper, mining old candy wrappers and a few coins, then an inner chest pocket revealed the treasure. I gripped the pink plastic cap with my teeth, and carefully exposed the few drops of liquid the thing contained. I sucked it down—disgusting, plasticky water, but water nonetheless. *Time is so precious…get going!* I heaved the packs onto my shoulders and forced myself into a strict upward cadence by counting my footfalls. Finally, after more than 300 steps, my foot crunched into a hardened patch of pure corn snow. I smashed it loose with my fist and trickled the tiny ball bearings of ice into my mouth. Never had anything that stung and burned so terribly—as the cold ice bluntly rehydrated my dessicated tongue and inner mouth—brought such relief. After about ten handfuls I actually felt quenched and ready to take the final steps to high camp.

When I looked straight up the steepest section of the day's ascent after a long stretch of sprint-rest cycles I saw Mark silently staring down at me. He'd made it, but he looked wasted. Not only was the final section steep, but much of it was icy, and the day was coming to an end. The sun was only 15 minutes from setting and I could feel the air quickly swinging back to sub-freezing temperatures. I staggered up, carefully finding the most secure knobs of rock amid ice and hard snow. A few yards higher I checked the sun's position again. *Almost all the way down!* I quickly scanned the Altiplano: booming thunderheads surrounded the volcano on all sides, their towering forms shifting from white to yellow and pink. I had to reach the small ledge where Mark was standing before sunset—I refused to miss that photo opportunity. I pushed upward even harder, making steady progress—then a small avalanche of rocks and snow trundled past my feet. Mark was running down toward me. "Here, give me your pack. I know you want to get photographs. Just 50 yards higher, there's a ledge—well, sort-of a ledge. You can make it before the sun sets!" Mark seemed even more excited about it than I was. He untied my camera backpack and we scrambled the last bit side by side.

My legs were boiling with pain by the time we reached camp. I dropped my pack, grabbed my tripod, and went to work. "I don't think this is the actual camp—we're maybe a hundred feet lower, but this should do. Pablo said the camp was right at 18,000 feet," Mark said between short gasps. I later learned that high camp is located at 17,900 feet and that our camp was about one hundred feet lower. Our site had one well-defined ledge, on which Mark had unrolled his bivy sack and sleeping bag. I climbed just a few feet higher and quickly shot a few rolls of film, then decided that putting off pitching camp any longer was a bad idea.

HACK!—HACK!—HACK! I whalloped the uneven sections of my 'bed' with my ice ax, accomplishing little in the way of effective grading, but quite a bit towards sending me over the edge of total exhaustion. With darkness looming, I had to resort to stacking rocks on the downward side of the slope to level the ledge. I unrolled my tent (now just a bivy sack, because I'd left the poles at base camp to save weight), unfurled my sleeping bag, and prepped my stove. "Hey Ed, man, I'm totally dehydrated…I don't think we drank enough down at base camp," Mark slurred.

"I'll be making water right away—let's just drink till…*what is it?*" I asked, plastered by the altitude.

"We piss gin clear," Mark returned quietly, after a pause of about a minute, "I hope we can get enough before we fall asleep. I'm making some right now. You got your stove running yet?"

"Just a minute. As soon as I get it primed." I unpacked my XGK, primed the tough stove, and set it alight. Within a few minutes a blue ring of flame popped up and down to the rhythm of the stove's sputtering hiss. I prayed that the vital

Cloud over The Fin

parts would remain hot enough during the first critical moments of ignition to burn efficiently and reliably. The stove soon roared like a jet engine. I filled my cooking pot with snow and began 'making water.' We relaxed and ate crackers and meat spread; serious cooking was more than either of us could handle that night. I grabbed one last shot of The Payachatas, drank two full liters of water, then collapsed under the weight my exhaustion.

Star trails over The Payachatas

CHAPTER FOUR

THE EAGLES' NEST

The Eagles' Nest; The Payachatas lie in the distance

"Look at this place…just like an eagles' nest, an eagles' nest at 18,000 feet!" Mark yelled to me on our first morning at high camp. My eyes were tightly sealed until the sun broke the day open with a bright flash, warming my face and casting a pink glow on the inside of my eyelids.

Other than some high altitude bed-head and cracked lips, I seemed to be okay. Then I sat upright; a thin-air headrush landed me flat on my back. My body felt completely sapped of strength. The enervation was relaxing, but I knew I had to stay put for the day.

"Hey, let's head up, I want to see how high we can get before the weather sets in," Mark said as he wrestled his feet into his boots.

"Mark, you go. I can't move. Yesterday totally wiped me out. I'm staying here for the day."

"You sure, man?" Mark asked, appearing fresh enough to run to the summit.

"Yeah, I have no energy. I only want to sleep, eat, and drink water."

"Take some pictures, too…this is a beautiful spot, one of the best I've ever seen." Mark donned his crampons, ate some chocolate, and stuffed his small summit pack with rope, food, and two water bottles.

"Here, drink all of this," I handed him what remained of my water, then set about melting more snow. "You want to wait about ten minutes for another liter?" I asked as I fumbled to pump my XGK.

"Thanks, but no. I have enough, and look at all this snow—water everywhere. Tomorrow I'll hang out here while *you* go for the summit."

"Good luck."

"Yeah, I'll see you later." Mark marched out of view behind The Fin.

The Eagles' nest brought wonderful shocks of novelty: basking in warm sunshine in a T-shirt at 18,000 feet; guzzling pure water above the plains of a high, parched desert; reeling in my exhausted, rubber-legged state; lounging on a ledge so far away from anything—with a view of everything. I could see so much from that high perch, from the snow-dabbed summits of The Payachatas, to the uppermost chunk of Sajama, to distant views east, to elegant volcanic textures thousands of feet below me. But it wasn't just the seeing, it was the feeling of the crisp winds, the warmth of the sun, and the hearing of…nothing at all. I wanted to have similar moments on other high ledges and other great peaks throughout the Andes. Which mountains, when, and how I would get there, I had no way of knowing—I just knew that I wanted more.

"The EAGLES' NEST!" I heard Mark yell a few hours later. I peeled open my eyes to see him crunching through the snow.

"Did you make it?" I asked.

"Yeah, I made it—to a bunch of rotten rock covered in melting verglas, above that I found deep snow undermined by running water. There was no

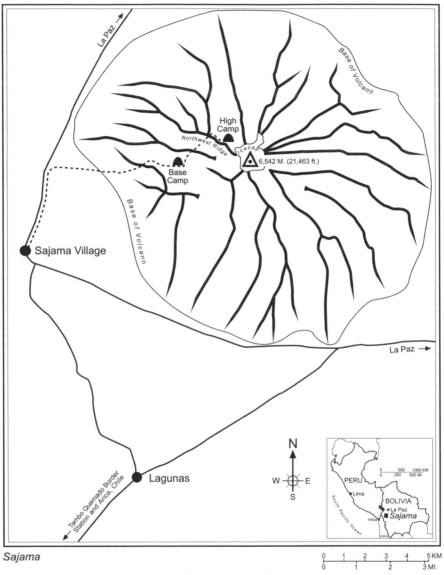

Sajama

0	1	2	3	4	5 KM
0		1		2	3 MI

Map shows basic topography, surrounding roads and villages, and author's route (- - - -).
Map created from 1984 space imagery of Sajama; stereographic projection.

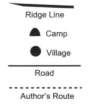

▬▬▬▬ Ridge Line

▲ Camp

● Village

──────── Road

- - - - - - - - - - - - -
Author's Route

Approximate Scale: 1:176,000
Map by Ed Darack

way I was going to continue. Looks like a lot of snow above. I'll give it another go tomorrow—with you?"

"Don't know. Probably not. I'm pretty happy here, and I don't think I have it in me to make any kind of real summit attempt."

"Let's make some food. I'm starving!" Mark said. I carved thick slices off the hard salami and cheese we'd bought in La Paz, and topped off the meal with meat spread, crackers, and chocolate. We gorged ourselves, then spent the rest of the day laughing and talking.

The next day Mark set off for a second summit attempt while I photographed the volcano's surrounding landscape. Mark returned by noon, having made it just slightly farther than he had the day before.

"The conditions up there are terrible!" he said with an amazed tone.

We spent the remainder of the day musing about other Andean peaks, discussing which ones we wanted to visit, climb, or just see. I knew so little about the Andes; the chain spans such a huge distance, so many individual peaks dot the range, and such a wide array of cultures call the Andes home.

"There's Aconcagua—the highest and most renowned. And then there are some mountains to the north of Aconcagua, big volcanoes I think, really high, really remote; few people ever climb them," I spouted during one of our conversations.

"I've heard of those peaks, can't remember their names, but I know what you mean, they're really desolate."

"What about prawns?" I asked, switching to one of our favorite topics.

"Prawns are good." Mark replied without hesitation.

"Barbecued…or sautéed in white wine and butter?" I returned.

"Barbecued. Definitely barbecued." Mark replied after a pause.

"Really?"

"…and beer."

"Fish tacos?" I shot back.

"Yeah, fish tacos. Fish tacos and cold beer," Mark continued, "that food sounds *so good* to me right now. I can't wait to get some." Our conversations drifted in and out of all sorts of topics until the afternoon storms arrived. We watched silently as clouds swirled above us and dropped fresh snow, adding further barriers to summit passage.

The Fin

We descended to base camp early the next day. Mark galloped ahead of me as I took my time tiptoeing through snow and ice. I noticed a lot more on the way down than I had during my ascent. Besides the stunning scenery, what intrigued me most was the fact that I found no signs of past human passage other than the impressions of our own boots. The peak was first climbed in 1939 by Josef Prem and Wilfrid Kühm (both of Austria), and relatively few expeditions have visited Sajama since then. Even base camp shows no signs of past visitors. When I reached camp I asked Mark what he thought about the absence of human detritus. "The winds," Mark said. "The winds hide all traces of people up here. Pablo and Eduardo said the winds are unbelievable on this mountain, especially this time of year…I guess we got lucky we didn't get hit by a wind storm. Come on, have some of this water." Mark's hair was soaked and his cheeks were beet red from submerging his face in the spring. I dropped my pack and felt my tongue knot up. I knelt down and dunked my face in the icy water without another thought.

"So, do we head down today, or leave in the morning?" I asked Mark after quenching my thirst.

"Bus won't come through for two more days. Don't you want to stay here another night?"

"I do…I definitely do," I said while staring at the west face.

"So do I."

I slept like a corpse that night, waking with enough energy to tackle the huge problem of carting all of my gear down without the aid of Pablo and Eduardo. After struggling for an hour trying to fit my equipment and food into (and onto) my main pack, I was resigned to stuffing everything into my mule bag. Once I zipped it up, I stared at the large, dirty monstrosity, wondering how my back would survive the beating that was sure to be doled out by the frameless, awkward pig.

Three hours of knee trouncing, ankle twisting, downward lunges later we joined the dirt road that led into Sajama Village. Clouds veiled the sun and its warmth, and the wind finally started living up to its reputation. I dropped my bag; the cool, evaporative air instantly chilled my sweaty skin. I pulled off my soaking-wet shirt and felt a stinging jab in the base of my lumbar region. "Oh my god," Mark said when I turned my back to him.

"What? What is it?" I asked.

"That bag rubbed a bunch of skin off your lower back in two quarter-sized spots!"

"You're kidding, right?"

"Oh, man, it's bad. You should see it!" I stared at my shirt. Dark stains of blood marred its fabric. I aimed my back into the wind and stretched my hands to the ground, breathing deeply as I felt the air begin to seal my wounds.

"Pretty good trip, huh, Mark...can you smell me?"

"Yeah, I can smell you."

"Good, because I can smell me too; I like it."

"You smell disgusting; like a dead pig."

"Yup!" I reaked horribly; sweat dripped down my grimy skin, blisters stung my feet, and each heartbeat sent a wave of aches through my joints. I peed what looked like dark syrup. I was a mess, but I loved the views and the feeling of the air so much that I wanted to continue, pained or not. I dumped the last of my water on my head, threw my bag onto my shoulders, and trotted down the road.

A half hour later Mark and I arrived at the village. We celebrated by eating chocolate and drinking beer.

"What about those prawns, man?" Mark asked.

"Yeah, and how 'bout some T-bone to go along with them."

"Barbecued; with some tequila to wash it down."

"Yeeup." We pitched camp that afternoon then ate an early dinner with Pablo and Eduardo, who told us that the trail we'd noticed that ran straight up the small hill was originally beaten by Incas carrying sacrifices to their gods. I slept for 14 hours, waking well past sunrise for the first time in six days.

"Look, a transport's coming," Mark said as we packed our gear. We ran into the village square and threw our bags onto the empty truck. As we rolled away we vowed to return to the beautiful volcano.

At the border 'bus station,' plumes of dust streaked into the eastern sky. We hid behind a small stone building for shelter from the dusty gale.

"The bus'll be here later in the afternoon. We have to sit around in this dust storm for a few hours," Mark said after a brief inquiry.

"Let's hope it's on time," I added.

"I know. I can't wait to see Arica, especially the beach." We sat on our bags, closed our eyes and leaned against a cobbled wall, hoping to grab some rest.

"Where are you two from?" came a voice over the wind. Mark and I looked up at a short Bolivian border official standing above us.

"You speak English...uh, we're from California—the United States," I responded.

"Yes, I know where California is. I have been to Los Angeles many times," the man said, then stared at us.

"Is everything...okay?" I finally asked.

"Oh, yes, fine. I just don't often see people from California, that's all." It didn't take long for this guy to recount his life story to us, particularly how he hated his job. "I used to be a pilot. I had my own plane back in the eighties. I used to fly lots of stuff and people."

"Really?" I asked, wondering what kind of 'stuff' he flew.

"Narcos," he elaborated, at long last.

"Like, uh, *drugs*?" I asked.

"Yeah, that too, but a 'narco' is someone who is in the business. I used to fly around what you Americans call the 'drug lords.'"

"Well...what happened?" I asked, now very curious.

"They chased me down with a fast helicopter, I crashed my plane. And now...I do...*this*." The guy looked disdainfully at a small office containing ledgers, stamps, and an ancient typewriter.

"Who is 'they'?" I asked.

"The DEA, you know, your government and the Bolivian army. Can't get another plane. Do you like cocaine?"

"Never tried it." I wondered if the guy was trying to set me up.

"It's really cheap down here. You can get high for like five bucks. Man, you could make a lot of money bringing it back up to California."

"I'm sure I could..." I looked at Mark, who was trying to hide his laughter.

"Okay, my friend, here comes your bus. That means that I have to get back to work stamping passports. Don't let the road down to Arica scare you."

"Thanks," I said, wondering why I would be scared by a road.

"I'm sure it's pretty steep. Probably a lot of hairpin turns," Mark said as the guard walked back to his little office. We waited till the bus passengers had their exit visas stamped, then got on the bus and started down to lower ground.

An extended wait at Chilean customs gave us an opportunity see the Payachatas from a new angle. The mountains are called the Parinacotas from that side; we viewed them from the shores of Lago Chungara—both the peaks themselves and their rippled reflections on the wind-stroked water. "You see those mountains, right up there..." a Chilean border guard, eager to practice his English, struck up a conversation with me.

"Yeah," I responded.

"We hear explosions up there sometimes. Land mines—the vicuñas, they step on them, and BOOM! They go DIE!" he said while waving his hands wildly in the air.

"Really?" I said. The guard peered into my eyes, with a stare that could only come from a guy who worked at a high altitude border station for too long.

"Yes, my friend. *Really*."

"Hey Ed, let's go. They're loading up," Mark said. "What was that guy talking to you about?"

"Oh, I don't know. Land mines and vicuñas. The guy says there are mines out here. And the vicuñas step on them and 'go DIE!'"

"Yeah, this was a heavily disputed border for a long time. The town we're headed into used to be part of Bolivia. In the past, both Chile and Bolivia got uptight and started planting land mines. I read about it someplace...can't remember where, though," said Mark.

The road from Chungara to Arica is probably the best location in the world to shoot a television advertisement for car brakes. The grade is the steepest I've ever seen for a paved road, and it twists along a roadbed that seems, in some places, tied around itself. When I closed my eyes, my guts seemed to spin around. When I kept my eyes open, my hands cramped from gripping the seat in front of me.

"So what's the plan for the rest of this trip?" Mark asked.

"I don't know. I really don't have any idea. I guess we'll get to Arica and figure it out from there," I said, thinking that all I wanted to do was relax on a beach and eat prawns.

"Valle de la Luna. You should go to the Valle de la Luna," came a British-accented voice from behind my seat. I turned to see a guy craning his neck above our seats. "I overheard you two. You have to go there. It's absolutely the best place in South America."

"Really?" I asked.

"Yeah, first you go to Calama; you can remember the town's name because it sounds like 'calamity.' Then catch a bus to San Pedro de Atacama. In San Pedro, guides run these little tours into the Valle de la Luna, that means 'valley of the moon,' by the way. The place is absolutely exquisite. It looks...well, it looks like the *moon*, or what I imagine the moon looks like."

"Valle de la Luna, huh? Is the place good for photography."

"An absolute photographic paradise." The bus stopped at a roadside restaurant and the three of us ate dinner together. The Brit, named Ian, quickly had me convinced that my next move would be to the valley of the moon.

I watched the blazing orange sun drop below the Pacific Ocean as I fell asleep. We woke a few hours later to the scent of the sea; we'd 'landed' in Arica.

I lifted my huge duffel; it felt like a bag of down pillows. I gawked at Mark. "I feel like superman. Being back at sea level is great! How long this will last?"

"Who knows...let's find a place to sleep, then get something to eat. I have the appetite of ten people right now."

Mark and I spent two days in Arica eating seafood and drinking beer. Mark saw me off on the bus to Calama, then continued to Iquique to go surfing. He ultimately made it to Bariloche, Argentina for some rock climbing. I spent a week in the Valle de la Luna; it turned out to be exactly the photographic paradise that Ian had claimed. A series of bus rides back to Lima, some flight plan juggling, and a few passport stamps later, I was back in Davis, sweating out 'reality.' Mark came home a few weeks later. The first order of business for us was to agree to return to the Andes...my only question: *when?*

BOOK II
OJOS DEL SALADO

Landcruiser under Ojos del Salado

Chapter Five

SMUGGLING

Arica Morro, Chile

When would be nearly four years later. A number of significant events took place during the months following my return from Sajama, some encouraging for my life of mountaineering, and quite a few discouraging. The worst blow was the total dissolution of the Nanga Parbat expedition. A few of us lost a good deal of money, and the entire team suffered a ton of frustration. *Another year, another year,* I repeated to myself. My relationship with my girlfriend disintegrated past the point of no return, and money got so tight due to problems with my business that I resorted to a summer job as a seasonal tomato truck driver in the flat, hot central valley of California.

At the end of tomato season I traveled to Baja California, where I nearly lost my life in a horrific car accident. I struggled back to Davis to learn that what I'd thought was a painful hip bruise was, in fact, a broken femur. Hospital drama ensued, including a reconstructive procedure that lasted more than eight hours. The chief surgeon told me that my injury might never heal correctly, and I could face the need for a hip replacement within the year. He ordered me to stay on crutches for 14 weeks.

I got fed up with my situation within just a few days of post-hospital recuperation, so I quit using my crutches far ahead of schedule. Ten weeks after the accident I boarded a flight to Venezuela, intent on climbing Monte Roraima. A large Tepui (similar to a mesa), thick jungle and roaring rivers surround Roraima. The mountain is renowned for its spectacular waterfalls and often cloud-shrouded summit. Fording swollen rivers with a good-sized pack was difficult, as was the non-technical scramble up steep, wet slabs, but I felt that the exertion would be good for my hip. I made it to the top, a little slower than average, and even camped on the summit for a couple of nights before making the 25 mile hike back to catch my ride to civilization.

I wound myself around a number of pursuits following the Roraima trip—I wrote and published magazine articles about a variety of topics, I developed a few inventions, I kayaked the full length of Baja California, and I published my second book. But I didn't make any clear plans to return to the Andes. Perhaps I was avoiding the challenge, realizing that a good, solid attempt—one where hardship, pain, and suffering leads to relished success—would require such commitment that I'd have to sacrifice my sphere of comfort and really dive into the endeavor with full-blown commitment. Total commitment was harder for me to grasp as I got a little older and 'wiser.' I remember driving my beat-up Volkswagen Beetle from California to Alaska in three-and-a-half days to climb Denali. I was 19 then, and summiting that peak was the greatest goal of my life. I failed on my first attempt, so the next year I drove the same crappy Beetle back to Alaska, and succeeded in reaching Denali's summit. That was real commitment.

A few years later, however, with so much clouding my life and my outlook, I found it difficult to grasp true commitment and conviction, to be 'misguided' by it, to clearly establish a salient goal and resolve to chase it to the edge of self-destruction. I needed some 'mistake,' some unforseen turn of events to convince me once again that I could sluff off my caution and jump headlong into a big unknown.

I was deep into a promotional tour for my second book, *Wind • Water • Sun*, zig-zagging around the west coast of North America in a crazy fit, trying to make a living. At the end of that tour, I was scheduled to visit a friend who was working in Africa for an aid organization. I wanted to trek, photograph, and climb the Ruwenzori Mountains of the East African Rift Zone, but the prospects for that trip disintegrated due to unforseen problems with my contact in Africa. I was left dangling, and in need of a difficult challenge.

The obvious challenge? I would return to the Andes, alone, and climb as many of the range's highest mountains as possible. Aconcagua came to mind first, but those desert peaks far to its north also tempted me.

Ojos del Salado and Cerro Pissis, the second and third highest points in South America, sit about 400 miles north of Aconcagua. I wondered if I could climb Aconcagua, Ojos del Salado, and Cerro Pissis in one long trip. Every planning aspect of such an expedition shot through my head at once—confusing, but invigorating. Airline tickets, ground transportation, gear, food, money...*always money*, I thought. I would finish my book tour in less than a month, at the perfect time to make an attempt on Aconcagua, and I hoped, Ojos del Salado and Cerro Pissis as well.

As soon as I'd located these mountains on the map of South America, my brain started to itch. I had definitely heard of Ojos before, and I thought that Pissis sounded a little familiar, probably from the classified sections of old climbing magazines. I sifted through a few and found that someone named Bob Villarreal had been placing ads looking for partners to climb these and other neighboring peaks for years. I called him, hoping to get some information for my trip. Thankfully, he more than obliged—giving me countless hours of his time about where, when, and who. Turns out Bob Villarreal knows more about the mountains of the Puna de Atacama, including Ojos del Salado and Cerro Pissis, than just about anyone. Of course, I had a question for him: Why?

"Because I love the desert. And the Atacama is a desert's desert. That place is so high, so lonely, and so...*strange*. You really have to want to be there, I mean you *really* have to want to be there." Bob's vivid descriptions put the hook in me for climbing those giants.

Bob told me that I'd be in South America at the right time to climb Ojos del Salado and Cerro Pissis. I'd find the routes on both Ojos and Pissis, he continued, fairly straightforward and non-technical. My main concerns would be water and access, especially for Pissis, a peak that is as remote as remote gets.

"I'll figure it out when I get down there," I said brashly during our final conversation. I was flush with excitement for the high unknown.

66

The next order of business was procuring an airline ticket—the least expensive means of transport by far was to fly to Lima, Peru, and then take a bus south to Chile. Ojos would be my first goal, then, if possible, I would make an attempt on Pissis, after which I would continue farther south to Aconcagua. Although Aconcagua would probably be the easiest of these three peaks—and the one I probably should have planned to attempt first—I didn't want to backtrack. And besides, after climbing Aconcagua I wanted to continue even farther south and trek and photograph the mountains of Patagonia and Tierra del Fuego. One long run south from Lima, followed by one long return run to catch my flight back home.

A few weeks later I received a healthy advance from my publisher for future sales of *Wind • Water • Sun.* The tour had gone well; the book was receiving excellent press, and sales were good—providing just enough money for the journey to South America. I bought 250 rolls of 120 format Fujichrome Velvia film for my Pentax, 80 rolls of 35mm Fujichrome Velvia for my Nikon, a new tent, a new backpack, a new sleeping bag, new hiking boots, used high altitude boots, trekking poles, and maps.

I continued to hone my knowledge of the high Andes by sifting through old library books, magazine articles, and web sites during the final few weeks before departure. While much has been written about Aconcagua—its geography, geology, mountaineering, archaeology, and human history—I could find only fragments of information about Ojos del Salado, and virtually nothing about Cerro Pissis. During my search, I couldn't decide which peak excited me most. Aconcagua had been a dream mountain of mine for years; the fact that it was not only the highest in South America, but in all of the Western Hemisphere (and Southern Hemisphere, too) was geographically alluring to me. But Ojos del Salado, that lonely, hidden volcano high in the desert, seemed like such an enigma, as if treading its flanks might somehow instill an elusive sense of mountain wisdom in me. And then Pissis, well, it's so remote that I imagined the experience would be like mountaineering on Mars. I couldn't even find a blurry photograph of Pissis.

I stuffed all of my gear into my trusty mule bag just hours before my plane was scheduled to leave. Included in the big black bag (the same one I had used on Sajama) was a huge Gitzo 410 tripod and a Studioball head for my Pentax. The tripod assembly added more than 15 pounds to my load, and I dreaded carrying it on my high altitude hauls, but I knew it would be worth it—at least I hoped it would. In addition to the huge mule bag (which weighed a good 90 pounds), I crammed my film into a stuff sack for carry-on number one, and both camera systems in my main camera backpack as carry-on number two. Loading the camera backpack required some creative packing (and re-packing). Included in the relatively compact bag was a motordriven Nikon FE2 with an 80mm to 200mm f/2.8 lens and a bulky tripod mounting bracket, a

50mm f/1.4 lens, a 24mm f/2.8 lens, a teleconverter, a macro tube, an assort-ment of filters…and the Pentax system: the beefy 67 body with a TTL pentaprism viewfinder, a 45mm f/4, a 105mm f/2.4, a monster 300mm f/4 lens, an assort-ment of filters for the 67 lenses, spare batteries, and cleaning implements. All summed, the bag weighed over 40 pounds; with film I was carrying 55 pounds of camera gear (not including the tripod). *Somehow I'll get all of this up to high altitudes….*

I can barely remember the ride to San Francisco International Airport that marked the beginning of the trip. I was sick with anxiety and fear. I don't think I absorbed much in the way of engine sounds, bumps on the road, the car radio, or even the conversation with my friend. I stared at my airline ticket and wanted to throw it out the window; I had the urge to quit before I ever got started. Life had been so comfortable, so relaxed during the prior weeks. I had completed such a major undertaking—the book of my dreams had been pub-lished, and I had just burned around most of the western states of the US and a few provinces of Canada promoting it. But now some real work was about to begin.

I stared at my bags and then at the flight information screen at the airport, heaved the pigs onto my shoulders—taking a whiff of my sweaty armpits in doing so—and walked off my trepidations.

Once in flight, I mulled over my near-term plans: arrive in Lima, get straight to a bus terminal, and then make a bee line to Chile. From past experience I knew that I wouldn't have any problems catching a bus from Lima to the town of Tacna, which lies just north of the Chilean border, and from there I planned to take a taxi across the border to Arica, Chile. I would then head down to the town of Copiapó, a mining and agricultural center that lies in the heart of the Atacama desert. Copiapó serves as the primary jump-off point for Ojos del Salado and other Atacaman giants. Armed with Bob's information and my knowledge from the Sajama experience, I felt confident and ready…I would just have to pull everything off smoothly…not get ripped off…not get sick…not chicken out…. *Easier said than done.* I ordered a Bloody Mary, laughed at some of the goofy contraptions in the airline's inflight magazine, and settled in for the long trip.

I tried to sleep during the Miami-Lima leg of the flight because I knew that quality rest would be elusive for the next few days. But I couldn't get my mind off the promise of adventures ahead. My anticipation and excitement mounted…I drew mental pictures of Ojos del Salado, as I had done with so many mountains in the past. *What will make this one different?* I wondered. *What about water? And just how was I going to get from Ojos to Pissis? How was I even going to get to Ojos? Forget it, just figure it out when I get there….*

But I couldn't just forget about it. I was speeding toward these peaks at 550 miles per hour. As the airliner jabbed through turbulence, I decided that my main goal would be to get to Ojos del Salado, give it an all out effort, and then see how I could get down to Pissis, 52 miles to the south of Ojos. *Walk?...no water! No way, not with all the camera gear.* Bob had mentioned a friend of his in Copiapó who could drive me into Pissis base camp, but he would charge 400 dollars per day, and would require at least three days. There had to be another way. If, after making a solid attempt on Ojos, I couldn't get to Pissis, I'd go straight to Aconcagua.

As the jam-packed plane descended toward Lima about an hour before dawn, flight attendants passed out customs forms. When I read the instructions my blood turned icy. I was allowed to bring five rolls of film into Peru; beyond that I would be required to pay a hefty import duty. I carried 330 rolls of film. I stuffed a spare T-shirt onto the top of my unprocessed rolls to try to hide the film. I left the customs form blank, conspiring to play stupid. I was about to become a smuggler. A film smuggler.

I breezed through immigration, receiving an automatic 60 day visa. Then I looked ahead at the customs officials. There were three of them. I quickly sized up each one: a distraught and mean looking woman—*no*; an angry young man—*no*; and a middle-aged guy with an 'I don't really care about anything' look on his face—*yes*. I queued up in his line and clutched my film bag tightly. The guy kicked my mule bag a couple of times, poked my camera backpack, then asked what I had in the white sack.

"Uhhhh, clothes, I mean *ropas*..." I stumbled through some Spanish.

"Open." The official said. I obliged, showing him the green T-shirt that sat on the top of the film. He peeked in, then looked at me. *I'm so in the clear*, I thought. Then he reached in and pulled out the shirt, revealing hundreds of shiny foil containers of expensive medium-format film. Something about it looked really drug smugglerish; I became very nervous, very quickly. "What is?" he asked, poking the film.

"Filma. Por photographia." I didn't know if those were the right words or not, but they sounded good. To drive home the point, I made a gesture with my hands like I was snapping a picture.

"Okay. Bueno," he said with a grin; he stamped my customs form and I walked free.

The day had barely begun by the time I'd changed 60 American dollars to Peruvian Soles and limped through the glass doors of the airport. The hazy white glow of pre-dawn Lima and a horde of fare-hungry taxi drivers greeted me as I stepped to the curb. I was tired, running on the last of my adrenaline, but I prodded myself to keep moving. As I looked over each of the dozen men hustling for my business I thought about going straight to a hotel for some rest. *Sleep would feel so good*, I thought. I *almost* went for the easy out. "¿Terminal de autobus?" I pried out of my mouth to the least obnoxious of the group.

"¿Donde?" he replied as the others fell silent.

"Tacna...Tacna."

"Sí. ¡Vámanos!" He hurled my mule bag onto the top of his small taxi and we sped onto the empty streets of early morning Lima.

A few years had passed since I'd last visited Lima. I was more relaxed now, less on edge—I didn't clutch my camera bag quite as tightly, nor did I keep such a keen eye on the lookout for thieves. I took more time to observe the city itself, the buildings, the walls, the streets, the aqueducts, the trash, the smells, and the sounds.

Mark once told me that he sensed desperation in Lima. He and I had a rough time on our arrival in this city four years ago—we'd landed at night and wound up in a hotel in one of the worst sections. Leaving the confines of our hotel building—even for a few minutes to buy a soda—was a dangerous proposition. I remember watching a pack of young children chasing trash down the street at midnight. I couldn't imagine that they were playing—none laughed or smiled. All I could surmise was that they were scavenging...trying to eke out some crumb of survival.

I hoped I could find a bus that would depart soon. I wanted to get on the road, to feel the drug of sleep deprivation as I watched the landscape change from urban to coastal to desert to agrarian and back to desert. Beautiful landscapes that I recalled from my first trip to Peru.

The taxi driver and I unloaded my bags at the Ormeño Bus Lines compound a half hour after I arrived in Peru. I was making good time. Now I had nothing to do but wait: the next bus wasn't scheduled to depart for eight

Lima from the air

hours. *Okay, I'll just sit here*, I thought—as if I had a choice. I spent those hours pacing up and down the streets outside the compound, drinking orange soda, and eating 'American style' potato chips.

That first overland leg lasted 22 hours, broken only by one significant stop at the town of Nazca (famous for its huge prehistoric lines etched on the desert landscape) for a dinner of rice and fried fish. I was riding first class, an express bus that sort-of had air conditioning and was captained by a driver who wasn't afraid to pass around blind corners and push the limits of every moving part of the rig. In addition to the dinner stop, a first class bus ride in Peru includes a few movies played on ceiling-mounted televisions—movies exclusively pirated from the United States. Regardless of their questionable legality, I furthered my language skills that evening by reading the Spanish subtitles on "Water World," "Mousehunt," and "I got da hookup" featuring Master P, as I listened to each movie's English soundtrack.

The bus arrived in Tacna at eight o'clock the next morning. It's during moments like unloading a ton of precious mountaineering and photography equipment amid the hustle of a gritty third-world bus station that one wishes for some companionship. I took a deep breath, heaved my belongings onto my back, and loped into the guts of the murky station. Although sleeplessness clouded my thoughts, I knew that I had to navigate a small maze of bureaucracy. *Find a taxi, get a ticket, pay the...bus tax?* I wondered. *Is that all? What else?* Surprises always lurk, especially in places like the Tacna bus station; I relaxed and prepared to face those surprises as they came.

The crowds seemed thinner and the officials less inimical than I remembered from my first experience in the Tacna bus station. But that didn't mean I wanted to stick around. I dropped my bags on an empty bench, held up my arms, then called out "¡Arica! ¡Arica!" as I slowly turned around. A portly guy in need of a shave bounded up to me. Instantly he had my mule bag over his shoulder, and was waving for me to follow him to his taxi. Four other patrons waited next to his rusted, faded blue Chevy Nova. We strapped my large bag to the roof, crammed the film bag between the other passengers' belongings in the trunk, and I was to hold my camera bag on my lap. Then my capacity to trust a stranger was tested as it had never been tested before. The driver demanded my passport so that he could officially register me; then he ordered me to return to the bus station to pay my departure tax—separating me from my precious belongings *and* my most vital piece of identification. Fear paralyzed me. I didn't know what to do. *Leave all my gear and my passport with these strangers?* The idea belied every bit of travel wisdom ever uttered. The other passengers glared at me, anxious to get moving. I finally threw up my arms, conceding to the peer pressure, and ran inside.

My trust was well rewarded. For six bucks I was racing south toward the border of Chile, sharing the front seat with my cameras and a colorfully dressed and well-fed Quechua woman. She seemed friendly. I smiled at her, as if to say, "Hey, Americans aren't pigs..." She gave me a courtesy gesture, then hid under her black hat. *How nice,* I thought, *she's probably going to Chile to visit her friends, or maybe her sick mother.* As we approached the Peruvian exit station, however, my seating companion started squirming. An argument broke out between her and the driver. After a few seconds they quieted down and stared at me with looks of panic. Then the 'friendly' woman pulled out a clutter of cigarette packs—that weren't filled with cigarettes—and started stuffing them into my socks. Once again, I was about to become a smuggler, but this time of

71

something a little more potent than color reversal film. "¡No! ¡No!" I yelled at them, yanking the cocaine-filled packs out of my socks and tossing them into the air. The rear passengers, an Argentine tourist and two Peruvian men, ducked their heads and smacked the coke into the driver's lap. The car swerved back and forth along the highway as the driver struggled to organize the 'cigarettes.' He barked what I interpreted as vituperative remarks at me, his face glowing red. Then he undid his belt buckle and rammed the cocaine down his pants— just as we pulled up to the border station.

I endured some sweaty moments wondering if I should say something to the Peruvian authorities about the smugglers. *Best to play dumb, I'm just a tourist, the police can see that...if they catch them they'll know that I had nothing to do with the crime,* I thought. I kept my trap zipped, and after an hour's worth of interrogations, we piled back into the taxi—without the woman smuggler. She'd simply disappeared, and nobody made even the slightest fuss about it. But my passport had its exit visa, and most importantly, I had that passport back in my own hands.

I passed quickly through Chilean customs, breathing a sigh of relief that all of my day's 'official duties' were behind me. When we arrived at Arica I jumped out of the taxi with my camera gear and grabbed my mule bag off the roof, then disappeared into a crowd of people. I never wanted to see that driver again. He got no tip from me. 20 minutes later I stretched out on a bench in the Arica terminal and waited for the departure of an express bus to Copiapó. Just 18 hours of travel remained before I would arrive at my main base of operations for the mountains of the Puna de Atacama.

Sajama ▲

Arica ●

—20° S—   —20° S—

BOLIVIA

CHILE

PARAGUAY

Tropic of Capricorn   .Antofagasta ●

Llullaillaco ▲   Asunción ●

Copiapó ●   ▲ **Ojos del Salado**
                    6,885 Meters; 22,588.6 Feet
           ▲ *Cerro Pissis*

BRAZIL

S   URUGUAY
o
u   ▲ *Aconcagua*
t   ● Mendoza
h   Santiago de Chile ●   ● Montevideo
                                     Buenos Aires ●
P
a
c   **ARGENTINA**
i
f   —40° S—
i   —40° S—
c

P
a
t
a   S
g   o
o   u
n   t
i   h
a
                                                     A
                                                     t
                                                     l
                                                     a
                                                     n   *Malvinas Islands*
O   t
c   i
e   c
a
n   O
                                                     c
                                                     e
                                                     a
                                                     n
    80° W   60° W
                          Cape Horn

Ojos del Salado Location Map   0   250   500   1000 KM
                                  0   250   500   1000 MI

Scale: 1:25,641,026
Azimuthal Equal-Area Projection
Map by Ed Darack

73

CHAPTER SIX

LUCKED IN THE DESERT

What's up?

The half-full bus departed late in the afternoon for an all-night trip to Copiapó. I watched the beautiful flag-topped Morro of Arica disappear behind a bare hillock, then I began musing about past desert adventures. I remembered the Atacama more from a conceptual standpoint than from a visual one. Of course I could recollect the images I'd taken of the Valle de la Luna—envision them mounted in plastic, illuminated by a fluorescent lamp on my light table back in my drab apartment in Davis—but in my mind, the overall world of the Atacama was one of simplicity, silence, and emptiness. It was so intensely forlorn, so barren, so detached from anything I could ever have imagined to be real. The fact that this landscape was sliced by roads—roads on which large air conditioned buses plied—seemed delusional, bizarre, and just plain wrong. I soon forgot about roads altogether and just stared into the distance, eventually passing out for the longest stretch of uninterrupted sleep I'd had since leaving San Francisco—about an hour.

Atacama

I arrived in Copiapó early the next morning. Copiapó seemed quiet, removed, and unhastened. I felt so comfortable with my first impressions of the town that I dragged my gear off to the side of the main terminal building, unzipped my mule bag, and set about assembling my tripod. I rested on a bench for a short while, lifted my arms to let a cool breeze give me an air shower, then set off to find a room with a comfortable bed.

Residencial Chañaral, a modest hotel tucked away just down the street from the bus terminal would be my home for next few days. My room cost six dollars per night, had its own shower and toilet, and was dead quiet.

But it wasn't even noon yet. I thought about the desert air; I thought about the mountains within my grasp; I thought about acquiring my permits for Ojos; I thought about drinking some beer and eating a hot dog. Sleep, in spite of how little I'd had of it over the past days, would be impossible. I sprung to my feet and bolted out the door.

"¿SERNATUR?" I asked the first person I met on the street. He pointed toward the city plaza. *Lelia…Lelia is the woman's name,* I remembered her name from a conversation I'd had with Bob Villarreal. Lelia was my main contact for up-to-date information and a permit for Ojos del Salado. She ran the Copiapó office of SERNATUR, Chile's version of the National Park Service.

Copiapó's central plaza is lined with broad shade trees and has the optimal number of benches. My road buzz was just wearing off; my ears weren't ringing any more and my wildly shifting appetite was settling—on whatever I laid eyes on, which in the square was a cart full of ice cream. I inhaled three vanilla bars.

I felt beads of sweat on my arms. The day grew hot quickly in the desert, but there was another reason why I was sweating: I was out of shape. I wasn't in poor shape, but I definitely wasn't in summit shape, either. *I'll just train as I go along*, I thought, wiping my forehead.

"¿Lelia?" I asked a woman as I entered the SERNATUR office.

"Sí," she responded. I told her about my intention to climb Ojos del Salado, and added that I needed a ride to base camp, possibly with another team. Lelia made some phone calls while I filled out the climbing permit application. The information would be faxed to the main SERNATUR office in Santiago, where an official would record my name, address in California, address in Copiapó, passport number, and emergency contact, and then fax my official permit to the Copiapó office the following day. The application process was free and easy. Finding a ride to base camp was another story. "No…no one is

Oasis in the Atacama

going up there now but you. There are some other climbers, but they are already there." I pondered my alternatives as I paged through a large binder stacked full of articles about Ojos del Salado from German, French, and British magazines.

I thanked Lelia for her time then set off to explore the city of Copiapó, hoping that walking the streets would inspire some creative plan for getting to base camp. The best I could come up with, however, was to go to a car rental outfit. I would have to rent a 4X4 Toyota Hilux—de rigueur for travel off the beaten path in the Puna de Atacama, and something of a status symbol in that part of the world. An expensive status symbol: the best price I could find was 800 dollars per week. I planned to be in the Puna for about three weeks including acclimatization and climbing time…2,400 dollars was about double what I had in my pocket for the entire trip. Nope, renting a car was out of the question. But I'd come so far and I was so close. I walked back into SERNATUR office later that afternoon to ask Lelia if she had any information on the Cerro Pissis approach, and I inadvertently said the magic words.

"Bob Villarreal told me…" I began.

"Bob! You know Bob?" Lelia cut me off mid-sentence.

"Yeah, Bob is the one who told me about you," I said, sensing that some doors were about to open. Lelia looked over to a younger woman in the back of the office; the two dove into a spirited conversation that ended with them laughing. The younger woman approached me.

"Sorry, no English…my friend goes to Ojos del Salado two days from now. I ask for you go with him. He was park ranger. He go up there once a year." She immediately got on the phone and spoke with her friend for less than 30 seconds, hung up, then drew a map to Alex Richard's house. "Go now. He waits to see you." I threw up my hands at this great fortune, and lunged toward the door.

"Thanks…I mean, uh…muchas gracias…" I said, grinning. I bolted across the central plaza, trotted past my hotel, made a few wrong turns down dead-end alleys, but finally made it to the busy street where Alex's small fortress is located. "Hello…Alex! Alex Richards!" I harked out after knocking uselessly on the barbed-wire-crowned wrought iron fence. After a few minutes and a few more shouts, a gracious-looking woman popped her head out of a side window.

Alex emerged a few moments later. "Won't you come in for some tea?" he asked. "Come, look at my fossils…." While his wife, Gloria, prepared tea, Alex gave me the grand tour of his house/desert natural history museum. Plants, bones, archaeological artifacts, and fossils that would make any museum curator twitch with envy were casually on display on his patio. And each had a story that he was happy to recount.

After a half hour of exploring his collections, we sat down for tea and discussed the trip to Ojos del Salado. Alex laid a stack of tattered maps on the kitchen table—maps I never knew existed. They depicted every aspect of the Puna de Atacama, and many looked hand drawn from direct field observation. I sifted through all of them, glancing over the geology, landmarks, and names of places few have ever visited. Of greatest interest to me, however, were the charts that centered on Ojos del Salado. Stacks of photographs followed, with a story for each one. "You want to climb Ojos del Salado?"

"Yes. You are going up there, right?"

"We are going to Laguna Verde, up by Paso de San Francisco, at the border with Argentina. We can leave you there, and then you can get a ride to the Ojos base camp. We leave in two days, early in the morning. We have two cars, and enough room for you and your equipment."

"Sure...of course!" I felt relieved, but then wondered how I would handle ascending 10,000 feet in a few hours. I finished my tea and set off to buy food for the climb.

Without a doubt, the best place in Copiapó to stock up on supplies is the massive "Ekono" supermarket. This place has everything imaginable for a grocery store, including huge jugs of water. I filled my cart with an assortment of canned and dried foods, then raided the packaged meat and cheese department, wondering how long the large cheese blocks and sticks of salami would hold out—not nearly as long as my canned tuna, I wagered.

21 days worth of food—and a few liters of boxed Chilean wine—set me back just over 100 dollars. I loaded the huge haul into a taxi and had the driver aim for my temporary home. With the food, water, and my pile of climbing and photography gear, there wasn't a square foot left in my room for maneuvering; but by that point, the only maneuvering I cared about was climbing into bed—which I did, then slept for 14 hours straight.

I spent the next day roaming the streets of Copiapó, eating hot dogs, ice cream, and researching Ojos and Pissis in the SERNATUR office. I had a good hunk of the Ojos logistics licked—an attempt on Pissis, however, was looking farther distant on the horizon with every bit of information I gathered about it. First of all, it lies entirely within the borders of Argentina. But because the best approach to the peak begins in Chile, I would either have to endure a near-impossible travail of red tape, border crossings, and international haggling, or simply enter illegally. Secondly, there are no roads anywhere near Cerro Pissis, and there is only one person who can navigate the labyrinthine high desert route to the peak's base camp from Chile—Bob's friend Patricio Rios, who was too expensive for me. All of this in addition to an almost total lack of information about climbing the peak. Not only did I not know what the standard route was, but I had no idea if there even *was* a "standard route."

I thought once more about the possibility of walking to Pissis from Ojos, but because most of the land between the two is over 15,000 feet high, and because the two mountains are separated by more than 50 air miles (many, many more walking miles), I not only gave up on the walking option, but I abandoned the idea of attempting Pissis altogether. So Ojos it would be, and only Ojos. Pissis would wait for another time. Once I had given Ojos my best shot, then I could begin to plan for the Aconcagua stage of the trip—but that was at least three weeks away.

That evening I consolidated my food, gear, and water, then ferried all of it to Alex's house. I'd done a good job of packing, but Alex looked worried. "Tomorrow...tomorrow we find out if we can get it into the trucks. You can get water at Maricunga and at Paso de San Francisco, so we can leave some of your jugs down here," Alex said pensively, as if calculating how much and where I would get water when I needed more. Maricunga and Paso de San Francisco are checkpoints manned by Carabineros—Chilean national police who have a reputation for honesty and helpfulness when it comes to dealing with tourists. But I still didn't like the idea of relying on them for something as vital as water...*budget mountaineering....*

Atacama road

CHAPTER SEVEN
TOO HIGH, TOO FAST

Dirt road, Salar de Maricunga, mirage

I didn't need an alarm to wake me on the morning of my departure for Laguna Verde. I jumped out of bed at exactly five o'clock, then quickly made my way through Copiapó's empty streets to the Richards' compound.

Alex was watering his plants when I arrived. "Early…good," he said as he opened the gate, "my friends will come soon. Put your things by the car. And here, have this." Alex handed me a small rock, densely speckled with pastel blue, bright green, and turquoise—a chunk of copper ore, one of the treats of the Atacama. Within an hour our group was organized and packed. I was actually able to sandwich all 40 liters of water into Alex's Suzuki Samurai.

We slipped out of Copiapó around seven, as the city began its morning rush. The lead car, driven by Alex, carried Gloria, my gear, and me; the second car carried two couples who were friends of Alex and Gloria. The group took this trip once a year, every year—a casual drive onto one of the highest, driest chunks of the planet.

Chilean Route 31 is one of only a few roads that traverse the Andes. Dirt and gravel for most of its length, the highway passes under such giants as Tres Cruces, Incahuasi, and Ojos del Salado. "Why is this road even here?" I asked.

"Mines…mines. Gold…a lot of gold…other metals, and now water. It goes over Paso de San Francisco to Córdoba, a very beautiful city in Argentina."

A redoubtable stretch of steep front ranges tore into the air directly in front of us. The range appeared two dimensional; flattened by distance and the soft light of an overcast sky. I searched for some visual hold from which I could gauge the size and scale of these peaks. The third dimension finally edged forth, allowing me to peer into the mountains, not just at them. I had to strain my neck to see the summits of this relatively low Andean range. I welcomed myself back into the Andes.

A long, protruding ridge camouflaged by the homogeneity of the mountains' color and texture marked the beginning of the climb onto the Puna de Atacama. The valleys, canyons, and mountain faces inside the range, however, were anything but homogenous. Like scenes from Death Valley and the Valle de la Luna, we rode past brilliant accretions of yellows, burgundies, oranges, and greens, knotted geologic strata, solitary piles of shattered rock, and plains of sun-kilned mud, horrifically split by gaping, geometrically-regular cracks.

A mule and a small patch of green…and a tin-roofed shack and a wooden fence. "Prospectors…maybe just someone crazy…I don't know. They have a little water from a spring, that is all they need," Alex told me. I was entranced by the prospectors. Their existence in the desert reminded me of small

Valle de la Luna

outposts on barren stretches of Baja California's Sea of Cortez coastline, except that the Sea of Cortez offers an almost limitless supply of fish…*how would you get food out here?*

We stopped for an early lunch under a lone shade tree. I took a short walk while the others ate. The early morning overcast had dissolved, leaving a clear blue sky. The air was dead calm at the bottom of the canyon. The silence bothered me; it seemed out of place. I wanted to hear air wailing over the canyon's sharp rocks. I wanted affirmation for my notion that wind ruled this small canyon. I closed my eyes and turned an ear toward the sky. Finally, some whistling…an eery salute from the high Atacama. *Come on up, I've got a few things to teach you*, I imagined it saying.

Valle de la Luna

I thought of my final evening in the Valle de la Luna on my last trip. I'd perched myself on the back of a steep ridge of hard earth, above a surreal mélange of sand dunes and triangular fins of brown rock. I'd just finished photographing a full moon rising over the sunset-washed Licancabur Volcanoes, and darkness was descending quickly. As soon as the light passed, the infamous Atacama wind roared, reaching gale force within just a few minutes. I crouched on the bare earth, gripping my equipment. The storm lasted for more than an hour, then it disappeared. How much more fickle would the air be over Ojos, a mountain that sits more than twice as high as the Valle de La Luna? How much harder would its winds blow? Could they push me over the edge of survival?

We piled back into the four-by-fours and navigated slowly up ever-steepening terrain. Our vista widened with the ascent. Distant peaks crowned visions of up-close precipices and ridges. Soon our views were limited only by the slight haze in the air.

We turned off the main highway onto a shortcut road, then torqued up a tightly-knit stitch of switchbacks that ended at a high pass. Alex shifted into lowest gear; the motor whined on the upward trudge. The sounds of the engine spinning down to idle and an accompanying strong head-rush marked our arrival at the pass. I stepped out of the car and nearly fainted from hypoxia. We had rocketed to 13,500 feet in just a few hours—hardly a prudent acclimatization regimen.

Tres Cruces, a broad, tricuspid neighbor of Ojos del Salado, anchored our view to the east. I peered down at Laguna Santa Rosa, a turquoise lake surrounded by dirty-white salt flats. Winds puffed at us sporadically from every direction; a few uneasy cumulus clouds roved the summits of the peaks above Laguna Santa Rosa. The air felt charged—incredibly dry and ready to pop with static.

Haze tinged the air. "The winds carry much dust into the air off Salar Maricunga," Alex said as he pointing to an expansive salt flat.

As we drove down to the shore of Laguna Santa Rosa, moving pink dots caught my eye. "Flamingos!" Alex said with a big smile. He parked next to a small refugio near the water, then we hiked to the shoreline. I sat on the ground with my camera and watched the birds lope through the cold, salty water. I wondered how those birds lived in such a hostile place, how they dealt with the cold, with the thin air, with the scarcity of food. Flamingos at over 12,000 feet seemed crazy to me. *Pink flamingos wading in a turquoise lake surrounded by salt flats high in the mountains of the driest place on the planet?*

"We go to Mina Marte now," Alex said. After climbing a small hill outside of Laguna Santa Rosa, the road shoots a straight-arrow course directly at Tres Cruces, the sixth highest mountain in South America. We turned south after a few miles, granting a continuously changing perspective of the enormous triple-summited mountain. Three volcanoes mashed into one, plastered with dark lava flows, snowfields, and swaths of ash and cinder. Tres Cruces seemed so complex to me, I felt I could look at it for weeks, maybe months, and see an entirely different mountain every day.

We paralleled a trickling ribbon of water lined with swaths of low, sturdy grass. "Look! Vicuñas!" Alex shouted as he turned onto the side of the road. Two of the brown-and-white-furred animals shot inquisitive stares at us, then resumed their chewing. We stopped less than 40 feet from them. They didn't care—until I got our of the car. Then they sprinted into the distance.

We pulled up to the entrance of Mina Marte about 15 minutes later. The mine seemed dormant: neat, well kept, but idle— no dust and no noise save for that of the wind. A security guard emerged from a small shack. He seemed happy to have company, but constantly nagged us for cigarettes. Midway into a conversation that I couldn't understand, I noticed a long line of 55 gallon drums. I took a closer look—the drums contained cyanide. Mina Marte is a "leach mine" where relatively low-grade ore is soaked in pools of cyanide to leach out the desired mineral—in this case, gold.

Vicuñas!

Mina Marte

Cyanide

Back on the road toward Laguna Verde and Ojos del Salado, Alex pointed out too many features and recounted too many stories for me to remember in my hypoxic state. We regained the main highway just outside of the Maricunga check station, then climbed higher onto the Puna. "Salto Grande...the big waterfall out here," said Alex, pointing down to a ten-foot cascade of the Río Lamas that is the Niagara falls of the Puna de Atacama. After seeing pink flamingos, rivers, and drums of cyanide in the desert, a waterfall didn't faze me. I laughed at the irony of what I'd been taught about such things as deserts and waterfalls.

I glimpsed Ojos del Salado for the first time about an hour after we visited Salto Grande. Set far back from the road, framed by dark, French-curved desert mountains, the peak resembles a leaning trapezoid with a complex summit. "Ojos del Salado," Alex said quietly as we rumbled past the mountain's broad shoulders. "Highest mountain in Chile. Very dangerous. Many people have died up there...cold, very, very cold and windy." I didn't utter a word to Alex's warning; I simply stared at the peak, squinting to make out snowfields, ridges, subpeaks—anything that would hint at a route to the summit. What impressed me most wasn't Ojos del Salado's height, but its breadth. I saw it as a peak of exploration, a high volcanic playground where I could engage its subtleties as well as climb it.

Laguna Verde is larger and more complex in shape than I'd expected. Ringed by cliffs of welded tuff, it has a complex and sinuous shoreline. We parked on the southwestern edge of the lake, near a tin-roof shack and a natural hot pool. The elevation at the lake is 14,200 feet above sea level. I checked the time: 11:00 in the morning. We had gained about two vertical miles in four hours. But while Alex and the others would soon be returning to low ground, I'd be staying. I breathed rapidly and shallowly; my pulse beat weakly and irregularly. Gaining so much altitude so quickly—and not soon descending—was beyond risky, it was stupid. But I had few alternatives. I could have had Alex take me down to a lower elevation where I could acclimitize at a more healthful rate, and then try to hitchhike back to the lake. But with that plan, I risked being stranded on the side of the road for days. Because Laguna Verde is the staging area for most expeditions to Ojos, my best bet to find a ride into base camp was to remain there. And if I couldn't get a ride, base camp is close enough to Laguna Verde that I could

Salto Grande

hike in. My body would just have to pull through a few days of trauma—'shock acclimatization' I called it. I had done it a few times, but I had never 'shocked' myself over 10,000 feet in less than half a day. "We go now to the Carabineros...for your permits." Alex prodded me to take care of my paperwork before the altitude made me totally useless.

The Paso de San Francisco border station lies about a mile east of Laguna Verde. Three armed but friendly Carabineros greeted us. Alex spoke with them for a few minutes before he introduced me. I noticed a large tank of oxygen in the corner of the front office. I felt a bit relieved at the sight, but even more so by Alex's next words: "They are going to check on you to make sure that you are okay. Don't worry, if you get very sick, they will take you down to lower elevation. You need to turn in your permit and let them hold your passport until you are done climbing." I unfolded my permit and handed it over with my passport. Jorge, the clerk, made some notes in a huge ledger, then offered some oxygen. I declined, wishing to tough it out without 'cheating.' "You are sure?" Alex asked.

"No, gracias." I replied.

"Okay, it is for you, if you want," Jorge added. I thanked him again, then staggered out the door to the car.

Gusts of wind raked Laguna Verde when we returned. The roof of the shack crashed and twanged loudly, but I moved in anyway, staking out one of the shack's two rooms with my mountain of gear. I thanked Alex, Gloria, and the other two couples for their company and for the ride. They gave me a few sodas and sandwiches, wished me luck, then drove off. It was a quick goodbye; I'd hoped to spend more time with them at the lake, but the thin air prompted them to head back to lower ground.

Alone in the little shack...I didn't feel scared or even apprehensive, but I did have the first pangs of a far worse emotion—loneliness. I thanked Alex and his wife over and over in my mind, wondering when I would see them again—always hoping that they knew how grateful I was.

After about 20 minutes, however, I became totally emotionless as I pushed myself to prepare for my coming trauma. I lined up all of my water bottles, set up my stove, piled my food within reaching distance, checked my headlamp, and downed some aspirin. Then I shut my eyes and tried to massage away the thumping in my temples. *Three days…at least three days before I'll even begin to be acclimatized.*

Ojos del Salado

Ojos del Salado Regional Map

Map details Ojos del Salado and environs. Map shows pertinent roads, population centers, huts, and physical features.

▲ Peak

● Population Center

♦ Hut or Outpost

International Boundary

Panamerican Highway

Secondary Routes

Scale: 1:4,000,000
Azimuthal Equal-Area Projection
Map by Ed Darack

Mountain Altitudes in Meters (and Feet):
Ojos del Salado: 6885 Meters (22,588.6 Feet)
Cerro Pissis: 6,882 Meters (22,578.7 Feet)
Cerro Bonete: 6,759 Meters (22,175.2 Feet)
Tres Cruces: 6749 Meters (22,142.4 Feet)
Llullaillaco: 6,723 Meters (22,057.1 Feet)
Cerro Cazadero: 6,658 Meters (21,843.8 Feet)
Incahuasi: 6,621 Meters (21,722.4 Feet)
Cerro Nacimiento: 6,436 Meters (21,115.5 Feet)
Cumbre de Laudo: 6,400 Meters (20,997.4 Feet)
Cerro Veladero: 6,159 Meters (20,206.7 Feet)
Volcán Antofalla: 6,100 Meters (20,013.1 Feet)
Cerro Copiapó: 6,080 Meters (19,947.5 Feet)
Cerro Colorado: 6,080 Meters (19,947.5 Feet)
Nevado San Francisco: 6,020 Meters (19,750.7 Feet)
Cerro Aguas Blancas: 5,760 Meters (18,897.6 Feet)
Volcán Lastarria: 5,700 Meters (18,700.8 Feet)

CHAPTER EIGHT

VIP HITCHHIKER

Waiting for a ride at Paso de San Francisco

In my pre-climb enthusiasm I always seem to convince myself that I'll acclimatize much faster than I ever possibly could. But I was never more wrong in my life than with my prediction of how my body would handle the two-mile-high vault to Laguna Verde. Not that I'd expected to have an easy time—I knew that life would be rough for a few days, maybe upwards of a week. I just never fathomed that my condition would be worse than any definition of 'horrific' I'd ever read, heard, or could even conjure.

The ordeal began as all my past bouts with AMS (acute mountain sickness): headache, nausea, shortness of breath, rapid pulse, lassitude, and loss of appetite. By sunset, the blood vessels in my head punched so hard that I imagined my skull might crack. I'd never before endured such a ferocious headache. I felt dizzy to the point of puking. Sweat seeped from my brow. My eardrums felt as if they would split. My vision was blurred from the intense pressure I felt in my orbitals—I clenched my eyelids shut. I feared I was developing the most dreaded of all altitude-related afflictions: cerebral edema (HACE), where the interstices of the cranium are inundated with fluid, squeezing the brain to the point of death, often within twenty-four hours. But my head throbbed so violently that I was soon unable to worry about anything at all. Nor could I stand up and walk—much less get to the Carabineros for help. I couldn't sit up. Nor could I open my eyes. Any movement—even the slightest flick of a single strand of hair—hammered carbon-steel spikes of agony into my skull.

Another edema demon showed up for the party: peripheral edema. First my hands and feet swelled, as did my lower legs and forearms. Then I felt my face get warm and puff up like a balloon, as if blood had burst through my capillaries, slowly inflating my cheeks like cookie dough in the oven. I swore it hurt just to think. *Will I die?* I wondered, *in this ugly little shack on the high Puna? At least the pain will be gone.*

The wind tore ceaselessly across the bare landscape, adding to my misery with the clanging of the tin roof, the howling rush of air, the distant roars, and the wisps of small eddies spinning into the shack.

It felt like hours passed, and the pounding showed no signs of alleviation. I began to acclimatize to the pain instead of the altitude. I padded my hands along the floor in search of a water bottle. I peeled open my eyes to aid in my quest—nothing but absolute darkness. I sensed only the screams of the wind, the bite of the cold, and the brutal pummels of the altitude.

I found the bottle and raised it to my mouth and sipped; I couldn't believe the water hadn't frozen solid. The frigid trickle numbed the back of my throat, briefly relieving my headache. My hands trembled uncontrollably as I tried to recap the bottle, but the cap's threads had already iced; I pushed the bottle off to my side. The thumping returned, fiercely emboldened by its brief rest. I collapsed into the fetal position, shakily massaging my temples, praying to any god for some relief from the altitude's iron grip.

Every muscle in my body quivered. I moaned as I breathed. I heard voices—no, just one voice—fléchettes of pain pierced my face; I realized my lips were moving: the voice I'd heard was my own. Who knows what I'd been saying. Probably jibberish, at best. Vertigo overcame me; I felt as if I were floating precariously above the cement floor, ready to fall to my death if the imaginary equilibrium that held me in my mid-air perch was upset by even the slightest movement. If ever life sucked, this was it.

I noticed a faint shadow off the edge of the door-jamb; I realized that I'd survived the night, albeit without sleep. I no longer hallucinated, nor did I mumble unintelligible jibberish. And the pain, while still intense, was *almost* manageable. I sat up and my hands instinctively began fumbling with the stove. The wind had died; I cherished the silence as I primed the burner. *I guess...I guess I'm not going to die...right?*

Laguna Verde

The stove lit easily, but the heat was useless to me: my water had frozen solid. "Stupid idiot!" I swore at myself for not keeping a bottle inside my sleeping bag. "You'll never light a stove at altitude that easily again in your life!" I choked the fuel supply and laughed—I'd only have to wait a few hours for the water to melt on its own. I leaned against the cold tin wall, gathered some spit in my mouth, flumed down four aspirin, and waited for the sun to warm the high desert.

Emerging from the shack in the middle of the afternoon, I slurped a half cup of warm soup to soothe my AMS, then concentrated on photography to help me forget about my condition. The brightness of the day stunned my irises; the delicate muscles cinched tight, sending more bangs of pain along my nerves.

I walked cautiously, avoiding quick movements. But even the gentlest motion of my legs sent thuds of misery into my head. *Just ignore it, laugh about it,* I thought. I tried to imagine how I'd put my physiological torment into words...I realized that not even the most insightful poet could accurately convey the agony. Certainly no practitioner of prose could either...maybe a new language of pain should be developed for this genre. But only a few die-hard sadists could truly appreciate a *lingua horribila*. Another problem: no one actually "remembers" pain. I concluded that bringing the experience of "shock acclimatization" to life for a non-moun-

Sunrise, Laguna Verde

taineer would require drawing upon an experience to which many adults—whether they'd been to altitude or not—could relate: a hangover, but with an added twist.

Find the cheapest, darkest tequila available, I thought, *don't eat or drink for a day or so to empty out your stomach...drink every last drop of the tequila (at least a 750 ml bottle)....* I paused to watch the wind-grazings on the surface of Laguna Verde. I noticed how arcs of ripples slammed into one another, creating beautiful—if frazzled—nodes of interference. I elaborated my hangover description in my head: *when you wake up, strap yourself onto a mechanical bull for a few hours.* "Yeah," I said aloud, "total genius," *and then stick your head in a paint shaker, screw it down as tight as it'll go—with the pressure points right on your temples—and turn it to the maximum setting. Stay there until some-one happens along and shuts it off.*

I laughed out loud at my mental images until my thumping head silenced me, then I quietly scouted the salt flats for good photography vantages. Those light winds that had been raking tiny ripples on Laguna Verde soon burgeoned into flesh-icing blasts that whipped the lake into a small tumult. I didn't stray farther than 50 feet from the shack that afternoon. I felt too weak, nauseated, and pained. Working the heavy camera temporarily deflected my attention from the AMS, but after only a few frames I struggled to make even simple adjustments. My day's work lasted about 20 minutes. I wrestled and cursed the wind all the way back to the hut. When I found a small bench fixed onto the

Morning steam, hot pool, Laguna Verde

wind-sheltered side of the shack, I plopped down and guzzled water. *Way, way saltier than the ocean*, I thought as I stared at the lake. Wind pawed whitecaps on the surface of the radiant turquoise water; the scene reminded me of blustery days on the Sea of Cortez. I swirled a bottle of my precious store-bought *agua pura*, ever dumbfounded by the sight of a wind-riffled body of water high above the clouds in the heart of a desert.

I mentally reviewed the photographic scenes I'd composed earlier, disappointed by the images; none struck me as remarkable. But the panorama before my eyes amazed me. Visually mesmerizing in its entirety, Laguna Verde teases would-be photographers as the lake's interrelated features defy attempts of photographic isolation.

After resting for about an hour, I had the energy to take another short walk, but this time I could muster only the strength to carry myself—no camera. I peered into the natural hot tub that sits a few steps from the shack. I couldn't imagine dipping into it—getting out of the hot water into the icy wind would probably have thrown me into shock. I could tell by the bits of trash ground into the surrounding salt that it was a popular destination—*for people with towels and cars with heaters,* I thought.

"Wow, the wind's really ripping…huh, strange that there is a lake here…I guess not, there's some snow up there," I mused to myself as I scanned the region in the driving gale. "There's another salt flat, and a pretty distant high peak…oh and look, a mummified cow." I staggered a few feet from the hot pool to a truly permanent resident of the Puna. Why a cow would ever visit a place more than 14,000 feet high, smack in the middle of the Atacama was well beyond my guessing ability. But this cow did make it to Laguna Verde, and there it sits, as a monument to the region's life-thieving air. I squatted next to the carcass. Her expression was shocking, as if liquid nitrogen had been dumped onto her, freezing the poor beast as she stretched her neck and gasped for one last bite of life. I couldn't find any signs of rotting; not even the sturdiest microorganisms are built to thrive in that place. Tattered bits of sun-bleached skin draped over the cow's bones—tough hide beaten by a far tougher wind. Most of the animal remained intact, but completely dried. When viewed from a few feet away, the collapsed, desiccated corpse has the look of carved and polished rock. I poked her neck; the feel reminded me of the dead wood of a bristlecone pine in the White Mountains of California. *Open air mummification*, I thought. I gulped in fear at the idea that I could be headed toward the same fate, but my mouth was too dry to swallow; the rear of my throat clogged, nearly choking me. I backed away from the carcass, listening to my shoes crunch the salty earth over the din of the rushing gale. *Another one?* I thought as I eyed what appeared to be the remains of a horse. Most of the animal's flesh had been torn away by the elements, leaving only tattered bits of dried-skin flapping over its bones—and not a trace of hair.

Turning away from the horse, I glanced down the Paso de San Francisco road. I considered hiking to the Carabineros station for some company. But the wind drilled harder, as did the pain in my head. *The wind…my head hurts with the wind.* I wondered if the intensity of my head's aching was related to the wind's strength. Each heavy gust of air was quickly followed by another rush of beatings on the inside of my skull. *Maybe the pressure, maybe the high wind lowers the pressure and…forget it—it just hurts.* I shuffled back to my hovel, closed my eyes, and waited for some peace.

Open-air mummification, Laguna Verde

I felt well enough that evening to cook some prepackaged rice and mushrooms. But I didn't feel well enough to eat more than about a quarter of the dinner. Chewing, like every other bodily movement, squeezed my head's nerves. I pushed the rapidly-cooling bowl off to the corner of the room to get it out of my sight; my warm meal froze solid within minutes. *Deal with it tomorrow....*

I drifted in and out of sleep throughout the night. Banshee screams of wind taunted me constantly. At one point I feared the gusts would tear the corrugated roof off the shack's walls and send the crumpling remains flying into Argentina. I clutched my ears to escape the gale's fire-siren blarings, and wished for just five minutes of quiet.

I wondered out loud why I was on the Puna de Atacama...sleeping on a vomit-stained cement floor...constantly fighting the wretching whims of AMS...ever fearful that my condition would lapse into cerebral edema. I fared slightly better during the second night, but I still felt as if my health was balanced like a dime on a wobbling needle. Then I remembered what inspired me to travel to South America. I remembered Sajama—the Eagles' Nest, and The Payachatas; I remembered the fleeting view of Ojos I grabbed while en route to Laguna Verde; I remembered the feeling of working myself into a lathery sweat in frigid air. The pain of shock acclimatization was just part of passing through the gates. The ordeal would end soon, then I'd move upward. As long as I kept my priorities straight and my outlook focused, the wind and the tin roof clangings would be nothing more than mild background noise.

I opened my eyes on the third morning at Laguna Verde to see a dark silhouette standing in the doorway. "Hello?" I ventured.

"Hello," came the reply, in a man's voice. He stepped inside my room and crouched beside me. "Is everything okay?" he asked in strained English. I recognized him as one of the Carabineros from the border station.

"Yes...sí," I responded while combing back my oily hair with outstretched fingers. My friend eyed the squalid conditions in which I dwelled, then started laughing. He picked up the frozen block of rice with one hand, pointed to it with the other, and shot me an inquisitive smirk as if to ask: "You were actually eating *this?*"

"Sí ... sí," I nodded with shame; we laughed in stereo.

"My friend, I back one minute." I sat up, feeling dizzy for a few seconds, then concentrated on solid, steady breathing as I waited for the Carabinero to return. "Té de coca...bueno por *la puna.*" He handed me a box of Bolivian tea made of crushed coca leaves—the same base from which cocaine is derived. Coca leaf tea is renowned for its ability to alleviate the symptoms of AMS, or as many in the Andes call it, *la puna.* It's illegal in Chile, or so I was told, but since the people who could actually enforce that law were providing the contraband, I didn't care.

"Gracias...*soooo* mucho," I said, laughing at my Spanglish. Carlos, the Carabinero who'd brought me the tea, was soon joined by his partners: a tall thin guy named Israel, and "Coolio," who constantly asked me if I knew Madonna. The trio had been patroling; and since not too much happens in that part of the world, a lone, sick American would-be volcano climber living in a tin shack at 14,000 feet must have been quite a novelty for them. They inspected my equipment, focusing most of their attention on fluorescent Eurostuff such as my headlamp and trekking poles, then stood side-by-side at the doorway and stared at me. I pushed the envelope of my Spanish skills to make conversation—basically saying "big winds," and "I like water." Most of our discussions consisted of charades mixed with pidgin Spanglish. Satisfied that I wasn't in need of rescue, the Carabineros gave me an open invitation for dinner and as many hits of bottled oxygen as I could stand. I saluted the trio with a tepid cup of 'cocaine tea,' and watched my new friends pile into their Hilux and speed away.

Distant Volcano

I stood on a ridge of deep-hued volcanic ejecta later that afternoon. The winds were up to their usual routine—blowing really hard—but I'd managed to hike a good 500 feet above Laguna Verde before the gusty thin air got the better of me. I found a boulder and rested in its wind shade.

A tiny orange dot caught my attention. I peered into a small valley and focused on the elegant shape of a grazing vicuña. I dropped into the valley and felt a rush of warmth and quietude. *Stay out of the wind...that's one of the cardinal rules of high Atacaman travel.* I followed the vicuña, once getting close enough to make eye contact. After an hour of pursuit I must have been a thousand feet above Laguna Verde, gasping for air with each step. The vicuña knew I was weakening. He held a stance at the crest of the ridge, his body silhouetted against a deep blue sky. I saluted him with a wave of my hand. He bounded out of sight and I headed back toward the lake.

I'd been making steady progress, but my AMS beatings forced me to lie flat on the ground. Looking toward the shack, I saw another Hilux zoom up. I closed my eyes and fell into a blurry dream about the new visitors. *Who are they? More Carabineros? Coming to take me to jail for drinking coca tea? Or someone stealing all of my water?!* A chill swirl of air bumped me awake. *Dinner,* I thought. *Food and water are vital right now.* I'd consumed so little of either during my days at Laguna Verde that I knew I'd have to force down as many liters and calories as possible. I rushed to the shack.

"¡Hola!" I yelled when I arrived at the front door.

"Hallo!" Came the reply in what I thought was a German accent. A middle-aged man and woman appeared from another room in the hut—a room that had a natural hot pool as its centerpiece. Despite the shack's miniscule size, I'd never learned of the hot pool that bubbled just a few feet from where I'd spent the previous two nights. Just another sign of my brain's reduced functioning.

Ralph and Claudia were climbers from Austria who'd been touring Chile for six weeks. They were considering an attempt of Ojos, but didn't feel they were yet strong enough.

"We have attempted the San Francisco peak yesterday, just near the guard station, and we didn't make it. We're going to stay here tonight, maybe see how we feel in the morning," Ralph said.

"...and this wind. It is just terrible. It gives me the worst headache!" Claudia echoed my thoughts about the wind-headache connection. I boiled a pot of water while the couple pitched camp next to their rented Hilux. I welcomed their company—especially the safety of having the truck so close at hand in case my condition took a turn for the worse. We ate dinner together on the floor of my room and discussed the possibility of the three of us traveling to Ojos base camp together.

"We must wait and see if Claudia's condition improves. You seem not so alive yourself," Ralph said.

"No, I'm not ready to move up to a higher altitude. Not even close," I replied, massaging my temples with one hand while shoveling food into my mouth with the other.

"Maybe you should go down to a lower altitude for a night, then come back here, then you can go to base camp." Ralph outlined a smart plan—except I didn't have access to a truck, and only wanted to go down with them if they planned to come back up to Ojos base camp. "We may go down a little lower, and if you like, come with us."

"Thank you. Have you ever had altitude sickness this bad?" I asked Claudia.

"No. It is so awful. Ralph only has a small headache and some nausea now

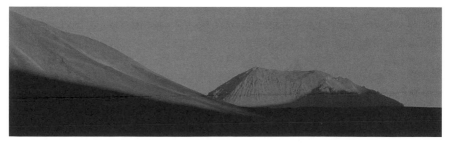

Incahuasi at sunset

and then. But me...*uhhhh!* This wind! It blows so hard and my head is hurting like it wants to explode! It is so cold, too. I've never been to a place where it is like this. And how are you?"

"Not well, but I came straight up here from Copiapó, with no acclimatization in-between."

Incahuasi

"You are lucky not to be dead!" Ralph boomed. "I think also that the bright sun affects us. It is like we are up here climbing on another planet. The air here is different."

"I'm glad I'm not dead," I laughed. "And I'm glad I'm here now. Hopefully just one or two more days and I'll be fine...."

Two more days came and went, and neither Claudia nor I felt any better. Even Ralph began slipping into an AMS rut. And the winds howled more vociferously than ever. Sleeping went from elusive to impossible. None of us spoke more than a few words at a time. We developed what I called the 'Laguna Verde gaze'—we didn't actually stare, but half-slept with our eyes wide open. Claudia endured spates of uncontrollable vomiting after each meal; by the end of the second day she conceded defeat to the Puna. She and Ralph opted out of an Ojos attempt.

I tested my health by striking off on small hiking forays on the slopes above the hut. I barely passed each trial. Eating, sleeping, ex-

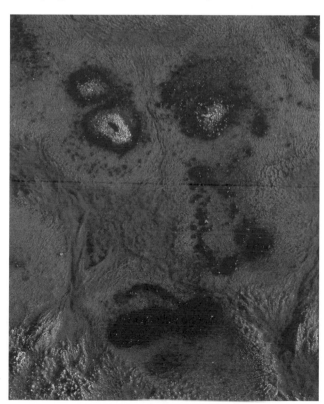

High altitude algae man in Laguna Verde

ercising, drinking…nothing worked. By the end of day five, I realized that my strength hadn't improved one bit. Furthermore, while not as bad as my first night, I felt that my health had slipped well below the physiological zenith I'd reached during the second and third days.

"Tomorrow we leave for Maricunga. It is about 2,000 feet lower than here. I think you should come with us," Ralph said as we tried to devour chunks of greasy salami for dinner. I felt trounced by the Puna. I craved a good night's sleep and just a few AMS-free moments. "You can stay at Maricunga for a night or two, then find a ride back up here. You can hike to base camp, or maybe catch a ride with another expedition."

"Sounds good. I'm not worrying about coming back up; I just really want to get out of here…." I droned.

We crammed our gear into the Hilux around noon the next day, visited the Carabineros to tell them that I would return soon, then aimed the truck toward lower ground. We noticed our strength—and sanity—returning within the hour. "Ooh, I can breathe again! And my headache is going away," Claudia exclaimed.

"And I'm starving," I said, unable to focus on anything but the thought of barbecuing a huge slab of marinated tri-tip—and eating it. We arrived at the Maricunga Carabineros guard station late in the afternoon, where we planned to spend the night. Ralph and Claudia would return to Copiapó the following day, and I would search for a ride back to Laguna Verde. The guards offered us water and an empty bunkhouse. With beds and electric lights, the accommodation was a far cry from the Laguna Verde Hut.

Maricunga Carabineros station

I devoured a huge bowl of spaghetti before falling into a 15-hour-long spell of deep hibernation. I jumped out of bed within a second of waking up the next day. Ralph and Claudia had already packed by the time I stepped into the beautifully warm, windless morning. "Best of luck to you on making it to Ojos…Since we have arrived last night nobody has come through here. I hope that someone does soon and is willing to give you a ride. I think that this is not such an easy place to hitchhike," Ralph said.

"Thanks. Thanks for the ride and for the company," I said.

"No problem. I am so glad we came down here. I feel so much better, I can't wait to get to the beach now!" Claudia chirped as she jumped into the truck. I waved them off then took a morning stroll down the dirt road.

I'd lost precious distance and altitude in the move down to Maricunga—and I had no return fare. But I felt strong again; I breathed easily and I could think straight. I did some jumping jacks and wind sprints. I still felt great. *Nothing like good health*, I thought. I felt charged to make the summit of Ojos and carry my beefy Pentax system as high as gravity and my own physiology would allow. I fixed and devoured a giant breakfast, downed three liters of water, and embarked on a two-hour hike, skirting the base of the mountains that sat behind the guard station.

A long streamer of dust signaled the approach of a possible ride—but the truck was headed in the wrong direction. I returned from my hike just as the vehicle parked at the guardhouse. A guy in a bright orange windsuit emerged from a Hilux, pancaked in dust. I asked him if he would be returning any time soon. "I hope never." *Back to waiting....*

I dropped by the Carabineros' office after another round of food. I told them I needed a ride back up to Laguna Verde, and also that I could use a little extra water if they could spare any. I felt a bit intrusive—almost demanding, but with my strength and spirits so high, I would do just about anything to get on the slopes of Ojos.

The guards at Maricunga weren't quite as friendly as those at the Paso de San Francisco station, but they obliged me with my requests. One of them called the Paso de San Francisco station to say that I was at Maricunga, was healthy, and would be returning soon. Another man topped off my water bottles. "Have your things ready in an hour," the man at the desk said when he hung up the phone. I finished packing a half hour later. Two hours after that, another Hilux zoomed up to the station, and this one was headed in the right direction.

The driver, a Chilean government official, was associated with the mining industry. He traveled alone, carrying only a briefcase and a small bag of clothes. I sensed that he wasn't thrilled to be taking a business trip to the high Puna, but he seemed happy enough to have company. The official, named Alberto, smoked cigarettes and joked with the Carabineros for an hour before we got on our way. He didn't joke with me, but he did continue smoking—with the windows rolled up. After an hour of difficult breathing (for me, anyway), we turned onto a narrow road that led to a mining camp. "Dinner. Yum. Yum," he said, and motioned for me to follow him into the cafeteria. The sun

Atacama mine worker

was just setting and I counted a dozen scenes I craved to expose to film. While Alberto made a beeline for the food, I set up my Pentax and started shooting— and shivering. The dry air's temperature plummeted within minutes of the sun's disappearance. After shooting a few rolls of crimson alpenglow basting rust-colored volcanoes, my painfully cold hands and growling stomach won my attention. I jogged inside.

The mining camp had been built of portable 'modular space,' essentially box-like rooms attached to one another to form a small compound. Diesel generators provide electricity, and trucks supplied food, tools, and whatever else the miners need. Such operations require tremendous financial invest- ment; only the most valuable commodities are pursued with so much effort. In this case, that commodity is water.

I sat at a table with an English-speaking Chilean mining engineer named Eduardo. He seemed happy to have me as a guest; I was happy to have a hot dinner of chicken and mashed potatoes. "Water is really the most important commodity in the world. We are drilling straight down for it here; it will be pumped to the cities along the coast and the interior of northern Chile," Eduardo told me. "The water has been accumulating for tens of thousands of years from the snowmelt in the highest peaks of the Puna. We need this water badly. We can't grow food without water; we can't run our economy without water…we can't *live* without water."

We chatted for a half hour, about everything from Chilean politics to American pop music, and of course, climbing Ojos del Salado. "Watch out for the winds, my friend. They can kill you…they are so cold, so damn strong and cold…"

"Vámonos amigo. Vámonos," Alberto said with a cigarette dangling from his mouth.

"Thanks for the food, Eduardo," I said as I scooped the last of the mashed potatoes into my mouth.

"No problem, my friend. Be safe. Maybe I'll see you up here another time." Alberto and I sped down the dark road to Paso de San Francisco, arriving at the Carabineros guard station around nine o'clock that night. I didn't know if I would need to pitch a tent at the station or be taken back to Laguna Verde. The answer was neither. Carlos, Israel, and Coolio had a bed made and waiting for me. While Carlos stamped Alberto's passport with an exit visa, Israel and Coolio whisked me into their kitchen and served goat meat soup and more cocaine tea. Alberto popped his head in to say goodbye, then Carlos joined us.

"Like Poison?" asked Coolio with excitement in his eyes as he handed me my second big dinner of the night.

"Huh?" I asked, waiting for my soup to cool.

"Poison! You like Poison?" I stared at the three of them, sitting across from me at the table, shoulder-to-shoulder, decked out in identical olive drab sweaters.

I started to worry that my friends weren't going to turn out to be so friendly after all. "Poison! You know, POY-EE-ZZON!!" Coolio repeated, punching his fist high in the air before jumping to his feet and powering up a small CD player. The blaring sounds of an L.A. eighties glam-metal power trio filled the room as all three of my hosts starting mouthing the words to a song I would have sworn could only be played in a T-top Camaro.

"Oh, yeah…Poison…I…uh…know *Poison*."

"Yeah! We love Poison!" For the next hour the trio of would-be Karaoke stars sang along with music I hadn't heard since high school. They had a full range of CDs from that genre, and they knew every beat, every word, every strum of every monster power cord of every song.

I downed as much as possible of the soup, tea, and bread my friends offered, before bedding down for the night. With the mass of food and fluids in my system and the acclimatization boost from sleeping a night at Maricunga, I woke the next morning anxious to run to the summit of Ojos. Coolio and I piled my gear outside the guard station, readying it to be loaded into a vehicle that might or might not come—and if one would be coming, we didn't know when. One thing was certain, however, anyone who came had to stop and see the Carabineros to get their papers stamped.

After an hour of pacing circles around my gear, a shiny white diesel pickup truck arrived from Argentina. As soon as the driver stepped out of his truck to get his papers stamped, Coolio popped his head out of the guard house and winked at me. 20 minutes later, the Argentine, a Córdoban rancher named Felix, returned, closely followed by Coolio, Israel, and Carlos. The Carabineros stood guard as Felix single-handedly loaded all of my gear into the bed of his pickup truck. I tried to help, but the Carabineros wouldn't allow it. "Retorno en dos semanas," I said to the trio as I shook their hands and thanked them. Felix revved the engine and I sprung inside the cab, waving to Coolio, Israel, and Carlos as Felix and I rolled down the dirt highway toward Laguna Verde.

Felix didn't say a word for the first part of the ride. I thanked him for picking me up and he nodded, but that was it. I spotted Laguna Verde and pointed to the short road that led to the shack. Felix still didn't say anything. "¡Aquí! ¡Aquí!" I said as we approached the turnoff without slowing—then passed it.

"Those Carabineros are good friends to you." Felix said, surprising me with his English.

"You speak English?"

"Yes, my friend…I speak fine English."

"Aren't we supposed to go to Laguna Verde?"

"No. We're going to the Ojos del Salado base camp."

"Really? How's that?"

"Because your friends the Carabineros back there wouldn't allow me into this country unless I agreed to deliver you to your base camp."

101

"Oh…. That's…uh…great. Thanks." I really didn't know what to say.

"No problem. You see the Chileans sometimes take delight in making us Argentines work for them." Felix studied a map drawn by one of the Carabineros; he squinted at the hand-scribbled lines for a moment, shook his head in confusion, and then threw the scrap of paper on the floor. "Okay…I think…oh yes…here we are…" he muttered. We turned onto an unmarked dirt track that shot arrow-straight into the distance. 15 minutes later we pulled up to a large, weatherbeaten hut. Felix then dutifully unloaded my gear, stacking my bags, water bottles, and my tripod in a neat pile. "No! I must do it all myself," he said when I tried to lend a hand. "Okay. Done. I've satisfied my duty to the Chilean Government," he announced. "And you are the worst smelling VIP I could ever imagine, even for a Chilean VIP!" he concluded. My chauffeur then

Unnamed mountain to the north of Ojos del Salado

glared at me, eyed the gigantic volcano I had come to climb, glared at me again, shook his head, wished me luck, and tore off down the dirt track toward the main road.

I walked along the base of the two-story, aluminum-roofed hut. Piles of splintered, half-burned wood lay strewn around its periphery. The structure had a ghost-house feel; I could have been on the set of a cheap hacker movie if only the place were surrounded by a dense, claustrophobic forest instead of a bright, wide-open sweep of high desert.

The morning winds whistled across the loose boards of the large A–frame. I eased my way up a creaky stairway, then tiptoed across a rickety deck to the main entrance and turned the doorknob. SNAP! The warped door popped open. Sagging floorboards groaned as I stepped inside. I stood in a small storage room, its shelves littered with empty water bottles and old bags of food. I opened a second door, and entered a small sleeping quarter stuffed with climbing gear, dirty clothes, half-eaten bags of food, and more empty water bottles. I glanced at the floor—and jumped back: two women lay completely motionless and silent. *Are they dead?* I wondered. "Hello," I said timidly, as if gently prodding them with my words. Neither moved. I inched closer. "Hello," I spoke louder—still nothing. "HELLO!"

"Hmm," I heard from one. She turned her head to me, opened her eyes halfway, then slumped back into her sleeping bag. *Okay, good, at least they're alive.* I closed the door and began hauling my gear up the stairs, wondering who those two women were, where they were from, how they got there, and how they would get out of there—which led me to ponder for a few seconds how I would get out myself.

I studied the landscape between the hut and Ojos. Miles upon miles of volcanic terrain. *A long march,* I thought, then wished that the 'base camp' hut had been built a little closer to the actual base of the mountain. I guesstimated that an approach hike would take a week, maybe more, considering all the weight I was carrying. *Just forget about it, deal with it tomorrow, rest and acclimatize.*

A rooster-tail of dust rose from what appeared to be a battle tank speeding across the high desert. *A battle tank? Up here? Probably just a mirage or something,* I thought. After a few moments I looked again. *Definitely not a mirage...maybe a huge jeep...I don't know...what would a tank be doing up here?* I shrugged my shoulders and continued shuttling my supplies into the hut, thinking about how I'd cross the sea of volcanic ash and sand that lay between the hut and the mountain.

CHAPTER NINE

UNIMOGS AND FISH STEW

Ultimate Volcano: Ojos del Salado   *Ultimate four-by-four: Unimog*

Mirrored aviator sunglasses don't say much about the person wearing them—unless that person is the commander of a 1974 Mercedes-Benz four-wheel-drive *Unimog*, roving the highest reaches of the Puna de Atacama. I'd just finished loading my gear into the front room of the base camp hut when a white-smoke-belching, sun-bleached-olive-drab, way-high-off-the-ground, diesel-gurgling, ABBA-era military monster rolled up to the A-frame—the 'battle tank' had arrived. The driver emerged amid a cloud of dust—and kicking up dust in a place constantly blasted by earsplitting winds is no small feat. The mirrored aviator one-ways caught my attention immediately. The glasses reflected the bright Atacaman sun directly into my eyes, blinding me momentarily. The driver shut the door of the beast with military precision, then marched up the stairs with supreme authoritarian poise. He came to a halt just inches from me, a cold, robotic expression chiseled on his face. A few moments of quiet suspense passed. Then he introduced himself: Ricardo—but from then on I could know him only as 'El Comandante.'

El Comandante, as it turns out, wasn't a comandante at all, but a conscript in the Chilean army charged with portering a group of Santiago based climbers from Copiapó to Ojos del Salado. But with those huge mirrors hanging below his forehead, he appeared commanderish enough.

The women asleep in the refuge were part of El Comandante's expedition. The 'Club Alemán Andino' organized the group, which was comprised of sixteen climbers, three Unimogs, three Unimog drivers, and a ton—literally—of gear. The other two Unimogs sat parked at the Andino Hut, a refuge at the 17,100 level of the mountain. El Comandante had been returning from the Andino (also known as the Ruda Camp or Atacama Refuge) when I first noticed his tank-like Unimog and the banner of dust its big wheels pitched into the sky. After our introduction, he invited me to meet the two sick climbers, Eva and Ana. Our meeting was brief—the two women raised their eyebrows, smiled wanly, then flopped back asleep. I brewed coca tea while El Comandante fixed lunch. Ana and Eva thanked us for the meal, but could down only a few half-hearted slurps and a couple of nibbles. The looks on their faces reminded me of how I'd felt during my stay at Laguna Verde. I wondered how quickly they'd ascended to the high Puna; *a few more days than I,* I hoped.

I tried to guess the hut's altitude. The elevation seemed higher than that of Laguna Verde, but not by much. Bob Villarreal would later tell me that the refuge lies at 14,763 feet above sea level. He would also tell me that the building, which I considered 'base camp,' was once the Carabineros guard station—and the dirt track that led to the station had been the main road; engineers rerouted the highway in the mid-eighties. More bizarre yet, Bob told me that those piles of smashed wood surrounding the refuge stand as the sole remains of a tiny hotel that mysteriously burned to the ground in the late eighties.

Ojos del Salado, Unimog, 'base camp hut' (Carabineros station), ruins of Louis Murray Lodge

Called the Louis Murray Lodge, just one man operated this high, lonely hotel.

"How you go up?" El Comandante asked.

"I don't know…maybe I walk up in a few days," I said, feeling the onset of a slight headache as I chewed my cheese and crackers.

"I go dos días…in two…days…I go up. You come?"

"Oh, ¡Sí! ¡Sí!" I replied.

"Too far walk. Too far. You come with me in Unimog!" My luck to that point was stupendous; I felt blessed. I wondered if my high altitude hitchhiking charms would ever run dry. *How will I get back here from the Andino Hut? How will I get back to the Carabineros? And how will I get back to Copiapó? Every stroke of luck that takes me farther up this mountain means one more obstacle I'll have to pass to get back down!* I cried in my head. *Just relax, take it one day at a time,* I told myself.

Thin air and a full gut coaxed me into my sleeping bag in the early afternoon. I worried about a relapse of altitude sickness, that my scarcely perceptible headache would rev up to another session of full-blown AMS and kill the journey—I couldn't take another beating like the one I'd had at Laguna Verde.

Instead of crashing back into altitude sickness however, I simply fell asleep. A few hours after passing out, I was back outside, strolling along gently rolling plains of tan lapilli. The sun closed on the horizon; long shadows spilled across the wavy contours of Ojos del Salado and its surrounding aprons of ash and lava. I finally had a chance to appreciate the giant volcano I'd come to climb.

I walked along a steep flow of welded tuff, losing sight of the hut and the Unimog—and was soon alone with the bare elements of the Puna. I welcomed the wind, firm but not too rambunctious.

Even after nearly a week of living in the mountain's shadow, talking with people from around the world about ascending its slopes, and now staring straight at the huge peak, I knew practically nothing about Ojos del Salado. The volcano's name intrigued me: *eyes of the salt,* I loosely translated in my beginner's Spanish. *Ojos del Salado* actually refers, metaphorically, to the *source of the salt river.* I couldn't point out any ascent routes, I couldn't identify camps, I didn't even know if I could find the volcano's true summit. I'd read that volcanologists considered Ojos del Salado to be the highest 'active' volcano in the world. The superlative distinction raised a few questions for me as I studied the peak's forms that late afternoon. I squinted, searching for a rising column of smoke or steam; I perked my ears listening for explosive rumblings; I shifted my feet, trying to feel seismic trembling. I yearned to experience something quintessentially *volcanic.*

I questioned the definition of 'active' as applied to Ojos. The volcano certainly wasn't erupting; had it been, I definitely wouldn't have traveled its slopes. I remembered reading that sulfurous fumaroles located below the summit of the volcano occasionally hiss noxious gases. The most notable recent volcanic event occurred in November of 1993, when Carabineros at Maricunga reported witnessing a gray stream of smoke rising for a few hours from the mountain's crater. Do small fumaroles and a micro-eruption really support classifying Ojos del Salado as active? Personally, I think 'dormant' describes the volcano's status most accurately.

I leapt from scrutinizing Ojos del Salado's volcanic taxonomy to pondering the ranks of South America's highest summits. Geologists have firmly established Aconcagua as the zenith of South America; nobody doubts this fact. Contrary to many popularly held ideas about the peak's orogenesis, however, Aconcagua rose into the sky not layer after eruptive layer as a volcano, but upthrusted, as a complex massif built of folded and faulted volcanic strata, strata that had been lain down by surrounding volcanoes through the millennia. Aconcagua stands as South America's highest point, but not the continent's highest volcano.

Nobody doubts Ojos del Salado's volcanic origin. But controversy obscures the mountain's exact altitude among its lofty peers. A number of climbing/scientific expeditions from the United States, Europe, and Chile have ranked Ojos del Salado as the second highest mountain in South America, just a few meters higher than Cerro Pissis, 52 miles to the south. Geographers from Argentina, however, claimed that Cerro Pissis stood about 20 meters *higher* than Ojos del Salado. (Like Aconcagua, Cerro Pissis lies entirely within Argentina, whereas the Chile-Argentine border splits Ojos del Salado through the volcano's summit. Having both the highest and second highest mountains entirely within Argentina's border generates a great amount of pride for many Argentines, but many non-Argentines—Chileans in particular—believe these findings to be exaggerations). My mind began cranking as hard as it could in that hypoxic realm, comparing orographic superlatives....

The only mountains higher than the Andes belong to the Himalayan complex of Asia. I tried to recall reading or hearing anything about volcanoes in the Himalaya proper, the Karakoram, the Pamirs, the Hundu Kush, the Tian Shan—I mentally searched every range in the earth's highest mountain group...but nothing. I couldn't think of a single Himalayan volcano. I paced back and forth on the wind-polished land for a few seconds, kicking some stones and staring blankly at their hues and textures. Then I looked up and wondered, *am I looking at the highest volcano in the world, active or otherwise? Or is that Cerro Pissis?* Until I saw definitive evidence proving otherwise, I'd consider Ojos the higher of the two. The prospect of climbing the highest volcano in the world added yet more excitement to my anticipation of the days ahead.

Fingers of snow dashed the uppermost flanks of Ojos. As snow goes, the nieve found on the volcano's flanks is exquisitely unique. Not by its appearance, but by its location—on the highest volcano in the world, smack in the middle of the driest place on earth. *I have to get up there, just to see it, see the exposed guts of a volcano right next to fingers of snow and ice, preserved by the intensely cold Atacama air....*

I climbed up the backside of another outcrop of welded tuff to gain a better view of my surroundings. Shadows cloaked most of the north side of Ojos. The late afternoon sunlight grazed only a few upper swaths of the mountain's undulating topography. The low-angled illumination brought shapes, textures, and colors invisible in the flat light of midday into stark relief. I broke out my camera and started composing—metering—shooting. The western aspects of the upper three summits of the bulky volcano shone brightly, starkly contrasting with the shadowed sections of the peak. A full palette of volcanic creations stood saliently over the surrounding landscape in that light: flows, craters, scabrous cliffs, and ash fields.

An iceberg of wind pummeled me as dusk fell. I felt my hands freezing—stiffening—almost seizing at one point. I hastened to collect my gear, stash it, and bounded back to the hut. The air throbbed with the pulses of a near-jet stream gale. I stumbled down a slope of sharp, jagged talus that clinked like broken glass with each footstep. I rounded the phalanx of tuff, meeting the windstorm head-on. I could see the base camp hut about a half-mile away, surrounded by completely naked land. The place didn't seem to be a landscape, just a stage for the bare essence of nature's wrath. But somehow that shack stayed put, and I aimed for it.

The air seized me in its cold, leaden grip—I wanted to drop to the ground, bury my head and try to forget ever *thinking* about climbing Ojos del Salado. Even just breathing was difficult: if I faced the wind, so much cold air would slam into my mouth that my diaphragm would cinch tight; if I blocked my face, then the air rushing around my head would create a vacuum around my mouth. I walked head down, in a zig-zag pattern to 'tack' into the gale.

I staggered up the stairs just as the first stars pricked the waning light of dusk. I threw open the door and dropped onto my sleeping bag wheezing and coughing. I heard El Comandante laughing with Ana and Eva. When I opened the door to the main bunk area, yellow-orange candlelight flickered off the walls. El Comandante sipped tea in a corner of the room, while Ana and Eva, still lying in their sleeping bags, worked on bowls of instant potatoes mixed with corn and peas. "Sleep good?" Ana asked me.

"Sí." I described my ordeal in the wind. None of them knew I'd left the hut.

"Mucho peligroso...mucho viento," El Comandante said as he produced a pot of mashed potatoes for me.

"Gracias. Muchas gracias." I buried my head in the food, finishing it off in about two minutes. Ana and Eva stared at me with astonished expressions. "Lo siento," I said, feeling like a pig.

"¡No! ¡No! Bueno... ¿Tu gusta comida?" Ana asked, laughing.

"Sí. Sí. Muy bien—muy, muy bien."

El Comandante brought out another pot after I licked the first one clean. I slowed my pace a bit with the second serving, allowing myself to actually enjoy the taste of the food.

I woke well past dawn the next morning. My day's goals were simple: drink water, eat food, hike around and take pictures. In 24 hours I'd be moving up to 17,100 feet; I needed to be in shape for the altitude boost.

Wiping my eyes open, I stepped into the bright, windless day and pulled off my shirt to let the sun's raw light massage my back. After about 20 minutes, however, I felt a little too much warmth. I hid my skin under one of my smelly long-sleeved polypropylene tops, then doused my hands, nose, cheeks, and ears with sunscreen.

Parallel tracks, faintly scribed onto the surface of the desert, caught my eye. They struck off in the direction of Ojos—the 'road' to the Andino Hut. I forced down a liter of water, grabbed some candy, then set off along its path.

A half hour later I found myself lost inside a labyrinth of volcanic debris. Gently rolling mounds of ash and pumice stretched maybe two miles to the south before rising into a more wrinkled landscape. I walked to the edge of the transition zone. The region appeared chaotic, jumbled, puzzling—an insane collage of deep sand, huge boulders, and chalky, fractured cliffs. I sat on the ground and closed my eyes. I was well acclimatized, but the Puna is an incredible energy sink. As I was dropping off to sleep, I heard a mild rumbling sound. Fearing an eruption, I shot up and scanned for smoke, cinders, lava. The noise died. I continued searching, in every direction. The rumbling returned, only louder, higher pitched. I saw a flash of red out of the corner of my eye—a Toyota Landcruiser rocketed over a knoll 25 yards away; it was headed straight for me. I dove to the side of the road and hid behind a boulder. The driver torqued the rig around a tight bend in the track, throwing chunks of pumice in my face as he blared the horn. I saw at least four dropped-jaw blank stares of element-beaten tourist-climbers strapped into the old Landcruiser. I wanted to scream some barrage of vituperations at the driver, but I was overcome with the 'hey, you're up here too?' emotion. I wished they'd stop to tell me about life higher up, to give me some advice on what sections had ice, which had loose rock and scree, stuff like that. Or just stop and talk for a while…about Chile, about the Puna, about politics…about anything. But the driver just floored it down a straightaway, blasting the Landcruiser toward the main highway.

The bizarre meeting stunned me. *Why hadn't they stopped? Did the driver see this trip as so routine that he wouldn't even slow down?* The man behind the wheel must have been a local guide; he saw this beautiful place, this gorgeous morning, as just another day at the office. The expressions on the passengers' faces echoed the emotions I felt: disbelief. They appeared shell-shocked;

maybe from the altitude, maybe because of a lack of food, maybe out of exhaustion, but probably due to a combination of all of these tribulations. I imagined that they'd traveled to Ojos for an enjoyable guided mountaineering vacation, but their guide forced the 'power slam' tour on them instead.

Food dominated my thoughts during my return to the hut. I blazed through my menu of possibilities, but couldn't decide on even a single course that piqued my tastebuds. Then an unlikely thought hit me: *fish stew…that's it. Fish stew!* I'd dreaded those cans of 'atun' since I'd unloaded them from their grocery bags in my small room in Copiapó. In my haste, I'd glossed over the most important category of expedition planning: food. Like the inability to remember pain, I never can seem to remember the feeling of appetite loss. Roving through the aisles back at the Ekono, I hadn't even considered taste. I focused on volume and cost, foregoing that most important factor, *sabor*. Unless a meal smells and tastes great, my stomach won't accept the food. And I didn't associate good taste with those cans of tuna—until the hike back.

I remembered that El Comandante had bags of onions, garlic, mushrooms, bell peppers, and most importantly, tomatoes. The thought of a cool, pulpy tomato made me want to run back to the refugio. I didn't; but once inside I started chopping, cleaning, and peeling. An hour later I had my grand culinary masterpiece of the Puna de Atacama: fish stew—heavy on the tomatoes. The four of us gorged ourselves that afternoon and then again at dinner. I was ready for the ride to 17,100 feet.

El Comandante woke me early the next morning to load my gear into the back of the Unimog. I took a good look at the boxy four-by-four. Huge knobby tires held the over-beefed chassis far off the ground. The body seemed ultimately utilitarian, basically four walls of steel with a canvas canopy and a small passenger compartment. Nothing is meant for show on the Spartan Mercedes creature. Every last wire, screw, washer, and bolt has a purpose. And the machine obviously was designed for just one purpose: to go and go, and to not stop going until…I couldn't even guess. The Unimog appeared so solid that it seemed carved from a single block of iron.

I squeezed into the passenger seat as El Comandante twisted dials and pulled knobs the likes of which I had never seen before. None were marked, and all were large enough so that someone wearing Antarctic-rated mittens at 40 below could make mil-spec adjustments. The proud driver couldn't hold back an 'oh yeah, here we go' grin as he pushed a big red button to the left of the steering column. The Unimog shook like an out-of-balance washing machine when the guttural Mercedes-Benz diesel spun up. Asphyxiating white smoke billowed into the cab as El Comandante yarded on a small handle on the floor and gunned the throttle. He wiped a veneer of dust off his one-ways, clamped both hands on a two-foot-long shift lever, cocked his body, then slammed the shifter into what I took to be the 'go' position. My neck creased back as the Unimog lurched forward. I caught my breath and stared at El Comandante; we both nodded in total satisfaction.

We cruised at a steady clip until we reached the section where the Landcruiser had nearly run me over. El Comandante let go of the steering wheel as he used both hands to shift from the 'go' to the 'go slower' position, then wrestled the Unimog through a long section of deep sand. The truck slammed back and forth like a small boat in a hurricane as all four wheels dug aggressively into the loose volcanic material. Before long we found ourselves deep in a maze of lava flows, boulder fields, and more volcanic sand.

The character of the landscape confused me. In one respect, the topography's complexity was engaging. At a second glance, however, the landscape appeared hastily thrown together, completely unrefined. The jumble looked like a proto-landscape, as if the parts were dumped at the construction site, but the work had yet to begin.

We didn't travel along a roadway, but a vague 'route' through the labyrinth of crude earth. El Comandante wrestled the Unimog out of the sandy lowlands onto a ridge of harder ground after about 15 minutes of slogging. The roadway reappeared and we sped onto a high plateau. We'd traveled nearly four miles, but Ojos still appeared far in the distance.

About six miles after departing from the base camp hut we parked next to a small orange shipping container surrounded by tents, people, and two other Unimogs, the Andino Hut. A small crowd of Chilean climbers cheered as El Comandante emerged from the command seat and greeted the group. The Club Alemán Andino had successfully put 8 of their 16 climbers on the summit after a physically emaciating, psychologically draining ordeal. Each member of the group seemed starved for easier altitudes.

I walked to the back of the Unimog to unload my gear. *Water!...on the ground!* I yanked open the tailgate and furiously searched for the split container. I found the bottle; luckily, only a few gulps' worth had drained. But then I heard a hollow clattering noise: a completely empty jug rolled along the bed of the Unimog.

"We have water. You want some? We leave it in the hut," came the voice of one of the Chilean climbers. I brushed past the exhausted team and watched him flip an industrial gauge latch on the door of the ocean freight container-turned high mountain refuge. I stared at a pyramid of water bottles—all full. "There is also ice over that rise," Tomas, my new friend, told me. "With enough fuel, you can drink for a long time up here, huh?" he said.

"Did you make the summit?" I asked.

"No, I was on the second summit team. We went on the day after the successful team. We made it to the crater, just below the summit notch."

"What stopped you?" I interrupted.

"The wind. The wind up there was so powerful that it lifted one of our rope mates into the air. He was just 15 meters below the summit, and flew off the rock. Luckily he was roped in."

"Roped in? Roped into what?" I asked.

"The last 15 meters is steep and rotten; the route has a few fixed lines to help you along. Be careful of those old ropes, though. They may break."

"Thanks, Tomas." We unloaded my gear from the Unimog, stacking a pile of water bottles and bags on the side of the hut. The Unimogs, stuffed with climbers and smelly gear, gurgled to life in symphony; I covered my ears against the noise of the loud diesels. El Comandante waved to me, then led the pack down the mountain.

Goodbye

I didn't have a headache, but I worried that the jump to over 17,000 would bring skull pounding soon enough. I sat on my sleeping bag and forced down as much water as I could squeeze through my throat. I poked my head out of my tent periodically, staring at the mountain's summit. The dark sky and high cliffs cast a forbidding pall over my moods. I appreciated the beauty of the volcano, but now that I stood on its slopes, I realized the seriousness of living so high on such a remote peak. The altitude, the seclusion, the otherworldly landforms of the area led me to question if I'd gotten in over my head.

But being alone, knowing that I had no one to rely on but myself brought an unexpected feeling of satisfaction and calm. I had a job to do; I'd rest for a few hours, then get to work.

Ojos del Salado from the Andino Hut

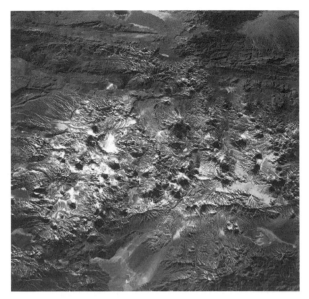

Space Shuttle image of the Ojos del Salado region

Another Space Shuttle view of the Ojos del Salado region

Chapter Ten

MEGAPACK

Nevado El Muerto

S hortly after El Comandante deposited me at the Andino Hut, I found that the refugio wouldn't be so lonely after all. Halfway into an acclimatization nap I heard the struggled whine of an engine spinning four wheels through deep sand. I popped my head out of my tent to see a Hilux slogging up to camp, carrying a lone American. The climber, a Coloradoan named Tom, jumped out of the truck before it came to a stop. Within five minutes he had his gear stashed inside the tiny hut and was waving to his departing driver.

"Wow! Finally here…Ojos del Salado!" he said to me after a quick introduction. "Can you believe they have this hut all the way up here?"

"Strange, isn't it?" I examined the weatherbeaten orange shipping container, wondering who transported the boxy refuge so high on the peak.

"I heard a South African mining company put this and another hut up here—"

"—Why?" I interrupted.

"For some reason one of their helicopters was flying around the summit of Ojos, and it crashed, killing everybody on board. I think there might have been a couple Chilean employees and a company executive flying that day. Anyway, from what I've heard, the mining company dragged this hut here and an even bigger one up to around 19,000 feet as some sort of memorial to those who'd died. The company donated the refugios to the Chilean government. A guide friend of mine told me that someone even built a hotel lower down by the old Carabineros station, but that place burnt down a few years ago."

"I saw piles of burnt wood down there," I said.

"Oh yeah? That's pretty weird, huh, a hotel way up here."

"Yeah, so, what about ocean freight shipping containers at 17,000 and 19,000 feet in the middle of the desert—on the highest volcano in the world?" We laughed until the thin air caught up with us.

"Say, do you use Diamox to help acclimatize?" Tom asked.

"No. No way. I never want to use that stuff."

"Oh come on. It's not like your cheating or anything. It works great. Here, take some."

"Nope…not gonna use it."

"Why? It helps *soooo* much!"

"I tried it once…" I began, feeling embarrassed by the story I prepared to tell about what many consider a wonder drug for allaying the problems of acclimatization.

"—And?"

"It was during my first attempt of Denali. I was at base camp and had never used the drug before, but wanted to stack the odds in my favor as much as possible for a successful summit attempt. A doctor told me that the drug was designed to be a strong diuretic, so, not wanting to dehydrate during the night,

I drank a ton of water before bedding down. I fell asleep quickly, then began having these wildly vivid dreams of open fields and barns. In my final dream, I walked to a wooden fence that was overgrown with wildflowers. I remember the colors, the winds, and the sun so clearly; the day felt so refreshing. I brushed the flowers aside, revealing a sturdy fencepost. I began peeing on it. I peed nonstop for minutes, experiencing one of the most relieved moments of my life. Then I woke up—in the middle of the night, after the temperature had fallen well below 0° Fahrenheit, during a snowstorm. I knew immediately that Diamox indeed worked very effectively as a diuretic, having caused sufficient biochemical reactions to turn every available fluid in my body into urine, which was then deposited, during my rustic dream, onto my now-soaked sleeping bag. I didn't sleep very well the rest of the night, as you can imagine."

"Oh my god!" Tom roared with laughter, "HA—HA—HA. You wet your sleeping bag on Denali. HA—HA—HA. Wow! That must have seriously bummed you out, dude. Geeeez, the last I time I wet my bed was when I was in…like…*kindergarten!*"

"So you're using Diamox?"

"Swear by it! I don't take whole pills, though—just a half or a third here and there. I start taking them about eight hours before going up to altitude. I *hate* spending time acclimatizing. My fingers tingle, and I have to piss a lot—when I'm awake, of course—but I never get altitude sick," Tom said, still laughing at my story.

"How many days did you give yourself to come to this altitude?" I asked.

"This is my fourth day. I hired a driver down in Copiapó to take me to the hut at Laguna Santa Rosa for a couple of nights, then to Laguna Verde for a night, and now here. I think I'll do pretty well. I feel good so far. Tomorrow I'm going to the high camp hut—oh, what's it called again…the…Cesar Tejos Refuge, that's it, the Tejos Refuge. I'll do a gear carry, then return here for the night; the next day I'll head back up to the Tejos Refuge, spend the night, then try for the summit."

"How are you getting down from here?" I asked.

"I told my driver, Rodrigo, to be here in four days; I guess that means I'd better get to the summit fast!"

"That costing you a lot of money?"

"A ton…like over a thousand dollars, but this is one of my dream peaks. It's totally worth it for me. I've already climbed Aconcagua; now I want this one…*numero dos* on this continent, *home boy*," Tom said with confidence.

A few hours later the wind kicked up and my head began thumping. Ignoring both distractions, I grabbed my camera and searched for photographs to be had. I found a vista overlooking a huge expanse of volcanic desert after just five minutes of hiking. Through my viewfinder I scanned, for patterned lava flows, for clouds, for distant peaks…so much of what the region offers. After shooting a few rolls I stood back and admired a broad view of the high Atacama. For the first time on the trip I felt as if I stood at a truly high altitude—a bloody nose altitude. Instead of gazing up to distant mountains, I glanced down at them. I viewed gathering storms from cloud level, not with a craned neck. I could see distant horizons, unobscured by the flanks of high-rising volcanoes. Still, the altitudes of many surrounding peaks far eclipsed the height of the Andino Hut. Nevado El Muerto, a girthy volcano to the east of the refuge, stood most saliently among these high mountains. With the exception of its neighbor to the southwest, Ojos del Salado, Muerto rises higher than any other peak in the direct vicinity of the Andino Hut. But Nevado El Muerto lassoed my attention not because of its height, but for the volcano's visual character: black lava flows pressed against wavy sheets of light-tan ash and cinders.

None of the mountains of the Ojos del Salado region could be considered icons of symmetry. None possess the perfect conical shape of the 'classic volcano.' These peaks appear tortured; static displays of earth-scale violence. Nevado El Muerto appears downright fearsome. Raspy chunks of jumbled black lava crown the complex behemoth's summit cone. Jagged flows dash its steep flanks like volcanic barbed wire. Muerto's slopes convey the orogenic nature of this part of the Andes: discordant, explosive, chaotic, brutal.

Tom and I pooled our culinary talents that evening for a dinner of half-cooked rice, instant potatoes, canned pineapple, and cherry-flavored juice. We cooked inside the hut, keeping the door cracked just wide enough to keep us from drifting into a carbon monoxide death. Leftovers of expeditions from all around the world cluttered the refugio: candy bars from Finland, Argentine sardines, US cereal, Korean crackers, and an Australian swimsuit calendar—two years out of date. Tom and I had a full range of blackened and dinged cookware to choose from, stacked tenuously high on the corner of a tilting, candle-wax plastered cooking table.

"Hey, look at this!" Tom shouted as I balanced a pot of water on my stove's burner. "A register...it goes back like five years! Hardly anybody's been here during that time" Tom whisked through the pages—vicariously reliving memories of past expeditions through their brief entries.

"Any of those written in English?" I asked.

"Some, but mostly in Spanish...some I have no idea about...some in German...a few in French...and looks like Japanese or something."

"Probably Korean," I said, as I poked a shiny white box of crackers.

"Yeah, I don't know. I can read some Spanish, but not German, and definitely not Korean. A lot of drawings in here too. Pictures of giant hairy monsters on top of the mountain...totally weird, man." Tom flipped through the register's pages, making different faces for each entry. "Looks like most people who come here don't make the summit. A lot of altitude sickness and cold and wind problems. You want to sign it?"

"Sure. But maybe on my way down." I picked up the register and scanned through the hundred or so entries—the number of expeditions increased dramatically through the most recent years. "Looks like as many people passed through here in the last year as did in the previous four combined," I said. Remembering the time I'd spent at Sajama; I hoped that the lonely Bolivian volcano's pristine base camp remained unfettered.

"I wonder what percentage of the people who come through here actually sign that thing?" Tom brought up an excellent point.

"Probably not everyone who passes through here," I answered. Then I remembered the SERNATUR office, and thought that they must keep visitation statistics. "Did you get your permit down in Copiapó?"

"Yeah, just stopped in, signed up, and got it. I had to get it, my driver wouldn't take me up here without one. You got yours, right?"

"I did. Turned it in with the Carabineros at Paso de San Francisco," I said.

"It's nice how anyone can just stop in and get a permit. No fees, no advanced planning, no nothing. I wonder how long that'll last...probably until they start figuring out that they can make some money at this game. I guess that happens when there's enough people coming around. That shouldn't be too long by the looks of the recent years in the register," Tom said with a snicker.

"You brought a tent, right?" I asked.

"Oh yeah, but I'm going to sleep in here tonight. I guess since you're in your tent I got this place all to myself." I looked with disgust at the hut's squalid condition. The bunk cushions sagged, graffiti from every corner of the planet marred the bedframes, stove soot covered everything, and I didn't even want to guess what had been splattered on the floor.

"You really want to sleep in this place?" I asked.

"What?" Tom stopped eating to look me in the eye. Mashed potatoes encircled his lips and chin. "You snobby or somethin'? This place is the Taj Mahal of the High Andes, dude. Check this place out...*pllll-ush.*"

"Well...you know. I've been staying in these huts for the past week, and I'm looking forward to my tent..." Tom stared at me for a few more seconds before going back to slopping food into his mouth.

"Yeah. Sounds good," he said during a brief lull in his storm of ingestion. I finished eating, cleaned my pots, then left Tom alone in his casa for the night.

The following morning dawned clear and calm. I laid in my sleeping bag and stared at the summit of Ojos. I gawked till my neck hurt. When I dropped my head I saw tiny black crickets hopping along the sand outside my tent. "WHHEEEEOOOOWWW!" Tom yelled as I tried to catch one of the small insects. The hut door flew open and out jumped my Andino neighbor, announcing to the world: "I'm gonna take the biggest piss of my life RIGHT NOW! Boy, those Diamox rule! No headache! But man, do I have to *go*! Tell you what though, no wet spots in my sleeping bag!"

"That was like eight or nine years ago, okay," I quipped.

"Wow, check that out dude!"

"What?"

"All these little black grasshoppers, man. Where'd they come from? It's like 17,000 feet and freezing up here."

"Yeah, I was just looking at them. I wonder what they eat. How do they get food?"

"Probably live off climbers' garbage or something. Who knows. Maybe they eat *hot lava*," Tom said as he zipped up his pants.

"Hey dude…Ed!"

"What?"

"You got a magnifying glass?"

"No, why…why would I have a magnifying glass up here?"

"So we can fry the little *muthas* like ants!"

"Just get your stuff together and move up to the next camp. These guys have a hard enough life as it is."

"So what do you think they are? Grasshoppers or crickets?

"I don't know Tom, they're lava-hopping ash crickets."

"Oh, okay, sounds good. Hey…look, another truck's coming our way. More people to join the party!"

I jumped out of my tent. Sure enough, another Hilux struggled toward the hut. I shook off my headrush, relieved myself (less conspicuously than Tom had), and greeted the arriving truck. A tall wiry guy with a huge bush of curly hair and an equally frazzly beard stepped out of the front passenger seat. A sturdily built woman with an ultra-serious look on her face climbed out of the back. They were Jerry and Pavalina, Bulgarians who'd moved to Los Angeles after the fall of the Iron Curtain, and spent most of their time and money absconding from their jobs in L.A. for the world's farthest flung corners.

"I have been in South America for one month now. Pavalina has just joined me to climb Ojos del Salado. I have already summited Aconcagua, and now we see if we can get to the top of Chile." Jerry spoke methodically, but I sensed that at his core he was a smartass. Pavalina, on the other hand, glared at me as a prison guard might eye an escapee. The driver helped the couple unload their gear, agreed that he'd return in ten days, then raced off.

"You are here alone?"

"Well, not any more, I suppose."

"Oh yes…yes, you suppose…alone just like Jerry here. Climbing the Aconcagua mountain by himself—"

"Pavalina…" Jerry rattled off a barrage Bulgarian vituperations at his wife, who immediately returned fire. A five minute screaming match ensued. "Yes, well, we are here now. You have been to the summit?" Jerry asked as if nothing had just happened between him and his wife.

"Not yet. I'm doing a carry to the next camp as soon as I get my things ready. And you two?"

"Maybe tomorrow or the next day we go up," Pavalina answered.

"Okay then, I guess I'll see you up there." I finished the conversation, then packed for the supply-carry to the Tejos Refugio. Ten liters of water, double plastic mountaineering boots, crampons, an ice ax, a bottle of fuel, and a week's worth of food would be the day's haul. I adjusted my trekking poles, heaved my medium-heavy pack onto my shoulders, and set off.

I followed a crude road scribed along the easiest path to the Tejos Refuge. A Hilux couldn't make it; the volcanic sand is deeper than the truck's clearance. Only a Unimog or a tracked vehicle like a bulldozer could climb the steep, sandy grades along the road's path. It felt like I was cheating, walking along a *road* on a mountain that rises over 22,000 feet high. *A road to high camp?*

I tried to set a slow but sturdy pace, forcing myself not to sprint. I lapsed a few times and knocked the wind out of my lungs by jogging. Bent over, I nearly cried from the shock to my chest. I thought about my lack of training before coming to Chile—and I cursed my laziness. 'Training while doing' and 'off the couch' had been my pre-trip mottos. *Stupid...totally stupid*, I thought as I took a long rest just a few hundred feet above the Andino Hut.

After cresting the first hill, the 'road' faded into obscurity as the route traveled through more deep sand, hard-packed rocks, and boulder fields. I lost sight of the Andino Hut after what seemed like an hour of travel. I gauged my upward progress by referencing formations on the slopes of Nevado El Muerto. I surprised myself by my speed. The excitement of ascent overcame the pain of lactic acid in my legs. I fell into a perfect rhythm of trekking—moving my legs, my poles, and my lungs in harmony, with economy.

Soon I reached a small plateau dotted with boulders ranging in size from microwave ovens to small houses. The rocks were colored deep crimson and black, and pocked with elongated vesicles. Many of these boulders appeared wrinkled, if not downright mushed. They looked as if they'd been hucked out of a vent, and hit the ground still molten.

The wind kicked up violently as I wound my way through the garden of boulders. Moving in and out of the huge rocks' wind shadows kept me busy maintaining my balance. The slope tapered nearly to a billiard table level. I navigated a few downslope sections before climbing the final hillock that crested at an overlook of the Tejos Refugio. I scrambled down a 50 yard incline, then walked across a half-ice, half-sand section. Alerted by a trickling sound beneath my feet, I noticed that water flowed gently between the sand and thin sheets of ice. I stopped in the middle of the wide, shallow stream and looked around at fields of white—snow almost completely surrounded the area.

Another 50 yards and I dropped my pack on the side of the Tejos Hut. After catching my breath and quenching my parched throat, I stood back and gawked at the strange sight. The refuge wasn't one shipping container, but two, welded into an 'L' shape.

Much larger than the Andino Hut, the Tejos Refuge looked solid enough to survive a direct hit by a cruise missile. A huge latch held the entrance door locked-shut. I needed both hands to disengage the mechanism, then had to throw all of my weight backwards to open the heavy steel door. Unlike the Andino Hut, I found the interior of the Tejos to be well kept, even inviting. The refuge featured a large, comfortable bunk room, a sizeable kitchen area with table and chairs, and a set of shelves—stocked, of course, with leftover food and water from past expeditions. Even more surprisingly, I found wiring for lights, and a sink! Even the floors, imitation hardwood, had been well kept. I stacked my supplies neatly in an empty corner, then went back outside.

I wanted to lie in the soft sand and bask in the high altitude sun. I felt gentle, warm pulses of endorphins flow through my shoulders, knees, and hips. I closed my eyes; I felt like a big blob of warm wax melting into the sand. Hypoxia, exertion, and the sun's rays acted together as an opiate. I opened my eyes to grasp a firm view of the summit from that altitude. The near-black sky and dark cliffs, the patches of glazen snow, ridges and tiny valleys…I committed all of these views to memory before drifting off to sleep.

"Hey dude! You okay? Hey…HEY? You dead?" I opened my eyes. A blurry view of Tom greeted me. I lifted myself off the ground and rubbed sand from my scalp. "Oh, man…don't do that to me, partner. Whew. You're just lyin' on the ground like a dead guy! A dead guy, man!" I didn't know how long my nap lasted, but it wasn't long enough to prepare for a Tom-type wake up call.

"No, Tom. I'm fine. I'm just taking a nap. Just taking a nap in the sun…out of the wind. Thanks for asking, though."

"Some hike, huh?" Tom continued.

"Beautiful. You feel all right?" I asked.

"Feel great. I think I'll be on the summit of this thing in two days. How 'bout you?"

"I feel pretty good. A little dizzy and slightly out of breath, but good. I'm not sure when I'll be able to make a summit attempt, but I want to be safe…I want to go slowly," I said, reflecting my relaxed mood.

"Yeah, we're at like 19,000 feet. Anything can happen. HAPE, HACE, you know, all of those. You gotta be careful, especially if you're not using Diamox."

"I'm going down. I'll see you a little later, Tom," I said as I knocked on the thick steel skin of the refugio.

"Okay, partner. See you later."

I guzzled some water and sprinted across the 'Río Tejos.' Because my head wasn't hunched over as it had been during the ascent, I noticed my surroundings differently. I saw more, including a large snowfield that I hadn't seen on the way up. I stopped and whirled my arms around like a windmill, stretching the muscles in my shoulders as I peered at some strange snow sculptures. *Nieve penitentes?* I thought, staring at a cluster of ice spires that seemed to be growing from the dry volcanic earth. They were knife-sharp, densely packed, sabot-tipped. I'd read that some of these ice formations dated back thousands of years. I wanted to lay my hands on their ancient forms, to peer into them, to spot bubbles of suspended air held captive since biblical times. I studied the area for photographic vantages before throwing on my pack and heading toward the Andino Hut.

"You have gone to the Tejos Hut?" Jerry asked as I strolled into camp.

"Yeah, got some supplies cached up there; now I'm ready to make my move up for good tomorrow."

"For good...huh...for good...you hope not *for good,*" Pavalina said as she emerged from the hut holding a cup of steaming tea. "Here, this is for you. You don't want to dehydrate. You must stay well."

"Thank you...thanks." I was surprised...shocked. Maybe Pavalina wasn't as cold and hard-edged as my first impression had led me to believe.

"Yes, drink the tea you tough American cowboy. Hopefully your American friends back home won't find out. Only grandmothers drink tea back in America, right?" Jerry mouthed sarcastically.

"Yeah, I actually don't usually drink tea. Never got into it. But don't forget where you are living now, too."

"Sorry. We don't have any Budweisers here with us, or we'd be more than happy to share. You'll just have to manage with the tea. Did your friend Tom make it?"

"Yeah, he made it. He definitely made it."

"Good. Maybe he'll stay up there," Pavalina said, making no attempt to hide her disdain.

"Oh, just shush Pavalina. At least he made it up this far," Jerry shot at her bluntly. I waited for another spat to erupt, but the fight never came.

"How you guys feeling?" I asked as I slurped my tea.

"Okay, maybe. Pavalina isn't doing so well. I think tomorrow is another rest day for us, then we'll try to go to the Tejos Hut the day after."

"There's room for you up there; room for sure." I said.

I rolled over just before dawn, shaking my head. I wanted to find out if I could give myself a headache. I couldn't. I sat upright and shook my head again. No headrush, no headache. I flipped on my headlamp and began packing. I slipped my overloaded camera backpack and extra clothes into the main compartment of the Dana. I rolled the huge tripod into my sleeping pad and buckled it under the top hood flap. I stuffed food and other gear into every available pocket. I crammed my white film bag with more food, five liters of water, and my cookset, and lashed it down tightly onto the back of the

Dana. I stuffed my sleeping bag into the pack's bottom compartment, and tied my tent onto that compartment's outer flap. I propped the entire assembly up with my two trekking poles, stood back, and scratched my head in wonder. All told, I estimated that the thing weighed 110 pounds.

"Oh my god! Just look at this pack! You are not going to carry this, are you?" Pavalina gasped as she emerged from the hut.

"I guess I am. I guess I have to." I closed my eyes, dropped my head, and began breathing deeply. I walked to the megapack, squatted down, passed my right arm through a shoulder strap...closed my eyes again...then heaved harder than I ever thought possible. No muscles, ligaments, tendons—or nylon—tore, and somehow I snapped my knees in the 'stand upright' position and buckled my waist belt. I'd successfully loaded 'It.' "Can you hand me my poles?" I asked.

"Oh, yes...here." Pavalina snatched my poles from the ground and handed them over. I adjusted the poles to perfection and locked down their wrist straps. Then I hunched over and felt the full weight of the pig stress every bone and joint in my body.

"I cannot believe you," marvelled Pavalina. "The pack is bigger than you!"

"Not quite, but almost. I hope I can make it. I won't be able to set this thing down until I get to the Tejos Hut."

"Why?"

"Because I don't want to lift this thing onto my shoulders again for the rest of my life!" I laughed.

"Ooooh god...ooooh god. That looks so...so...terrible! Jerry, you must come and look at this."

"What?" Jerry poked his head out. "Oh, it's not bad. He'll make it."

Encouraging words. I smiled at the 'Bulgarian Connection' then lumbered off...one-step—one-rest—two-step—two-rest, and on and on and up and up....

Nieve penitentes

Ojos del Salado, Detail

| 0 | 1 | 2 | 3 | 4 | 5 | | 10 KM |
| 0 | 1 | 2 | 3 | 4 | 5 MI |

CHILE

Ojos del
Salado

Santiago de Chile •

ARGENTINA

South Pacific Ocean

South Atlantic Ocean

| 0 | 250 | 500 | 1000 KM |
| 0 | 250 | 500 | 1000 MI |

N
W — E
S

Scale: 1:168,960
Map by Ed Darack

◗ Camps With Huts

▲ Peak

— ·· — ·· — ·· —
International Boundary

_____
4 X 4 Route

············
Climbing Route

To Murray Hut
4,500 Meters
(14,763.8 Feet)

Nevado El Muerto
6,470 Meters
(21,277 Feet)

Andino Refuge
5,210 Meters
(17,093.2 Feet)

CHILE

Tejos Refuge
5,800 Meters
(19,028.9 Feet)

Ojos del Salado
6,885 Meters; 22,588.6 Feet

ARGENTINA

CHAPTER ELEVEN

LIFE IN A
CARGO CONTAINER

My tent, my tripod, and the Tejos Refugio

Climbing to the Tejos Hut with that massive, ridiculously out-of-balance backpack was easily the most torturous and oppressive five hours of exertion of my life. I struggled to breathe the dizzyingly thin air; clammy sweat drenched my clothes; my shoulders burned under the pack's deep chafings. Most baneful, however, were the grinding sensations I felt in my joints. My knees, ankles, back, and hips had suffered before, but I'd never worried that a hip would pop out of socket, that a vertebral disk would mash into fragments, or that a patella would burst. I felt like an old burlap sack, stuffed full of bones…overstressed, brittle bones strung together with bungee cords and frayed duct tape.

But, I made it—up the sandy hill, across the boulder-strewn plateau, through the Río Tejos. I arrived at the refugio and gave the cargo container a stiff whack with a trekking pole. I smiled at having hauled my Pentax and its giant tripod to nearly 6,000 meters, on top of the weight of my climbing and camping gear…now I only needed to get all of that stuff *off* my back. Setting the pack down was as difficult an ordeal as lifting it. I tried to squat, but I couldn't hold my balance. I considered falling onto the sand like a felled tree, but…my precious camera equipment. With the pain of my shoulders and hips reaching a boiling point, I knew I had to make a move—any move. So I squatted—lost my balance—and tipped backwards. Just as I looked straight up at the blue of the sky I rolled to my right and thumped on the ground. Nothing graceful about it, but the pack had been landed.

Gravity felt as if cranked way down in intensity during my first moments of backpack-free strolling. I tried to walk off the creaks in my bones and the binds in my joints. No luck. I swayed my hips in small circles. I massaged my lumbar region. I kicked my legs high into the air—I even popped my ankles. Those routines worked—a little. I followed with some stretching and a few high altitude jumping jacks…very few. My musculoskeletal system snapped back into tune by number five. Or maybe that 'snapping back' was just my thin-air imagination.

After pitching camp I shouldered my camera pack and headed east across a flat bed of ash. Five minutes of easy walking brought me to a field of low penitentes. I peered closely at an ice form that stood alone, a few feet in front of a pack of interconnected penitentes. I tapped the penitente's hard surface; it resounded with a deep thud, like a piece of polished ironwood. The form's smooth surface, crystalline clarity, and almost total lack of suspended air bubbles gave it an ancient appearance. The penitente seemed to me not an item of the active present, but a memorial to conditions thousands of years past, preserved in the cold, sterile air of the high Atacama.

I approached the main group of penitentes. Some individuals appeared broader, taller, and possessed more complex features than the pack's lone sentinel. Some were bulbous, some tall and thin, some even had holes in their midriffs. I found the only common trait to be their dart-like general outlines. Elegantly formed beams of ice connected penitentes to each other along an extensive lattice. The ice, sprouting from the mountain's dry volcanic ash, seemed not only alive, but enduring—gracefully tenacious.

I was struck with a dizzy spell when I stood up; I lost my bearings momentarily. I'd eaten only a few bites of a candy bar all day. *A good enough excuse for being tired*, I thought. I really wanted to lie down and take a nap, but I hadn't hauled my camera to that altitude just to let it sit idle. I shook off my headrush and mounted the Pentax on its tripod.

I composed a shot, metered it...closed my eyes—quickly praying that my precious camera had survived the ascent—then I released the shutter. Kerplunk! The mechanism did its job in $1/15^{th}$ of a second—then again in $1/8^{th}$ of a second—and again in $1/30^{th}$ of a second. The Pentax worked flawlessly. I ran through a few rolls of film, exposing scenes of a shadow drifting across the penitente field. I glanced at the highest flanks of Ojos during my third roll change and stood back in excitement. Translucent clouds surrounded the summit—a storm raged. Snow churned through the air, dusting the peak's highest slopes. The inclemency excited me, but it also made me hesitate in a spate of fear. *What if this is some freak, huge storm...I didn't plan for that!*

I quit worrying and composed another shot, using a wide angle lens to include both the ancient, quiet penitentes at my feet, and the ephemeral, rambunctious squall raging above. The lighting was perfect for conveying my impressions of that instant of time—very blue; very cold. After a few frames I stood away from the camera and peered at the azure radiance of the penitente field. A soothing, almost soporific iridescence beamed through the ice trove. The glow radiated the chromatic embodiment of *frigid*.

I ventured farther to the south, toward the 'edge of the plain,' where the relatively flat table of ash, penitentes, and rocks on which I stood dropped off toward the lower lands around the Andino Hut. The sun descended behind a long ridge to the west; icy katabatics fell from colder, higher ground. My exposed flesh numbed almost instantly. I dropped my equipment, yanked a balaclava over my head, and rammed my hands into thick mittens. I windmilled my arms to force blood back into my fingers. I stared at my tent...I wanted to crawl into my warm sleeping bag. I wanted to escape the elements and succumb to my gnawing lassitude. Then I shot a glance toward Nevado El Muerto. The light falling on its western flanks burned so aureate that even the darkest of its crusty black lava flows boasted blonde highlights. I forgot about sleeping bags, tents, and food, and walked trance-like to a small rock alcove overlooking the giant Nevado El Muerto.

The wind roared over the surrounding boulders and whistled across the tips of the penitentes. I nestled into a tiny, protective perch—Eagles' Nest dé·jà vu. I locked my 300mm lens onto the Pentax, stared through the viewfinder, focused…and leaned back against the cold rock. I felt giddy; peering through the clean air, pleasantly dizzied by mild hypoxia, holding my camera, and feeling the throbs of my relaxing muscles made me thank myself repeatedly for making the effort to climb Ojos del Salado.

I stayed in my nest until the last of the day's glow slipped off the summit of Muerto. By then the temperature had fallen well below freezing. Very high, very dry air maintains a day's residual warmth about as well as a chicken wire bowl holds boiling water. I staggered into the wind and set a course for my tent. *Step one…step two…okay, again…step one…step two…keep going.* Glowing twilight washed the area in a shade of blue similar to what I'd seen in the penitente field. I stumbled through a cerulean dream. The wind continued shouting, but I heard nothing; the air became life-drainingly frigid, but I experienced only the notion of cold, not the actual feeling.

"Hey Partner! Yeeehaaaa!" Tom's voice beat me out of my oneiric lapse. "Man, you're like CRAZY dude, carryin' that huge tripod up here. And what's up with setting up your tent? Why don't you come and chill in the *high palace of steel* with me?" I turned to my tent, unzipped it, and set my camera inside.

"Just a second, Tom!" I forced the words into the blustery air. "I have to take care of a few things. I'll come in and we'll make dinner—Okay?"

"Okay!" Tom yelled back, then he scurried into the refuge.

My tent leaned hard to one side under the wind's press. One of the guy lines had partially shredded. I added more rocks to the inside corners of the tent as well as to the tie-down points outside. But I still worried… about further damage to the tent, about a massive tear to the fabric…even the entire tent flying away with all of my things. 19,000 feet isn't quite in the jet stream, but it's close enough. I grabbed my stove and some food, then headed into the hut to see what kind of wisdom Tom had for me that evening.

"Tell you what, Ed, you know that big mountain up there? Huh?" he asked.

"You mean…*Ojos del Salado?*" I replied.

"That mother…is MINE baby. ALL MINE!" Tom punched his fists into the air and hopped around like a cranked-up cheerleader, then he plunked onto one of the kitchen chairs. "Whoa…my head's spinnin'…just a little."

"Are you okay, Tom?" I asked.

"Totally okay. Been poppin' Diamox all day, feel like a million bucks in Vegas baby. Besides, if anything goes bad I got Decadron." Tom's ace-in-the-hole was a diuretic that is sometimes used as a last ditch emergency med for HACE (High Altitude Cerebral Edema) and HAPE (High Altitude Pulmonary Edema). "Whatcha makin' there, hombre?" he asked, red in the face.

"I'm gonna drink some coca leaf tea and then make spaghetti. Want any?" I asked, noting my friend's twitching eyes.

"Yeah, gimme some tea. Heard it works wonders for altitude. Work for you?"

"It works…a little…I think. Probably just a placebo more than anything."

I lit the stove and stared at its yellow flames, which seemed hypnotic. I followed them from the base of the burner up their long, thin paths to their tips where black smoke streamed into the confined air we breathed. "Hey, I better open the door, to keep from asphyxiating us," I said.

"Okay Ed, you're the man," Tom slurred, before slapping his head into his hands. "Smells pretty good to me…I love the smell of burning gasoline in cargo containers at 19,000 feet, man. COME ON! Let's get high on the fumes, dude!" Tom's fingers muffled his voice; he sounded insane.

"When did you get up here?" I asked after bracing the door half-way open with a large rock.

"About three or four hours ago, I guess. I don't know. Does it really matter?" Tom whipped his head out of his hands and looked at me like as if he wanted to embark on a serial killing rampage. "I mean that's a question that my stupid ex-girlfriend would ask. Man I can't stand her! She's all freaked out on powerboats and electric woks and stuff like that. Like one time she asked me about one way streets on the George Washington bridge going to Brooklyn from Manhattan, and I'm like the GW goes to New Jersey, what are you totally nuts or something?" Tom seemed delerious.

"Sure you don't want some spaghetti?" I asked.

"No, I'm not hungry. I don't get all that hungry up in places like this. All I know is that I'm gonna go for it tomorrow."

The priming flames had well-heated my XGK. I carefully opened the fuel valve and the long yellow flames and gentle putterings of prime mode gave way to four rumbling blue claws.

"You see all those candles over there, man…let's start burnin' em, huh?" Tom pointed to a shelf stacked with partially-burnt candles. "You know, for light…I mean now that that thing is running with a pot on it, it's pretty dark in here."

I grabbed a handful of candles and placed them on the table. Tom lit them, then fell back into his chair. I could hear him gasp for air. His wheezings were loud enough to overcome the stove's roar.

"Hey Ed…"

"Yeah?"

"You into movies?"

"I guess," I said.

"Okay, how 'bout this one for you? *Force TOM from Ojos del Salado*. Starring TOM, produced by TOM, directed by TOM…TOM as key grip…whatever a *key grip* does…."

"Sounds pretty good, Tom. I—" I stuttered, "—I mean is that some take on *Force 10 from Navarone?*"

"Nope…totally original. Gonna go for it tomorrow. Hell, I'll be going for it in just a few hours. Like three or four in the morning." The candles lit up Tom's expressions with flickering yellow and orange light; he looked almost as nuts as he sounded. I began to wonder if I'd have to rescue him—or worse yet, fend him off if he really flipped out. I remembered the look of mania on his face as he told me about his ex-girlfriend and the GW Bridge...then I thought about my 15 pound tripod, noting that it would make a great weapon for self defense...I stared at Tom's face. It was plastered with a sinister, almost crazed look. *A stiff blow to the head with the tripod if this nutcase comes after me....*

Surely my thoughts of Tom's potential for crazed behavior were my own delusions. After all, I had been at altitude for over a week, was feeling the effects of the thin air myself, and I hadn't eaten much, either. I dropped some spaghetti in the pot then watched Tom stare blankly at the wall.

"So...why you up here all alone," he asked in an eerie tone after about five minutes of uncomfortable silence.

"Well..." I began hesitantly, "um...I really love the high mountains, and photographing them from up high...as high as I can get on them," I spattered off. "Oh, and the people I meet are...you know...*interesting.*"

"Yeah...I know...*interesting.* I know what you mean, dude," Tom said, pensively. I looked at him, then I looked out the window into the pitch black night. The winds howled ominously, buffeting the refugio with their gusts. I glanced at Tom, at his emotionless expression, at his beady little black eyes—flashing in the candlelight. *Tom is some escaped mental patient with a weird penchant to climb high mountains in South America,* I thought.

"But why are you up here *alone*?" Tom continued his interrogation.

"I guess I just never got around to inviting anybody...besides, its hard to travel with someone like me who constantly stops to take pictures, you know?"

"Yeah...I can't stand that. Makes me really pissed off. Always taking pictures of anything and everything. Reminds me of that guy my ex-girlfriend split me for. Some little photographer from L.A...little bastard. I hate him so much." Tom seethed with rage. "Hey man, maybe I'll have some spaghetti. How 'bout I get some salami to add to it," he said, his anger quelling a bit.

"Sounds good, Tom. I'll just throw some more pasta in." I hummed to myself as I stirred the pot. Tom disappeared into the main bunk-room. I looked for an implement of defense—just in case he returned wielding an ice ax instead of food. *Watch every word,* I thought. *Don't set this guy off.* I dropped more spaghetti into the pot. *The stove...the hot stove...throw it in his eyes if he comes at me. I just can't turn it off. I have to let it keep burning.*

"High altitude trailer park...we be in the DOUBLEWIDE, my man," Tom showed his more jovial side when he returned. "I mean, this really isn't configured in a 'wide' way, more like an 'L', but I guess you could still call it a doublewide, right?"

"Um...yeah Tom...sure...sounds good to me. You get that salami?" I asked as he appeared out of the darkness, holding—I froze, staring at what he had in his hands—a small bag of cheese and meat.

"Yeup! Got it right here, bro. Even got crackers and cheese. Want some?" he asked as he reclaimed his seat.

"No....no thanks." I said, feeling my neck hair settle down.

"No. NO? Whadaya mean, NO? Huh? This is good food, buddy."

"The spaghetti's almost done. Maybe I'll have some of those crackers for dessert." Preparing dinner seemed to take forever. I wanted out of that steel loony bin. I grabbed the pot and strained the water into the dirt outside the hut. "Tom, got a bowl?" I asked.

"Yeah, hold on. Here." Tom handed me a small Sierra cup, well crusted with old food bits and stained with something that looked like dried blood. "Al dente, huh. *Really* al dente, my man. Aren't you gonna shut down the stove?" Tom said as he chomped his dinner.

"Oh...yeah." I twisted the flow knob and choked the supply of fuel to the burner, thinking that I could take care of Tom with my bare fists if he went berserk. "Okay, well...*bon appetit.*"

"Bon jour!" Tom lifted his Sierra cup to me in a toast. "Hey, did you see how those guys got this thing up here?" Tom asked midway through his third scoop of pasta. I shook my head. "It looks like they took rail from a railroad track and welded it into skis, and made a giant sled out of each of these containers. They just dragged them up here, then welded them into a big 'L'. Must have made one hell of a scraping sound every time it went over one of those big rocks!"

"That's interesting Tom...oh well, looks like I'm full. I'll see you tomorrow morning." I aimed for the door.

"Wait!" Tom shouted as I stepped into the night.

"Huh?" I turned.

"Thanks....for the spaghetti...and...and the company," Tom said with a forlorn look. I knew immediately that the guy was totally harmless. I felt stupid for thinking that he might attack me. "You gonna try to make the top tomorrow?" he asked.

"I don't think so. I don't feel so well, but maybe I'll go up for a small hike or something. You going up?" I asked.

"Yeah, I think so. I thought maybe we could go together, though. If you wanted to...I mean...I'll wait a day, whatever."

"Well, I'm not sure exactly *when* I'll be ready for a summit attempt, so I don't want to make you wait for me. I have a ton of food here to keep me going for a week. I'm not going to head up until I feel strong. I could head up in a day from now, or maybe not for five days. So go tomorrow, and if you don't make it and want to try again, then maybe we can head up together," I said.

"Yeah, okay...sounds good. I'll see you tomorrow then. Have a good night." I closed the door and scooted to my tent.

I lay awake in my sleeping bag for hours, occasionally peeking at the refugio's kitchen window. I couldn't see Tom directly, just his shadow on a candlelit wall.

He stayed up for hours after I'd gone to my tent. I wondered what he was up to. There wasn't enough light in the refugio to read a book or write in a journal, and he didn't have a portable radio…I suppose he just stared at the burning candles. And once he blew them out, he couldn't have rested more than an hour before I heard the door squeak open and saw his headlamp bobbing up the mountain. *That guy is such a freak*, I thought, *maybe not maniacal, maybe not homicidal, but just so weird.*

I forced myself to crawl from my warm cocoon a half hour before dawn to hump my camera to a large penitente field that lay to the west of camp. Although the wind had died long before I set off on the morning shoot, my tiny thermometer showed the temperature as 30° Fahrenheit, *below* zero. I tried to balance my breathing to keep from hurting my lungs. Shallow breaths didn't feed my blood enough oxygen; but deep gasps sent shards of pain through my chest as if I had sucked up a fistful of fiberglass.

Handling metal in this weather was tricky. I worried that my hands would freeze onto my tripod. *Will the camera work in this temperature? Will its lubricants freeze? Will the battery die?* I'd pondered the battery problem before leaving for the expedition. I purchased eight new cells (four lithium for cold weather, and four silver oxide) and a cold weather pack—essentially an extension cord that allows the battery to be kept warm in a pocket.

The morning's golden rays drifting down the slope above the penitentes cued me to prepare for shooting. I mounted the 300mm lens and adjusted the focus to razor clarity on my main subject, a fin of ice that stood alone in the dry ash. I forced myself to hold my breath while close to the camera; I worried that otherwise I might fog my lenses. My face must have turned beet red during some of the longer adjustments. The light arrived; I wound through film, always careful to advance each frame slowly to mitigate the chance of tearing it in its cold, brittle state.

After an hour of shooting I returned to my tent, slipped into my sleeping bag, and fell blissfully asleep. I needed the shuteye, if for no other reason than to rest my mind to handle whatever would happen next.

CHAPTER TWELVE

ALONE WITH THE WINDS

Nevado El Muerto, moonrise, from high on Ojos del Salado

I woke in the early afternoon to the snaps and groans of a gale pummeling my tent. The air was surprisingly warm; sweat lightly soaked the inside of my sleeping bag. I licked my lips. Hardened flaps of skin dug into my tastebuds as I moved my tongue over what should have been delicate tissue. My lower lip was split with three deep fissures. My upper lip seemed to have fared better, but chunks of sand had dried into its tissue. *A sign of dehydration.* I thought of the cow and horse mummies at Laguna Verde.

The inner cavity of my nose felt like a sun-hardened lakebed. I closed my mouth and forced air through my clogged nostrils—blobs of dried blood exploded onto my lap. I laid back and nursed a bloody nose for 20 minutes, then slammed a liter-and-a-half of water. I almost drowned myself midway through my gulps as I gasped for air—everything at high altitude, including drinking, has to be done in much smaller steps, much shorter intervals. Simply waking up at 19,000 feet in the Atacama is an ordeal.

I opened my tent to a flood of light and about a dustpan's worth of airborne sand in my face. I jerked the flap shut, put on my sunglasses, and laced up my boots. *One…two…three…*I counted, then whipped open my shelter and sprung into the bright day. The combination of grogginess, altitude, and wind made standing nearly impossible. I staggered around for a few minutes before making a beeline for the refugio.

I searched for Tom. His sleeping bag lay neatly on one of the bunks, but I found no sign of the emotional Coloradoan. *Still up there*, I thought, *I'll set up the camera with a telephoto and look for him later.* In the meantime, I would satisfy a burning curiosity to page through the hut's register.

I scanned entries of people from throughout the globe. The register was much like that of the Andino Hut in its international flavor. The content of those Tejos Hut entries, however, were very different from those of the Andino Hut. The Andino registry notes related the excitement of pushing toward the summit, but those in the Tejos Refugio book told of the ugly realities of treading high on the slopes of Ojos del Salado:

"My husband and I just finished a trip to Vinson Massif, the highest mountain in Antarctica," one entry began, "and the winds and cold temperatures were nothing like we had ever experienced, that is, until we came to Ojos del Salado. This place is unbelievably windy and cold. It is even worse than the worst day at high camp on Vinson. We can't believe it. We made it to about 500 feet below the summit crater, then had to turn back. It was just too much…"

Other entries told of parties splitting up high on the mountain, severe altitude sickness, and a few told of deaths. I shut the cover of the well-worn book and pushed it off to the far side of the table.

Walking outside I scanned the bright patches of snow high on the mountain. I braced myself against the door of the hut and squinted, trying to pick out tiny details of the mountain's highest slopes…a trail, a faint path, anything that would reveal a route to the summit. I wanted the peace of mind of knowing the lay of the route; more importantly, however, I wanted to spot Tom to see if he was okay. I easily picked out some switchbacks on the slopes above the hut, but couldn't resolve anything beyond that.

A thin layer of fleet cirrus cast shadows on one of the larger snowfields, quelling the snow's glare and allowing me to see a faint line traversing the field. I ran to my tent and grabbed my Nikon. I quickly had the 80-200 zoom with a 2X teleconverter fixed dead on the route. *A dot!…but was it moving?* I backed away from the viewfinder, rubbed my eyes, then peered through the high grade optics again. Sure enough, the dot moved—not smoothly, not consistently, but it moved. *It has to be Tom*…but then I noticed more moving specks. I backed away and stared with my naked eye. Of course I couldn't see anything. "Who is that? Who's up there?" I yelled to myself in a miffed tone, wondering how they—whoever *they* were—got so high on the mountain without spending even a night at the Tejos Hut. I loosened the drag on my ball head and panned the camera around the snowfield and started counting: 14 dots in total, moving down the mountain.

Scrape…whisk…scrape…whisk…. The telltale sounds of trekking poles moving over volcanic sand grabbed my ears. "Hello there, Ed…whew, you're alive!" Jerry yelled out.

"Of course he is alive. Why do you say such things?" Pavalina decried.

"Yes, he is okay, look. Looking up toward the Slovenians with his camera," Jerry said as he dropped his pack and shook my hand.

"Slovenians? That's who's up there?" I asked.

"A giant bunch of Slovenian doctors and their friends," Pavalina spewed.

"How come they didn't stay here for the night?"

"Thought they could just race up from the lower hut. I wonder how high they got?" Jerry asked.

"At least to that high snowfield." I pointed to the large swath of white. "Are you guys staying here or just doing a carry?"

"No, oh no. Jerry could stay, but I have not the acclimatization to be here for a night. I still don't feel well, so we have to drop some of our gear here and head back down. You are feeling well?" Pavalina asked.

"Okay. A little low on energy, some headaches now and then, but mostly just resting and enjoying this place. I think maybe I'll take a short day hike a little later…. Just to see," I said.

"Hey look. Here comes someone…alone…I think the other American…Tom, your buddy." Jerry pointed to a lone figure, ungracefully descending the slopes a few hundred yards from the hut. The three of us headed toward him.

"Hey! Hey Tom…that you?" I yelled. The climber stopped, lifted his trekking poles into the air, and swung them back and forth.

"YEEEEEAAAAAHHHH! It's me…Tom!" came a slightly muffled bellow.

"Oh god, this one is so…so…*crazy*," Pavalina uttered under her breath. Tom plopped to the ground and clasped his hands together between his legs. He looked like a big kid who'd been playing in a sandbox all day and was waiting for his mommy to bring him some juice. Jerry, Pavalina, and I looked at each other then ran up to him to see if he was okay.

"I just don't know about this guy. Why is he up here?" Pavalina asked as we hopped between boulders.

"For the same reason that you are here!" Jerry shot back. Pavalina stopped in her tracks, threw down her trekking poles, and began crying.

"I'm here for you, Jerry!" Another high-speed torrent of Bulgarian filled the thin air of Ojos del Salado. I turned my head and continued walking quickly to Tom.

"Hey dude! What's up, my man? Got some whiskey for me?"

"Are you okay, Tom?" I asked.

View north from near the Tejos Hut

"Yeah, of course I am." He flicked some rocks back and forth between his hands like a game of Paleolithic pong.

"How high did you get?" I asked as I picked his backpack off the ground.

"I don't know. Maybe halfway between the hut and the summit. I just sat down at sunrise and fell asleep. I got a little higher later on, then fell asleep again. I got this really bad headache, but it's goin' away now. Think I'm gonna head on down to the lower hut and catch a ride out with those South African people. They got three trucks and one driver guide waiting down there."

"South Africans?"

"Yeah, South Africans, a whole bunch of 'em up there."

"You mean *Slovenians*?" I annunciated very carefully.

"Yeah, whatever. Hey, let's get going on down. I wanna get some beer to-night. If those guys move fast enough I'll be in the bar within ten or eleven hours!" Tom said as he stood up. "Hey, what's their problem?" Tom pointed to Jerry and Pavalina shouting at each other.

"Oh, I don't know. Maybe we should take the scenic route back to the hut, let them have some time to themselves."

"No way, man. I love watching couples fight! Let's go check 'em out!"

"Oh! You are okay!" Jerry yelled with a big grin when he saw Tom.

"Did you make it?" asked Pavalina.

"Nope. Not even close. But I'm ready to party!"

The four of us relaxed for a few minutes at the Tejos Hut before Tom, Pavalina, and Jerry started down.

"See you tomorrow…maybe," Pavalina said to me as the trio trudged across the Río Tejos.

"Okay, I'll probably be here," I said as I considered taking a short hike.

"¡Adios, amigo!!!" Tom yelled. "Take it slow, man, get up this mu-duh!"

"Okay…okay, Tom," I said. The trio disappeared into a boulder field and I packed some water and food for my small jaunt. I started up the switchbacks at the base of the route; for what seemed like two hours I did nothing but stare at the ground and move myself higher…very steadily.

I felt the warmth of exertion pulse into my head from my chest…*my face is probably beet red*, I thought as I stopped for a rest. I sat on a rock, looked down toward the refugio, and felt a slight ring of vertigo. A jab of adrenaline pumped into my arms and legs. *I really gained some altitude*, I thought as I squeezed my eyes shut and massaged my temples. A few hundred yards to the east of me the Slovenians scampered down toward the hut. "Hello—hello!" some of the group yelled as they passed by. I wondered how high they got…I wondered if any made the summit.

The 'climbing' to that point was anything but. Mostly steep hiking that re-quired no more technical prowess than you'd need to walk up a steep San Francisco street during a rainstorm. I looked to the west and noticed a huge staircase of rocks. *A different route? Looks challenging…I'll check it out when I get down*, I thought before continuing higher. The trail petered out to noth-ing after about ten more minutes of ascent. I sat down and studied the route above before heading back to camp.

I faced the door of the Tejos Refugio an hour later. The wind kicked hard and dusk loomed, but I felt warm nonetheless. I dropped my pack and stared at the strange building. I studied the weathered paint, the ribbed construction; I inspected the ski rails that some determined souls had used to drag the con-tainers to that altitude.

The dead employees from the helicopter crash…the hut had been erected, in part, to memorialize the mining company employees, according to Tom.

Why had they been flying around the peak...sightseeing? Memorials in Latin American countries are typically elegantly simple affairs: crosses inscribed with names, sometimes adorned with colorful flowers. Even the more ornate shrines incorporate a crucifix into some part of their structure. I searched for a cross or a plaque...*nothing*. I'd never seen such a sterile, detached memorial as the Tejos Refugio. The history, as told to me, just didn't make sense. But maybe there's more to the story than any visitors know; maybe a lot more. I felt chilled, not from the air, but from my thoughts of the dead. How many had died on these cold, high slopes? What were their last thoughts? Did they die in peace? *I have this cold, high place all to myself for the night.*

I stared intensely at the door of the hut, at its big latch, its reinforced hinges. I felt enervated, exhausted...I wanted to sleep, but I couldn't—I couldn't pry my thoughts off those who'd perished. I swung the door open, lit one of the candles, then bolted to take pictures.

I grabbed my Pentax and headed for the edge of the plain to shoot more images of penitentes. I encountered the same cerulean glow as I'd experienced during my first night of shooting in that area, but in an entirely different field of the spiny ice formations. The blue faded as a sickle of pink light crept off the summit of Nevado El Muerto; a full moon rose. I shot the moonrise as many ways as I could devise, before the evening grew dark and cold. I searched for my headlamp...*not in my bag; back at camp?* I couldn't see the refugio, so I aimed toward where I thought it was and started walking—into a stiffening wind.

A faint outline of the hut appeared. I focused on the dim visage and searched for the flicker of candlelight...*nothing, completely dark. Did it burn out?* I wondered. I quickened my pace as I closed on the refugio. I swung open the hut's door and found the flame robustly glowing.

I lit a few more candles, then ran out to my tent and searched for my headlamp. *The damned wind.* It careened through the area in great gusts, creating more noises than usual. I knew how miserable that wind could make life for me. I needed to get to my light just to be able to cook, to dress in warmer clothes, to fix my tent if something broke, to find aspirin should a headache grip me— even to open my tent to relieve myself. I padded my hands around the floor, throwing clothes out of stuff sacks and spilling packs of food everywhere. I was so close to wailing in anger...I threw up my hands and clawed at my matted, greasy hair...then I found the light—right where it was supposed to be, in one of my tent's gear pockets.

Other than promote headaches, nausea, lassitude, and ataxia, altitude plays some less noticeable, albeit vexing tricks on the body, such as numbing perception. My olfactory receptors had all but been shut off; I couldn't remember smelling anything good—or bad—since I'd arrived at the Tejos Hut...but, I reasoned the effect derived as much from the cold as from thin air. The altitude also quelled my ability to taste. I experienced only the impressions of hunger:

globs of food stuffing my mouth, those globs in a semi-chewed state descending my throat, followed by a feeling of vague satiation. My body's tactile response had also been nulled. My fingers, toes, nose, and cheeks felt like anesthetized tabs of flesh. The most incommodious loss of perception, however, was my strained hearing. I felt as if a buffer sat between my ears and those nerves within my head responsible for making sense of sonic vibrations. I felt as if gum had been lodged deep within my tympanic cavity, pressuring my eardrums and jaw.

With my warped hearing and hypoxia, I constantly thought I heard human voices. As I stared at the candlelight that evening, I'd hear my name whispered. Sometimes I'd hear someone call me from a distance. I felt my heart race; my hands jittered on the table...my neck even started to hurt from jerking my head over my shoulder to see 'who' spoke to me. Sometimes I'd hear two—or more—people speaking with each other. Sometimes I heard laughing; sometimes screaming; sometimes crying; sometimes blood-curdling moaning. Sometimes I'd hear a friend's voice; other times a famous voice; often I couldn't recognize the voice at all.

Storm clouds as seen from Tejos Hut camp

I stared through a window. The nightscape seemed so empty, so incredibly vast and unforgiving. The landscape appeared green under the light of the full moon. The light soothed me; I fell asleep.

I woke up in complete darkness some time later, shivering like mad. The candles had burned out. I found my right hand stuck to a cake of dried wax. The moon had set; I could see nothing, absolutely nothing. The wind and the 'voices' it brought, however spoke more vociferously than ever. I jumped out of my chair to search for my headlamp. I cursed myself for being at the Tejos Hut. I was sick of the place, of the feelings of weakness, of the headaches, and especially of the voices.

The first light of dawn had arrived by the time I zipped myself into my sleeping bag. *Sleep doesn't really matter, right? I'll 'sleep when I'm dead' and that might not be too far in the future, right?* I decided to make a go for the summit, if for no other reason than to feel alive again. But life at the Tejos Hut was about to become even more bizarre.

Waning gibbous moon rising over Nevado El Muerto

CHAPTER THIRTEEN

NEVER-NEVER LAND

Hubble Space Telescope zooms toward the central Andes

I snapped-to quickly. My heart hammered blood throughout my vasculature and my deep, voluminous breaths poured oxygen into my lungs. My thoughts became sharp and focused, my steps were powerful and regular, and my eyes and hopes were trained on the summit. 15 minutes later, the big orange hut was a tiny orange dot and my body's pulsing warmth was beating back the morning's steely chill. No headache, no spasms, no joint aches. All systems go.

The sun broke over a ridge to the east and drenched the slopes around me with golden rays. I pulled off my balaclava and unzipped my jacket, feeling the air temperature race higher. I looked toward the summit: dark rocks surrounded by darker skies. Not a single cloud or even the weakest breeze. I turned to measure the expanse of desert stretched out below my feet. I felt as if I had the entire Atacama in my grasp.

Life wasn't so rosy a few hours later. I had to breathe two or three times for every step I took. And each step wasn't really a step up, but three quarters or a half step, when factoring 'slippage' on the loose volcanic ash.

My pace slowed even further during the next hundred feet of climbing. I was well over 21,500 feet, but the snowfield crossing, an integral part of the ascent, stood well over 300 feet distant.

I reached the snowfield crossing by mid-afternoon. The snow itself appeared to be glazed with ice, making it more of an icefield, where a slip could land me a good thousand feet below. I felt like trying to run across without crampons. I almost lunged for it…but then I regained my senses.

I sat down, strapped on my crampons, pulled out my ice ax, and stood up…then noticed the rock staircase I'd seen the day before. The route was even more appealing than when I'd first noticed it. At least a thousand feet remained between me and the summit. I pondered my options…then I noticed storm clouds approaching. *Forget this*, I thought, *head for the rock route tomorrow.* I pulled off my crampons and shot back down toward my tent.

I found the hut's door wide open when I arrived. Jerry and Pavalina sat at the kitchen table, drinking tea with two other climbers. "Hey there, cowboy! Make it?" Jerry asked.

"Nope," I replied, feeling happy to have company.

"Oh, well, maybe you'll try again, huh? Maybe with us."

"I have it in me for one more shot…one more, then I have to throw in the towel and find a shower," I said.

"Here, take my seat. You deserve it. So how high did you get today?" Jerry asked as he stood up from the table.

"Thanks for the seat. I don't know for sure, I think about 6,500 meters, or more, maybe up to 21,500 feet, near the top of the big snowfield up there." Only Jerry and I spoke. Pavalina rested her head against the wall, and the two men accompanying the couple stared vacuously at the kitchen table.

"Introduce them, Jerry. Introduce them!" Pavalina said in a pained tone.

"Yes, Ed, this is Patrick and this is Jaromir."

"Nice to meet you," I said. "Where are you from?"

"I am from Czech Republic," Jaromir said as his expression flashed from blank to vivacious. I looked toward Patrick, and waited for his response. "Patrick is not feeling well at all. Not at all," Jaromir added.

"Patrick is from Germany. A big strong German fellow, but not strong enough for this place," Jerry commented, smirking.

"No, I am not feeling so good," Patrick gasped with a deep guttural bellow. His face appeared translucent, his eyes were cranked wide open, his lips were dried and cracked. He looked to be a half step from death.

"These two have come up here very fast. Very fast," groaned Pavalina. "I cannot believe how fast they came up."

"How long did it take you to come up here?" I asked Jaromir.

"I came up with Patrick yesterday to the Andino Hut from Copiapó, and today we have come up here."

"That's impossible!" I yelled. "From near sea level to almost 19,000 feet in two days! No way. I don't believe you."

"Look at him, he is a tough eastern European, like Pavalina and me!" Jerry boomed.

"Hey, man, look...do you feel okay? I've never heard of anything like this. Did you acclimatize at all before you did this?" I asked.

"My fiancée and I have just climbed the Licancabur volcano near San Pedro de Atacama, farther to the north of here. We felt fine there. That is a mountain just below 6,000 meters. We climbed it in one day—up and down from San Pedro. We were acclimatized to the altitude of San Pedro, I think it is around 3,000 meters," Patrick spoke up.

"How long ago was that?" I asked.

"A little more than a week ago, I think. I am very dizzy now. I cannot talk anymore or I fear I will begin to vomit." Patrick dipped his head into his hands. I could hear him struggling for air.

"Are you all nuts? Do any of you care that this is absolutely insane? You are toying with death, you know that, don't you?" I shouted.

"Oh, come on, Ed. Real life is not like those soft little mountain safety books you read back in California. Pavalina and I have been through so much more. Look at Jaromir here, nothing even bothers him. He is fine. He is fine because he has never read any of those crazy books."

"SHUT UP Jerry! Shut UP! Ed is right, these guys are SO crazy," Pavalina screamed. "Look at Patrick, he is about to die. We are going to have to carry his body down from this place. We are going to have to give the dead body to his fiancée!"

"Where is Patrick's girlfriend?" I asked.

146

"She's in Copiapó. She didn't feel like coming up here," Pavalina answered.

I stared at Jaromir's eyes. His pupils appeared normal. His skin wasn't discolored. I couldn't believe he was unaffected by the extreme altitude shift.

"Jaromir, are you sure you feel fine?" I asked.

"Yes. Fine. I feel strong. I am going to go for the summit tomorrow after a rest here. I have been dreaming about this mountain for years. It is very difficult for me to get away from my work back in Prague, and I don't have much time. I would also like to climb Tupungato, down by Aconcagua. I have to make the summit of Ojos within the next few days." Jaromir spoke lucidly.

"How did you and Patrick meet?" I asked.

"Down in Copiapó. His fiancée didn't want to climb, and he didn't want to go alone. We bumped into each other in the SERNATUR office. So we hired a guide to take us up here. He's waiting at the Andino Hut with his truck."

"A guide? Or a driver?" I asked.

"A guide-driver. He drove us into the hut, and then pointed out the route."

"He didn't think anything of coming all the way up to the Andino Hut in one day, and then you guys coming all the way up here the next day?"

"He does the drive to the Andino Hut all the time, sometimes he brings three groups up here per week during the main season. He never asked about how well acclimatized we were," Jaromir replied, matter-of-factly.

"I wish I had your acclimatization ability! How do you feel, Pavalina?" I asked.

"I feel okay, not great, but much better than Patrick here."

"Look, a storm is coming in," Jerry said. We walked outside. Thick, white clouds enveloped the summit of Ojos; ribbons of high stratus coalesced into a large, gray blanket. Shadows disappeared, the wind died, and the temperature began sliding. "I think that the skies will be having some fun with us tonight!" Jerry added.

"Come on, let's get a bed ready for Patrick," Pavalina said. "If a storm really does come in, and Patrick gets worse, then we won't be able to get him out of here. He should at least have a good bed to sleep in."

"I think we should think about getting him out of here right now," I said.

"Okay, Ed. Let's fit him into your backpack and you can carry him down. All 90 kilograms of him...What is that in pounds? Let's see...that's like...Oh, I don't have my calculator...oh, 200 pounds, right? You should be able to handle it, right?" Jerry smirked at me.

"I think it'll take a few of us," I added, annoyed.

"If he gets bad enough then Jerry, Pavalina, and I will help him down from here. You can help if you want, but I think that we should be able to handle the rescue. I think he will start feeling better, though," Jaromir said.

Jerry and Jaromir walked back inside. Pavalina approached me.

"Pssst! Hey Ed! This is so crazy! We have to get Patrick down from here. He's going to die. I know it. Go in there and look at him. Jerry doesn't care and Jaromir is just so crazy! I can't carry that big German guy down by myself. I need your help. I saw you carry that huge pack up here. You could probably carry that guy down yourself—"

"—Listen, that just about killed me! And that guy is like twice the weight of the pack I carried. No way can I carry him!" I interrupted.

"But the two of us together? We can do it!"

"Let's just wait to see if his condition improves." I felt as if I was giving up…I knew that his condition probably wouldn't improve, but I just couldn't fathom bringing him down. "I don't think that its an emergency yet, but close to it. Once it gets serious, then we have to act—we are going to need Jerry and Jaromir's help, though," I added.

"OH GOD! You men are all the same. Just so STUPID! I just hate all of you men. Don't care about anything! Don't care about anything but yourselves. This is an emergency right now! He could be dead for all we know! He could be drowning in his own blood in his lungs right now, you stupid!"

"Look, calm down! Okay? I'm exhausted, you know. I don't feel so great myself. None of us do. This is living misery, living misery for…*I don't know what*. I don't even know why I came up here. All I know is that I don't want to go down yet. I want…to get to the summit," my voice tapered off.

"You see there, you men, just wanting the stupid goal. Meanwhile Patrick is in there dying. Think of his poor fiancée down there in Copiapó. What will she do when she gets him back in a bag? Huh? What about his mother? Think about her. She probably won't ever see him again! I have seen so much misery and death in my life. I don't want any more!" Pavalina began sobbing.

"Okay—okay—okay! You win, Pavalina. You win. You're right, let's get him out of here." Pavalina composed herself—within seconds she was back to looking like an emotionless Stalag security guard.

"Jerry, Jaromir! Come on, we're getting Patrick out of—*what the?*" I yelled, then stopped dead in my tracks. Patrick was standing on his hands, walking around the kitchen as Jerry and Jaromir laughed.

"You see, cowboy, look. He's a tough German guy. Pavalina start crying for you? Trying to get you to turn against me?" Jerry said with a huge grin.

"Hallow Ed! Nice to meet you, upside down and all!" Patrick said—red in the face. He flipped back over and shook my hand. "I guess that gets rid of my headache, huh?…wow!…a little dizzy now." My eyes widened; I felt the hair on my neck stand up. I backed into the corner of the room.

"Who are you people?" I asked, my voice wavering with fear, confusion, and absolute amazement.

"You see, Ed, here is the German superman! Ha—ha—ha!" Jerry exclaimed.

"You hungry for some Chilean soup, made by a crazy Czech guy?" Patrick asked me. "Look at this guy's state-of-the-art stove. Nothing we make in

Germany could ever compare to this masterpiece!" Patrick pointed to a burnt soup can that Jaromir filled with quarter-sized white pellets.

"What's that stuff?" I asked.

"Solid state fuel. Soviet issue, leftovers from the Dark Ages. Works great."

"It smells carcinogenic," I snipped.

"Oh, well, you know the Soviets, they never cared about anything like that. Just so long as it worked, and this stuff does. Always works. You can even use it in the rain to keep warm." Jaromir dropped a match into the soup can, igniting a light blue flame that danced above the lip of the can.

"Okay, I guess I'm hungry. Soup sounds good," I said.

"Excellent!" said Jerry. "I think we are all going to be great friends by the end of all of this!" The five of us squeezed around the kitchen table as Jaromir cooked a bowl of chicken soup. I couldn't help but eye Patrick; I felt suspicious

Storm enveloping Ojos del Salado

of his miraculous recovery. Many times, in the darkest depths of AMS, I could jump out my dire state for a few minutes and run, do jumping jacks, do pull-ups, just about anything—only to have the sickness slam me back to painful reality. Pavalina acted suspicious as well. We looked at each other and shrugged.

"Tomorrow we'll all stand on the summit of Ojos del Salado! Let's make a toast!" Jerry shouted.

We talked until well past nightfall as the weather continued to worsen. The hut shook in the wind, and snow fell steadily. But the company of others made each of us ignore the inclemency—and Patrick's condition. None of us noticed his slow deterioration that began some time after we ate Jaromir's soup. We finally paid attention when he lunged for the door—tripping over his feet and crashing onto the floor.

"Oh no! What is wrong?" yelled Pavalina.

"I think that Patrick wants to go pee-pee," answered Jerry.

"No, this is worse than before," said Jaromir. "I don't like this. Look at him. He's shaking."

"More than shaking, he's convulsing!" I said as I knelt down beside him. I rolled him over—his face had turned purple and his lips blue. His eyes shot open and he reached his hands toward me.

"Silke! Hilfe! Hilfe! Hilfe!"

"What? What is he saying?" I looked up to Jerry.

"He is saying he needs help," answered Jerry.

"Silke is his fiancée. He thinks that you are his fiancée, Ed. I think we'd better get him out of here!" Jaromir yelled.

"What's he saying?" I pleaded. "Does he have some condition he's trying to tell us about?"

"We should have gotten him out of here. I told you!" Pavalina shrieked.

"Shut up Pavalina. Shut up! He's speaking nonsense. He is out of his mind. Look, he has cerebral edema. He's hallucinating, convulsing like mad. It's like the devil is inside of him. He won't survive the night," Jerry said.

"NO! NO! NO! Hilfe! Hilfe! Hilfe!" Patrick screamed.

"Shut him up, smack him! Do something!" Pavalina yelled.

"Smack him? What? Why don't we just beat him on the head with a rock? Pavalina! Are you crazy, you don't smack him!" Jerry yelled back.

"Okay, everyone calm down! Pavalina, get his things. Jerry, you and I will carry him down. One of us for each shoulder," Jaromir commanded.

"I'm not coming back up here. Never again. I'm not! I hate this place!" Pavalina yelled, then started crying. "Jerry, we have to take our stuff down with us! I don't want to come back up here!"

"Okay, fine. Dump all the food and water out of our packs, we'll just take our equipment, nothing else," Jerry commanded.

"Ed, are you going to stay up here?" Jaromir asked.

"I need to help you two carry him down—"

"—but will you come back up here with me?" Jaromir asked as he laced up his boots.

"No. No way. Once I go down, I'm not going to come back up—"

"—Okay, then stay up here. I'll be back tomorrow. Just wait one day for me. I don't want to go up alone. We'll go together, yes?"

I looked out the window at the wretched conditions. *The three of them can get Patrick down just fine, It won't do any good if I go.* I tried to justify my urge to stay in the hut.

"Fine, but…are you sure that you three can carry your things and Patrick—and his things—down?"

"Who cares about his backpack…Pavalina, get his sleeping bag; and find his jacket and storm pants. Put them on him," Jerry barked.

Patrick flew into an intense spasm, curling into the fetal position, then he retched his chicken soup all over my chest. "Don't worry about it, Ed, we'll take care of everything with him, then you can help me take down some of his things after we summit," Jaromir said as I shook off Patrick's dinner.

"Fine, whatever. Just get him down safely."

"Good luck to you guys," I said after we'd dressed Patrick. Jerry kicked open the door and the four of them staggered into the howling gale.

"I'll see you tomorrow, Ed!" Jaromir yelled. "We'll go to the summit!"

"Yeah, I'll see you. Be safe. Hey, Jerry and Pavalina—good luck, huh. I'll see you back down at the Andino Hut, or maybe even in Copiapó!" The foursome disappeared into the stormy night. I slammed the door then watched through the window as the glow of their headlamps faded. *Alone again in the Tejos Hut.*

CHAPTER FOURTEEN

BLOWN OFF

Summit of Ojos del Salado

I waited the entire day for Jaromir's return to the Tejos Hut. He never arrived. I passed the time resting, eating, writing in my journal, and reading a trashy mystery novel that I'd found buried under a pile of leftover food. The storm that had raged through the night dissipated by midday, allowing me to traipse around with my camera for a few good photography sessions.

That day was my fifth at the Tejos Hut. Five days at an altitude just shy of 19,000 feet. I could feel that my body was chewing on itself just to maintain its basic functions. A human body simply cannot maintain normalcy for more than a few days at altitudes above 17,000 feet. Cells no longer repair and replace themselves quickly enough to keep pace with the rate of cellular damage and deterioration; no amount of acclimatization can overcome this reality. Cardio-pulmonary fitness can be ramped up for brief periods of time at this elevation, but in terms of overall physiological wellness, *Homo sapiens* simply wasn't engineered to run around in the Tropopause.

The very highest 'permanent' human settlement existed at just below 17,000 feet in Tibet. The inhabitants of this community, which was occupied for only three to four months per year, abandoned it in the early 1930s. Incidentally, after their occupation of Tibet in the 1950s, the Chinese built a town at 5,100 meters (16,732 feet) on the Quinghai-Tibet road. Called Wenquan, military personnel and support workers occupy this lung-wrenching settlement.

The term *Death Zone* was originally coined by a Swiss Doctor named Edouard Wyss-Dunant in his 1952 book, *The Mountain World*. Wyss-Dunant, who almost reached the summit of Everest during the 1952 Swiss Everest Expedition (the peak was finally climbed a year later by Norgay and Hillary), dramatically portrayed the effects of altitude on human physiology and defined a number of acclimatization zones. He termed the highest of these zones the *Todeszone* (German for Death Zone) and demarked it to begin at the 7,500 meter (24,606 feet) altitude level. At this altitude and above, Wyss-Dunant stated, not only could normal human functions not be maintained, but they rapidly deteriorated—even with the use of supplemental oxygen. He also described the zone between 6,000 and 7,000 meters (19,685 to 22,965 feet) as a region where very limited, short-term acclimatization is possible—but death always looms. The Swiss doctor also created a definition for the region between 7,000 and 7,500 meters: a zone where acclimatization was impossible.

The Death Zone has since been readjusted to 8,000 meters (26,240 feet), for a variety of reasons. Maybe the term needs to be amended again, and perhaps additional terms should be added: 'Super Fast Death Zone' for 8,000 meters and above, 'Fast Death Zone' for 7,000 meters and above, and 'Plain Ole Death Zone' for 6,000 meters and higher. Or 'Death Zone,' 'Deader Zone,' and 'Deadest Zone.' Regardless of monikers, the Tejos Hut lies at an altitude where a human's days are numbered—and I was definitely approaching my limit.

I made a huge dinner of spaghetti and mashed potatoes that evening. Then I stared at the bowl of glop as it quickly cooled. I raced to force the food down before it froze. Eating was never so difficult. I think I managed to consume just over a thousand calories per day during my stay at the Tejos Refuge. Those who study high altitude physiology insist that an average sized male needs to ingest around 5,000 calories just to maintain the physiological status quo. I pondered this fact as I slopped into my mouth the last hunks of food I could eat that evening...*Impossible...no way.* I ate less than half of what I'd prepared; one more bite would have triggered a puking fit—then I'd have to begin my night's force-feed all over again.

I woke about an hour before dawn on what I deemed would be the last possible day for me to make a summit attempt. This time, however, instead of heading straight up the standard route, I would angle off to the west, setting a course for the base of the rock staircase.

The sun beamed powerfully, warming my skin and the dark rocks. The staircase turned out to be more difficult than the standard route, but I enjoyed the climbing far better. I didn't find a scintilla of evidence of past human passage. Not a footprint, not a candy wrapper, nothing. I felt as if I was breaking new ground; I was certain, however, that I wasn't pioneering a novel route—too many people visit Ojos for someone to have not tried this obvious line.

I struggled onto a broad, gently sloping plain at the top of the staircase in the early afternoon. The wind was fearsome. I dropped to my knees to rest. I stared at the edge of the summit crater, adjusted my trekking poles, and moved slowly against the wind, gravity, and my growing fatigue.

I have this mountain all to myself...this is amazing, I thought during one of my frequent rests. The intense solitude gripped me; I loved the feeling. I had only myself to rely on. Just me in the raw elements; no thoughts of anything but moving upward, breathing, and drinking some water every now and then. Nothing complicated, nothing convoluted. *This...this is really what I came here for...nothing else could ever be this good.*

So little land on this continent stands higher than I am right now. Volcano after volcano marched into the crystalline distance. Peaks that appeared so daunting and huge from the floor of the Puna now seemed insignificant. *The horizontal versus the vertical...*I remembered one of the most jarring of all mountain geography lessons: even in the world's greatest mountain areas, the horizontal massively overwhelms the vertical. I say *jarring* because I used to imagine—as I often still do—that the planet's greatest peaks protrude dominantly above entire continents. The reality of mountain scale is that if the world were reduced to a five-foot diameter ball, not even the most tactilely gifted person could feel the miniscule ripple that Ojos del Salado—and all of the Andes—would form. And now that I was near the absolute of the area's vertical, I was staring straight at this lesson of earth scale rise/run ratios.

High cirrus motored toward me from the west; winds boomed down faster and harder. I felt apprehensive about moving farther up the mountain. The view was so beautiful...I wanted more—but the moment seemed so committing, so serious. I was treading a place that demands respect; a place that affords no protection from the whims of the atmosphere; a place that offers no hope for salvation should I screw up or succumb to my physical limitations.

I stood up after a long, contemplative rest. The wind gushed like a whitewater rapid during spring melt. I struggled to breathe as I had during the windstorm outside of the base camp hut. But the air near the summit is much thinner, and it roars much faster. The sun chiseled at any bit of exposed flesh; the wind felt as if it was not just blowing on me, but blowing *through* me; and the volcanic earth under my feet might as well have been the surface of a distant asteroid. The ground seemed truly rarified, somehow blessed. I felt slightly uncomfortable walking on the sharp rocks, as if I was committing some sort of volcanic sacrilege. *Lucky rocks*, I thought...*so high, such a great view...not covered in snow...how could rocks be so lucky? As close to another planet I could ever get without actually leaving this one.*

I stood inside the summit crater. *Fumaroles*...I remembered my cogitation about the volcano's classification. I searched for some sign of sulfurous vents, some noxious odor, some yellow-white steam. *Nothing.* If Ojos is an active volcano then its activity was in another place that day. But while I found no signs of current volcanism, the crater itself appeared as if it had recently erupted. The slopes surrounding the concave inner basin seemed poised on the brink of collapse. Rocks and boulders of all shapes, sizes, and colors lay haphazardly strewn about, as if weathering had yet to begin post-eruptive sculpting.

I walked a few steps clockwise and found a faint trail that coursed along the edge of the snowfield on the crater's eastern wall. I followed it with my eyes—the path led to the south, then disappeared into a small cleft in crumbly, dark volcanic rock—the summit crown of Ojos del Salado. I easily hiked the trail for about 50 yards, then the route's slope steadily increased as it shot directly toward the large notch that marked the last of the climb.

The winds hounded me as I climbed higher. The western lip of the crater gave me some 'wind shadow' protection when I hiked relatively low on its shoulders, but once I closed on the notch, I felt the wind's full force. *The last few steps to the top of the highest volcano in the world!* I stopped about 100 yards from the notch and shot a photograph of the chunky summit. The air's velocity at that point was too much. Fear burst through me—I couldn't see a place to hide; I couldn't bear the wind's incredible roar. I dropped to my knees and crawled.

The wind lulled. I stood and took a few steps higher. But the thin air had killed my judgment—I wanted to lunge for the summit. A weighty punch of air lifted me off my feet and flopped me on my side. I set off a small avalanche of clinkling volcanic rocks as I slid downslope. Chunks of sand blasted into my nostrils and mouth. *This is crazy! But the summit...it's so close!*

I crawled on all fours, keeping as low as possible. The wind must have been howling at a continuous 90 miles per hour with gusts well over 100. The bright day darkened as a thick band of clouds drifted between the sun and Ojos. I looked up—the raft of stratus sailed by just a few hundred feet above the summit. Its swirling innards made me dizzy. I stood so close to the cloud mass that I felt as if I could reach my hand into its churning form and scoop out some icy water. *Is this what the inside of a tornado looks and feels like?* I wondered. I hunkered down, questioning, *why am I here and not in some office enjoying a glazed doughnut?*

But the musing didn't last more than a few seconds. My brain was so beaten down by the altitude that I was far more concerned with how I was going to escape the air's fury than in contemplating my motivation for being on the mountain. I weighed my options...I really had none, because I had no time to wait out the inclemency. I stood at the base of the notch—maybe 50 feet from the actual summit. I looked up to see some fixed ropes flailing in the gusts. *A hazy moment of near-summit victory.* I was close, but that would be it, close. "You win!" I yelled at the summit, "YOU WIN! I'm going home now! ¡Adios, Cumbre!" I no longer cared about summit success. I only wanted down.

I slid along sharp rocks for about 40 yards to a point where the wind was still strong, but not enough to toss me into the jet stream. I stood up, looked over my shoulder—as if the summit was watching me—then bolted for the lip of the crater. The air was ominously calm as I reached the crater's edge. I jumped over the smooth lip, expecting an easy 'dirt ski' session to the top of the staircase, but instead got walloped by another round of gusts. When I opened my eyes I stared at blue sky—the wind had thrown me flat on my back.

I shook off the beating and then scurried like a rat over the jagged rocks. I spent about 30 minutes reaching the safety of the staircase. The nooks and pockets of the rocky formation shielded me from the gale. I found a bench-like rock and rested quietly. Then I took off my pack and boots. *Okay...I'm okay...I escaped,* I thought. For the next hour I lay sprawled out, basking in the warm sun, worshipping life and luck.

I noticed a lone figure approaching the refugio. *Has to be Jaromir...Patrick...is he okay?* I raced down to the hut and flung open its door. "Jaromir! Jaromir!"

"Ed?" I heard from the bunk room.

"Is Patrick okay?"

"Oh, yes...yes, he's fine. He should be back in Copiapó by now. Everything is fine. Did you summit?" Jaromir asked as he yawned himself awake.

"I didn't. The wind was too much for me. I thought I was going to end up in Argentina. I really want to get out of here." I was so relieved—at being off the summit, at knowing that Patrick was okay, and because I had some company.

"How did the rescue go?"

"Jerry and I carried him half way, then he hiked the last half as he regained full consciousness. But once we arrived we found that our driver was gone, and Jerry and Pavalina's driver wasn't due back for another few days."

"So...what did you do?" I asked.

"We put Patrick to bed, Jerry and Pavalina watched him, and I walked out to that big two story hut near the road, where I found our driver. I woke him and told him he needed to get back up to the Andino Hut to take Patrick, Jerry and Pavalina out to Copiapó. I rode with him to the Andino Hut, picked the three of them up, then decided to return to Copiapó because I was so exhausted."

"But...you're here now? What happened?"

"When we got back out to the main road I decided I wanted to give the peak a shot. So I jumped out and walked up here."

"Are...you...are you serious? You walked all the way out to that hut? Then all the way back up here? I can't believe it!"

"No, it's nothing. Tomorrow I think I'll make the summit. Do you want to go for another shot?"

"No way, I'm done with this mountain. I've been here for almost three weeks now. Just about one week straight at this altitude alone—and above. I have to go down. I'm going to sleep hard then head out in the morning. If there is anything I can do to help you out, though, just let me know," I said.

"Thanks. I think I have everything I need," Jaromir replied.

Jaromir had long since departed by the time I woke the next morning. I hiked back to the Andino Hut under the thickest, grayest skies I'd yet seen in the region. I didn't stop once during the descent.

I found the Andino Hut deserted. I grabbed one of the water bottles I'd cached, then signed the register. I pondered making a statement about the full week I'd spent at the Tejos Hut, but I simply scratched my name and the date.

The air stood cool and still. Gray skies signaled the approach of a big storm. A thick deck of stratus cloaked the top third of Ojos—I wrung my hands as I thought of Jaromir climbing in a whiteout. *I hope he turned around before the weather got too bad...but I'm sure he just kept going....*

I wondered how I'd get back to Copiapó. I had a ton of food, water, and fuel, enough that I could shuttle my gear to the main highway. I also needed to make sure that Jaromir returned safely. If he didn't show up by noon the next day, I'd have to search for him. In the meantime, however, I'd rest. I unrolled my sleeping bag, sprawled out, and truly relaxed for the first time on the trip.

I'd given Ojos del Salado my best shot. *Now it's time to recuperate.*

CHAPTER FIFTEEN

I JUST WANT DOWN

Ready for a hot shower and some real food—at sea level

I felt human again after the move to lower altitude. I could think clearly, I could move quickly, and I could inhale easily. Although my altitude was 17,000 feet—still very high—life seemed much easier after spending a week at 19,000 feet. Still, I couldn't wait to get back to sea level.

I watched the storm build throughout the day. It cast an unusually flat light on the landscape, making the bizarre forms and patterns of that high corner of the Atacama even more photogenic than usual. I had an almost endless supply of energy to power my insatiable urge to run from one vantage point to another, exploring and shooting photographs.

The reality that it could be days, or even another week, before I finally returned to Copiapó hit me that night during dinner. Jaromir would almost certainly be down the next day; I could hike out with him to the base camp hut…but not with all of my gear. Getting both camera and climbing gear out would require at least two, if not three, trips. Even then, I would only be at base camp…. *How would I manage from there?* I tried to get my mind off of my logistical challenges by making plans for Aconcagua, but those thoughts only frustrated me more. *Make plans? It may be the end of the climbing season before I'm even back in Copiapó!*

I fell asleep easily that night with two full bowls of instant mashed potatoes and gravy in my stomach. My last thought before sliding into unconsciousness was that I would rest better than ever at that lower altitude. Nope. About 15 minutes after switching off my headlamp and drifting into blissful rest, the first scratchings of the hut's permanent denizens woke me. I flipped on my light and stared into the glowing eyes of a big fat mouse standing inside my food bowl. The ensuing battle lasted all night long. In the end, of course, the mouse—and his small army of brethren—won. They kept me awake for many more hours than I was able to sleep, and the furry thugs managed to chew holes in five of my instant food packs.

I spotted Jaromir the next day at mid-morning and waved my trekking poles at him as he briskly descended the hill outside the hut. He stopped in his tracks and returned the salutation. I could almost see him smiling, even from a half mile away. "You survived that storm!" I cheered as he strode into camp.

"Yes, but barely. I got lost on the summit and ended up in Argentina for a while. I had to backtrack. I was up there for hours!" he answered.

"What do you mean you got lost on the summit?" I asked, as I handed him a bottle of water.

"When I got to the top of the snowfield I was in a whiteout. I didn't want to go down, so I continued up and to the left, when I should have gone right. I climbed over that steep band of black rocks and then walked for, oh, I guess like a few kilometers in a big loop, going into Argentina for a while, then making my way back around to the Chilean side. The entire summit region of the mountain is huge, absolutely huge. I finally made the summit and then I came down the normal way. I was in and out of the clouds all day up there. Not too much wind, but it was a real challenge finding my way around up there. Do you know the exact height of this peak?" Jaromir asked.

"One map I have shows that it's 6,860 meters, another shows that it is 6,880. I'm pretty sure that it's 6,880, although the Argentines claim that Pissis is 6,880 and Ojos is only 6,860," I said. "I've seen a whole bunch of other altitudes, one source claims that this peak is over 7,000 meters high."

"I read that Ojos actually has two summits, one in Argentina, and one in Chile. They are exactly the same altitude, though." We walked into the hut and sat down at the table. "So, how you getting out of here?" Jaromir asked.

"I don't know. I think I'll wait here to see if a ride comes today; and if not, I'll start shuttling my equipment to the base camp hut. How are you getting back? Is your ride coming back up here?" I asked.

"I think I'm going to start walking. That ride was Patrick's ride. He paid for it, and the driver and the car are now down in Copiapó. I didn't make any arrangements for him to come back and pick me up. I don't have the money for that. I am sure Jerry and Pavalina told their driver that they wouldn't be needing him once they got back to Copiapó, so that's why I walk...I don't think that there will be many more climbing expeditions coming up here, maybe none. You may be waiting for a long time," Jaromir said.

"I hope not. I really hope not." I stared at Jaromir's old backpack. It was the most haggard looking external frame pack I'd ever seen.

"You like my backpack?" Jaromir asked.

I laughed in disbelief. "That thing is held together by about four threads. How does it hold anything without ripping?"

"I don't know. It just does. I'm always repairing it, but that's how I was raised. We didn't have the things that you do. We just made do with what we had."

"And you made it to the summit."

"It was a dream of mine for many years. Now I go to Tupungato. Do you want to go with me?"

"I'm set on climbing Aconcagua."

"But there will be crowds of people up there. Doesn't that bother you?"

"Surprisingly, there were crowds of people up here, too. I'm sure the place will be crowded, but I don't mind too much. Anyway, I kind of like meeting people in these places. Really, though, I just want to carry my camera as high as possible—I hear that that mountain is incredibly beautiful. I think I'll try Tupungato another time," I said.

"There were more people up here than I thought there would be," Jaromir agreed. "But we have the mountain all to ourselves now. Maybe I'll see you down in Copiapó." Another storm was approaching; most of Ojos was socked in, and fresh snow lay on surrounding peaks.

Lastarria and lenticulars as seen from Llullaillaco

Cerro Pissis

oncagua's summit region from Nido de Cóndores

Sajama

Viento Blanco (White Wind) howling over Aconcagua's summit

Sunset light, clearing storm, Aconcagua

Hikers in Upper Horcones Valley

Valle de la Luna and Salar de Atacama

One of the Taito Geysers

Nieve penitentes below Ojos del Salado

Andean color

"We might get some snow, maybe even a whiteout. Look how low some of those clouds are," I said, pointing to a lone cloud whisking the summit of a small peak to the north of us. "Do you even know where you're heading? Are you going to the base camp hut, to the Carabineros, or…where?" I asked.

"I'm going to head out to the main road, from there I'll catch a ride to Paso de San Francisco to pick up my passport, then I'll get a ride back to Copiapó." Jaromir threw on his pack and marched north—not on the road, just dead north, making his own path.

"Good luck!" I yelled as he dropped into a small valley and trudged through deep sand. He moved quickly, even in difficult terrain. Within a few minutes he disappeared behind a bend in the valley.

15 minutes later, as I was paging through the register, I heard a strange whining sound…I figured that it was the wind. Then I heard it again, but louder this time. I bolted outside and searched the landscape. Swooshing and a few small crashes added to the high pitch whir. A truck? I wondered. I walked down the road a few yards and stopped to listen again. The wind was almost dead calm; the noises had to be coming from a vehicle, but I couldn't see anything. I turned to walk back to the hut, thinking I'd imagined the sounds…and a Hilux flew over a small rise. "He should have stayed! Jaromir should have stayed!" I yelled as the shiny red truck sped my way.

"Hallo!" Said a tall, thin guy sporting wire-rim glasses. "What are you doing up here all alone I wonder?" The driver spoke with a thick German accent.

"I'm waiting to find a ride out of here," I answered.

"Hmmmmmeeeeooooo," he said like a hungry cat begging for food. "Well then, we shall be here for a few days. If you want a ride with us, you shall have to wait. But we can arrange something. I'm Fritz, and this is my partner, Nils." Nils waved to me, then examined the hut as if he were a health inspector. "You are American?" Fritz asked.

"Yeah, American, and let me guess, you two are German—"

"—Bavarian actually," Fritz chopped.

"Say, did you happen to see a lone guy with a bright orange backpack hiking out of here," I asked.

"Mmmmmm-nooooo. I've only seen you. Why are you here?"

"I just tried to climb the peak; I almost made it."

"Oh, you were climbing! That is good. I did not know you were a climber."

"Yeah, of course I was climbing. What else would I be doing here?"

"Well, I have met many strange Americans doing strange things, I thought that you were not climbing, maybe doing something else."

"How did you guys find this place? I mean most people who come up here hire drivers. You didn't get lost at all?"

"The Carabineros drew us a map, but we simply followed the dirt tracks on the ground. In some places the routefinding was difficult, especially through the sand, but we made it. Oh, and look, here come the Frenchmen." Another Hilux popped into view. Overflowing with gear, the truck rode low to the ground. All four doors flew open at once as seven brightly-clad climbers jumped out. The French had arrived.

"Excuse me, but we were wondering if you have climbed this mountain?" the eldest member asked.

"I have, not to the very top, but pretty close."

"Oh, yes, and which way is it to the top?" I pointed out the route as best I could. "And is there a similar chalet higher up on the peak? We were told that there was."

"There is, well, I wouldn't call it a *chalet*, but it's a nice hut."

"Does it have a kitchen with running water?"

"It has a kitchen, but no running water. Just some beds and a table, with some leftover food and water. There is a small meltwater stream that forms each afternoon very close by."

One of the group's two women approached me, "Excuse my English, but do we require a stove for climbing?"

"Um…Yes! Definitely! Unless you want to eat ice instead of drinking water and all your food is already prepared," I said.

"Oh, well, we have only one stove, and it is not working. Maybe you can help us with the repair." The French group encircled me, each staring with exactly the same expression of lost puppydom.

"Well…sure. Let's…let's take a look at it," I said hesitantly. It wasn't long before I had the stove in about 30 pieces on the small table inside the Andino. All seven of the French climbers packed into the hut and spectated as if I were a physician performing life-saving surgery on their patron saint. The Bavarians, mashed into the far end of the hut, glared at the French.

The weather deteriorated rapidly. The sky grew darker by the minute and threatening clouds obliterated our view of Ojos. I glanced outside a half hour into the repair job to see snow falling. "I wonder if we shall be able to make climbing in this weather," the leader mused.

"Look, there it is! A cracked hose. We can fix that easily. I need a second knife." Five hands, each holding identical Victorinox knives, outstretched instantly. I grabbed the nearest tool and began cutting and mending. Within a few minutes I was pumping and priming, ready for the final test…"Does anyone have a lighter or a match?" I asked.

"Yes Ed, I have one." I looked up to see a smiling Jerry standing in the doorway—snow covering his hair and beard—pulling a lighter from his pocket.

"Where did you come from?" I asked.

"We are here to rescue you and that crazy Czech. Come on, let's get out of here. There's supposed to be a huge storm. It's already snowing, if you hadn't noticed! We may not be able to get out of here if we don't leave now."

"You guys came all the way back up here to get us?"

"Patrick and his fiancée rented a Hilux, there was no way we were going to leave you two up here. But where is Jaromir?"

"I don't know!"

"What do you mean, *you don't know?* Is he still up at the Tejos Hut? We thought for sure he'd be down by now. That's why we waited so long."

"No, he came down today, but then he left for the main highway—"

"—Well, we didn't see him as we drove up, where is he?"

"That's just it, he didn't go out on the road, he took the direct straight-line path back to that big hut down there."

"Oh, God, that such crazy Czech!" Pavalina joined the conversation. "Oh, Ed, you look terrible. You really need a shower!"

"We have to go find him. Come on, finish with the stove and let's get out of here!" Jerry commanded. I flicked the lighter, primed the stove, and watched it sputter to life. Cheers erupted from the French team. One by one they charged me with cheek kisses and long, drawn-out hugs.

"Okay, you're all welcome! I have to go now. Good luck!" I said.

Jerry and I hauled my gear into the bed of the Hilux, then jumped inside. "Hello, Ed. Good to meet you again," said Patrick from the driver's seat. He looked to have been given a new lease on life. "This is my fiancée, Silke."

"Hi there," she said. "Now can we leave, Patrick?"

"Yes, just as soon as Jaromir comes."

"He's not coming," Jerry snapped.

"What do you mean?" Patrick asked.

"We have to go find him. That guy just can't sit still. How long ago did he leave, Ed?"

"About two or three hours ago."

"So he could be anywhere by now! God. We'd better hurry. Okay, Patrick, let's go—now!" The doors slammed shut and we roared off in search of Jaromir.

"I don't understand, where is he?" asked Patrick again.

"He's walking out to the main road," I said.

"Walking out! Again! Why?"

"Because he didn't know that you guys would be coming back to get us."

"Okay, let's everybody keep our eyes wide open and on the look out for Jaromir, especially to the west of here. That's where he will probably be," Pavalina said. Patrick drove as if he were racing to the finish line of the Paris-Dakar.

"You must slow down Patrick!" yelled Silke.

"I must drive fast, we have to find Jaromir. Look at it out here, it is snowing hard…" Patrick finished his answer to Silke in German, realizing he didn't need to speak in our group's lingua franca.

We kept our eyes peeled all the way to the base camp hut. No Jaromir. I ran inside to see if he was there, but found no sign of him. We drove to the main highway to see if he was hitchhiking—nothing. "We should go to the Carabineros to get Ed's passport and check in, if Jaromir has come back to the road and found a ride, he might be there. If he hasn't been there yet, then we know that he is still somewhere between the road and the Andino Hut and we can just wait for him," reasoned Patrick.

We zoomed past Laguna Verde through the driving storm. Snow was beginning to stick to the ground. "I hope he is down at the Carabineros station…he won't be able to find his directions in this weather," groaned Pavalina. We parked at the Paso de San Francisco guard station and received a warm welcome from Coolio, Israel, and Carlos.

"¡Sí! Jaromir! ¡El Loco!" Coolio exclaimed, allowing us to breathe a collective sigh of relief. I talked with the guards briefly before Jerry dragged me away.

"Let's go, Ed. This storm is dumping like crazy. We don't want to get stuck up here. Do you?"

"Okay, let's go. Jaromir should be somewhere on the main road," I said as we ran to the Hilux.

Snow collected on the road as visibility shrank to less than 50 feet. "Oh, my god, look at this storm," Pavalina uttered. "I hope that Jaromir is right on the road, or we won't be able to see him."

"Okay, we're at the eastern cutoff for the base camp hut…no Jaromir." We continued at a fast clip. About 20 minutes later we passed the western cutoff for the road. Still no Jaromir.

"Where is he?!" growled Pavalina.

"He is okay. We'll find him. How are we with fuel, Patrick?" Jerry asked.

"Fine, these things get great mileage, plus there's a big fuel tank. If we need to we can go all the way back up to the Andino Hut, maybe twice, and still make it back to Copiapó."

"Look! What is that?" yelped Silke.

"It's someone at the mining camp turnoff," I said, recognizing my dinner stop from a few weeks prior. "Hey, there's an orange backpack. I think it's…"

"¡El Loco! The crazy Czech," interrupted Jerry. Patrick flashed his lights and honked the horn as we skidded up to our friend. Silke rolled down the window. Dust and snow flew inside the cab. "Hey you!" Jerry yelled, "what you doin' on the side of this stupid road?"

"Jerry? Patrick? Pavalina? Ed?…and Silke? Some miners gave me a ride this far from the Carabineros." Jaromir looked stunned to see us together, comfortably inside the Hilux.

"Yes, we're all here, now let's go. You must be cold," Pavalina said. Jaromir strapped his pack onto the mountain of gear in the truck's bed then squeezed into the back with Jerry, Pavalina, and me.

Patrick stepped on the gas pedal and we flew west toward sunny skies and warmer altitudes.

"What do you say we go to Laguna Negro Francisco…maybe spend the night there?" Patrick asked.

"I'm fine with that," I said, sensing that Patrick didn't want to go straight back to Copiapó.

"Okay, so long as we have wine, food, and cigarettes…which we do…so let's get over there," Jerry added.

The clouds broke open as we cruised past Tres Cruces. We stopped for some photographs and I volunteered to take the far back seat—out in the open air in the bed of the truck. Jerry jumped into the driver's seat and we rocketed to the Mina Marte cutoff, where we headed south. A few hours later the six of us were walking leisurely on the shore of Laguna Negro Francisco, trying to sneak up on a huge flock of pink flamingos. Evening fell and we retreated to a SERNATUR hut.

"No one is here? I guess we just move in, right?" said Silke.

"Yes, we own the place, then, right cowboy?" Jerry asked me.

"That's it," I replied. We opened the main door and found the accommodations absolutely decadent compared to tents and mouse-infested shipping containers. One room even had carpeting. We rolled out our sleeping bags, fired up our stoves, and broke out the wine.

"I see you staring at my cigarette, Ed. You want one?" Jerry asked.

"I quit smoking about two weeks before beginning this trip. I swore I wouldn't start again, but you're tempting me…really tempting me," I said. After a few more cups of wine, I broke down. "Okay, I'll have one."

"You know, cigarettes really are good for high altitude. They train your lungs to be more efficient with the oxygen that they get. I know this for a fact," Jerry said, deadly serious.

Don't go too slow

Flamingos, Laguna Negro Francisco

"Whatever you say, Jerry..." I took a deep drag and got floored by the rush. Jerry broke out laughing. We spent the rest of the night talking about adventures past and future, Germany, America, and life behind the Iron Curtain.

"Oh, yeah," said Pavalina, "it was so easy for me as a woman to travel in the Soviet Union. I went anywhere I wanted. It was never like your movies portrayed things in our country. Very easy for me. Life was better for most people back then. Nobody had to work. Everyone just got their food and shelter. Now everything is kill your brother, kill your mother, run by the stupid mob. That's why we moved to L.A."

"Don't talk about L.A. Pavalina. We will be back there too soon. Too soon..." Jerry said, somberly.

We arrived in Copiapó the next evening. Jaromir and I each checked into a two-dollar per night room in Resedencial Rodriguez, and the rest of the group moved into a similarly priced hotel across the street. We drank and smoked ourselves into oblivion celebrating Jaromir's summit success, my near-summit success, Patrick's amazing survival, Silke's relief over Patrick's amazing survival, and Jerry and Pavalina's choice of wine, cigarettes, and hotels—cheap and good.

The next morning my friends went their separate ways. I hung around one more day to repair my camera backpack and to plan the logistics for Aconcagua. I also stopped to see Alex, but he wasn't home during any of the three times I visited. I left a note for him with Lelia at the SERNATUR office, detailing the highlights of the trip, giving my address, and of course, thanking him and his wife one last time.

Ojos del Salado stood in my past; South America's highest point now ruled my thoughts. Well fed and showered, I climbed aboard an air conditioned 'Turbus' express coach bound for Santiago, reclined my seat, and rested for Aconcagua.

Cracked playa in Atacama Desert; foothills surrounding Puna de Atacama

BOOK III

ACONCAGUA

Clearing storm, west face of Aconcagua. Image taken from Plaza de Mulas

170

CHAPTER SIXTEEN

A MONK, A MOUNTAIN, AND MENDOZA

View of Aconcagua and clearing storm from Lower Horcones Valley

A concagua. A dream mountain of mine for so many years, Aconcagua stands as a peak of superlatives: Argentina's highest point, crest of the Andes, apex of South America, zenith of both the Western *and* Southern Hemispheres, summit of the Americas, crown of the New World, and earth's loftiest point save for the seven and eight thousand meter peaks of Asia.

I first mused about scaling Aconcagua when I was in grade school. Back then I mistakenly believed the name of South America's highest mountain to be 'Anaconda.' The word *anaconda* conjured so many adventurous images for me—adventures specific to the wilds of South America: dark jungles, long, sinuous rivers, mysterious tribes—all lying deep in the shadow of a great range capped by one brobdingnagian peak, *Anaconda* itself. Nevertheless, I eventually learned of the true—albeit tongue-twisting and less visually evocative—name of the Andes' highest mountain. But while I long savored the idea of summitting Aconcagua, I never augered much into the who's, what's, where's, and when's of that peak as I had with Denali, Mount Logan, Popocatepetl, and the giants of the Himalaya.

Before leaving for Lima, I'd gathered a few clues to making it to the summit of the Americas by paging through old magazine articles and by studying a topographic map of Aconcagua. However, as my research efforts had focused primarily on Ojos del Salado and Cerro Pissis, I'd gleaned only the most rudimentary logistical facts for an Aconcagua attempt. I had to get to Mendoza, Argentina, where I could procure the requisite climbing permit. I'd learn route information, costs, timing, and pretty much anything else I could gather from the people in the permit office, then take the journey's obstacles as they came. After three weeks on Ojos del Salado, I didn't have the energy to obsess over the minutiae of an Aconcagua expedition.

The bus ride to Santiago was crowded and long. About 18 hours after slipping out of the gates of Copiapó I stood in the waiting area of one of the capital city's main bus terminals, my knees creaky and my back pained. At three o'clock in the morning, the terminal was completely deserted. I had only one goal for the next day: get an international bus to Mendoza, just over the 'hill' from Santiago. I dragged my gear to a corner, gathered myself into the fetal position on the mule bag, cradled my camera pack, and fell asleep.

The formerly-empty lobby was gorged with people when I cracked my eyes open. Throngs of travelers whisked past me. I looked at a clock. I'd slept like dead wood for three hours. I stood up and heaved my bags to the nearest ticket desk. *Not here, there…not there, over there…a little farther.* I wound through a liquid maze of humanity, hopping from desk to desk, searching for what I'd thought would be an easy-to-find bus to Mendoza. No luck.

After a sweaty and nervous hour of dragging my coveted belongings around the jam-packed terminal, I finally secured my ride to Mendoza. But the bus wouldn't leave until the afternoon. That was fine; I'd waited in dirty bus terminals before. I played gastro-intestinal Russian roulette with some greasy empanadas, took a shower, then stared at the huge, variegated buses lumbering in and out of the station's main entrance as I waited in the shade.

The coach to Mendoza was packed with a colorful hodgepodge of characters. I tried to guess who was heading home and who was a tourist as I stared unabashedly at people. Nobody seemed to speak English. "Ocho horas, más o menos," a woman in a neighboring seat told me after I asked how long till reaching Mendoza. *Eight hours...I bet it'll be eight hours of great views,* I thought as we wound out of the terminal onto the packed streets of Santiago.

Of all the people I gawked at on the bus, the one my eyes kept returning to was actually the least vibrant of the bunch: a monk. He sat alone and talked to nobody. He looked at nobody. He intently read a book; the Bible, I guessed.

My attention turned to the hills...trees—people—cars—and agriculture fields blurring across my field of view. We broke free of the city's grasp in less than an hour; the scenes changed quickly from urban to agrarian, then to low alpine. At the town of Los Andes we connected with Chilean National Route 60 and headed east—and up—toward the crest of the continent's spine. As with the road to Paso de San Francisco, the route steepened as we traveled east. The climax of the highway's upward trend is a set of intricate hairpin switchbacks that looks like a huge seam of black webbing sewn tightly into the underlying rock. The rig swayed back and forth as the driver downshifted and wrestled the bus around constricted bights of asphalt. *One...two...three...*I started counting each 180 degree twist of the road. I quit in a spate of dizziness after 15.

The ascent culminated at Uspallata Pass—also known as Cumbre Pass—(3,863 meters, 12,674 feet), the point where the blacktop crosses the international boundary between Argentina and Chile. The giant statue, *Christ of the Andes,* marks the pass. The bronze figure was erected in 1904 to commemorate the resolution of a boundary dispute between Chile and Argentina.

We stopped at the Chilean border guard station to have exit visas stamped and to change money (one Argentine Peso for one US Dollar), after which we pulled into a large, enclosed parking garage. The Argentine authorities ordered us to open our bags for inspection. A spasm of worry jabbed me. *What if someone had stuffed drugs into my bag?* I remembered the crazy taxi ride from Tacna to Arica when the driver and one of his passengers tried to get me to smuggle cocaine for them. I knew that hiding drugs on unsuspecting tourists was a common way for traffickers to move their wares from country to country. I began to sweat, thinking of the movie 'Midnight Express.' *That was a true story!*

The guards slowly progressed toward my bags, taking cursory looks through each person's belongings. I stared at the monk; he gave me a reassuring look. "You are here to climbing the Aconcagua mountain?" he asked.

"How...how...how the he...*oops*...how did you know that?" I asked.

174

"Because I see the guards looking at your ice ax and crampons over there, and your face, you have the sunburn of someone who climbs mountains. All the American and European climbers come to this part of this country for one mountain and one mountain only: Aconcagua. It is the highest." The monk paused and looked at me for a few seconds. I shot a glance toward the guards who were checking my climbing gear and making faces at each other like they had seen much better. Not 30 seconds later the authorities moved on to the next passenger's bags. I turned my attention back to the monk. "And...you smell strange. You smell like you have been wearing sunscreen and sweating a lot, and not washing your clothes—this is how I know you are climbing Aconcagua," he finished.

I laughed. " Thank you so much," I said, flushed with relief.

"What for?" he asked.

"Oh...uh...I don't know..." I didn't want to admit my ridiculous anxieties to him, "...for speaking in English. How did you know I spoke English?"

"I did not know. But you look foreign, and most foreigners here speak English. That's why." He paused for a moment. "Many people have died on Aconcagua. I would like to bless you...for your safe passage to the mountain and back. Would you like me to bless you?" he asked. I'd never been blessed in my life, at least not formally.

"Yeah...yes...sure," I said, feeling that I could use any extra help I could get. He raised his right hand and scribed a small cross in the air, while he uttered a rapid and barely audible prayer in what I assume was Latin.

With all the passengers' passports stamped with Argentine visas, we started down the steep grade toward Mendoza. "Would you like to look at Aconcagua?" the monk asked after a few minutes of speedy travel. I sat on the right side of the bus; he on the left.

"Yes! I've never seen a mountain that high," I said. "But can you actually *see* Aconcagua from the road?"

"Come here. Look." The monk moved out of his seat. I braced my forehead against a window. Not a single cloud roved the baby blue afternoon sky. I peered between two foreground peaks to see a ghostly visage of a huge mountain. Aconcagua's snow projected a strange, soothing glow. Dark bands of rock provided texture and depth. *The south face of Aconcagua*, I thought, *one of the greatest mountain walls on earth*. I sat transfixed.

"Here, you look...I'm sorry. You should take a look." I felt like a jackass for hogging the view of such a beautiful mountain—especially from a monk. I backed into the aisle. The monk's eyes followed me as the last views of Aconcagua slipped out of sight; he seemed far more interested in my safe passage on the high mountain than in his glimpsing it.

"I have seen Aconcagua before, and I'll see it again. Don't worry," the monk said. "Sit down and rest. I think you need it."

"Thank you," I said, sinking into my seat. I felt calm and relaxed. I closed my eyes and thought about nothing.

The next thing I knew the driver was jerking my shoulder back and forth. "¡Mendoza! ¡Mendoza!" he barked, before jumping out of the front door. I sat alone on the bus. I rose and stretched, then dragged my stiff body into the cool nighttime air of one of Argentina's most renowned cities. I stopped in my tracks, remembering the monk. I searched for him; I wanted to thank him again, but he was gone.

"¿Hotel?" I asked the first taxi driver I found. The driver nodded, then grabbed my mule bag and mashed it into his small trunk. "Poquito dinero," I added, hoping he knew of a good, clean, cheap, hotel.

Five minutes later I unloaded my gear at the steps of Hotel Blanco. The desk clerk took my money—14 dollars for one night—and helped me drag my gear upstairs to my room. I kept my fingers crossed as he opened the door. I was in luck: a large, impeccably clean room with a high ceiling, a good-sized window, two beds, a bathroom with a shower (and to my surprise, a bidet) and a color television—with cable. I sprawled on the bed closest to the window and buzzed through channels as if I'd never before seen a television. When I found a station that featured American movies with Spanish subtitles I practiced my language skills into the wee hours of my first night in Argentina.

Early the next morning I narrowed my route choices down to either the Ruta Normal or the Polish Glacier. The Ruta Normal (normal route), otherwise known as the Northwest Ridge route, is a relatively non-technical climb that is the passage of choice for the bulk of the mountain's would-be ascentionists. The Polish Glacier is reputed to be more difficult (the supposed difference in difficulty between the two routes varies from minimal to quite substantial), and less crowded. Because I guessed that either route was well within my ability, my decision rested on two main factors: photographic possibilities and cost. My greatest cost would be renting a mule to porter my load of equipment to the base camp of whichever route I chose. Jerry had told me that the mule rentals were expensive, but that one mule could carry the equipment of three climbers. Meeting two people who'd want to share a mule was much more likely on the Ruta Normal than on the less-traveled Polish Glacier.

My most important consideration was aesthetics. I'd heard and read a few tantalizing descriptions of the Ruta Normal with its incredible sunsets, massive walls, and geologic intricacies. By contrast, I found little about the scenery on and from the Polish Glacier route—but that didn't mean that it was less visually appealing than the Ruta Normal.

Early February is deep in the heart of the austral summer. I walked a half block before I spotted a cab—just enough time for my shirt to transform from dry and comfortable to sticky and wet. Three cab rides and a lot of frustration later, I arrived at Parque San Martín, home of the permit office. I paid the fare and walked to a small building that looked more like a concession stand. 'Dirección de Recursos Naturales Renovables' a sign read. A woman greeted me—in English—and produced an application form before I could open my mouth. I listed my name, address, emergency contact number, checked the '21 days climbing' box (the other two selections were '3 days short trekking' and '7 days long trekking'), filled in the number in group box: *1*, expedition leader box: *Ed Darack*, and rescue insurance box: *none*, then I paused at the box for my intended climbing route. I looked at an Aconcagua poster hanging on the office wall. The top photograph of the montage featured an image of an intricately fluted rock wall glowing crimson. *Absolutely beautiful, absolutely what I want*, I thought. I imagined myself standing in front of that wall with that same lighting, behind my tripod-mounted Pentax 67. I imagined how good I'd feel lifting the weight of that precision equipment off my back after hours of trekking. Excitement tingled through me as I stared at that poster. "From what route?" I asked.

"Route Normal," she replied. So I scribed 'Ruta Normal' in the box. I paid my fee ($120.00, acceptable only in US dollars), then asked about the route— the dangers, the average duration, food...anything I could think of.

"Excuse me...are you heading up to Ahh—con—cag—U—wa?" came a British-accented voice as I gurgled water from a tap on the side of the building. I turned to see a guy wearing a big introductory grin.

"Yeah," I said.

"You're going up the normal route I take it?" he continued.

"That's right," I said.

"How many are in your group?"

"Just me...just me and a bunch of camera equipment," I said, wondering how high I would be able to drag my Pentax.

"Really? My friend and I are going to go up on the normal route, but we're looking to share the cost of a mule into base camp. A mule can supposedly carry around 60 kilograms, and each of us needs only around 20 kilograms hauled—we're going to hike into camp with a bunch of gear on our backs. Are you interested in splitting a mule three ways?"

"Are you kidding? Yeah!" I responded.

"We'll be going up tomorrow to Puente del Inca, that's where the muleteers are based. Will that fit in your schedule?" the guy asked. I thought for a second: *what schedule? I don't even have a schedule, other than to get my cameras high up on Aconcagua, and try to see if I can summit the peak.*

"Oh, yeah...Yes. Of course! But...I don't know how to get up to Puente del Inca," I added.

"Uspallata Express. It's a bus line that makes the run every morning at six. They probably have tickets left. Get over there in a hurry. If you don't get the

Aconcagua Location Map

| 0 | 250 | 500 | 1000 KM |
| 0 | 250 | 500 | 1000 MI |

Scale: 1:25,641,026
Azimuthal Equal-Area Projection
Map by Ed Darack

CHILE   ARGENTINA

72° W

-31° S

Panamerican Highway

Cerro Fredes ▲   ▲ Cerro de la Totora   Cerro Corralitos ▲

                                                    San Juan ●
                        Cerro Pircas ▲

                        ▲ Cerro Mercedario

-32° S

Cerro Jorquera ▲   ▲ Cerro Cielo

                    Aconcagua
                    6,959 Meters 22,831.4 Feet
                        ▲
San Felipe de   ● Uspallata
Los Andes
        CH-60   AR-7
                    Puente del Inca   ● Mendoza

-33° S

● Valparaiso   ▲ Nevado El Plomo

                        ▲ Tupungato
Santiago   ▲ Tupungatito
de Chile ●
                                    ▲ Loma Negra Guadalupe
                    ▲ Volcán San José

-34° S

Rancagua ●   ▲ Volcán Maipú

South Pacific Ocean

Aconcagua Regional Map

0		100	150	200	250 KM
0	50		100		150 MI

Map details Aconcagua and environs. Map shows pertinent roads, population centers, and physical features.

▲ Peak

● Population Center

• Hut or Outpost

– – – – – –
International Boundary

———————
Panamerican Highway

———————
Secondary Routes

Scale: 1:4,000,000
Azimuthal Equal-Area Projection
Map by Ed Darack

Mountain Altitudes in Meters (and Feet):
Aconcagua: 6,959 Meters (22,831.4 Feet)
Cerro Mercederio: 6,770 Meters (22,211.3 Feet)
Tupungato: 6,570 Meters (21,555.1 Feet)
Nevado El Plomo: 6,050 Meters (19,849.1 Feet)
Volcán San José: 5,856 Meters (19,212.6 Feet)
Tupungatito: 5,682 Meters (18,641.7 Feet)
Cerro de la Totora: 5,615 Meters (18,421.9 Feet)
Volcán Maipú: 5,323 Meters (17,463.9 Feet)
Cerro Pircas: 4,366 Meters (14,324.1 Feet)
Cerro Fredas: 3,803 Meters (12,493.4 Feet)
Cerro Jorquera: 3,743 Meters (12,280.2 Feet)
Cerro Cielo: 3,245 Meters (10,646.3 Feet)
Cerro Corralitos: 3,162 Meters (10,374 Feet)
Loma Negra Guadalupe: 1,124 Meters (3,687.6 Feet)

179

first bus, then they have another around noon. What's your name, anyway?"

"Ed…and you?"

"I'm Paul, and this is Gary." Gary hadn't uttered a word; he looked haggard. I smiled enthusiastically at him, receiving a simple nod in return.

"I'll see you tomorrow." I found a taxi, bought my ticket for the early bus, and headed back to Hotel Blanco. I felt like I was ready, almost.…

I sat on the side of my bed early that afternoon staring at my trusty black mule bag, wondering how on earth I ever zipped the thing closed back in Copiapó. I was almost afraid to open it. Not only did I have my backpack, tripod, climbing equipment, clothes, sleeping bag, tent, stove equipment, and fuel crammed into the thick nylon sack, but my leftover food from the Ojos trip was squeezed in there as well. I don't think there was a cubic millimeter of free space remaining. Even my pots were stuffed with gear. After delaying the chore by sipping wine and watching television, I wrested open the zipper. An hour later I had my tripod put together, my backpack loaded, and my food organized—two weeks worth. I had so many leftovers from Ojos del Salado, I didn't need to go to the store to resupply anything. Then I set about arranging my cameras and film. I worked like mad, unpacking, cleaning lenses, sorting the exposed film from the unused rolls, and testing batteries. I stood back at last and admired my work…then I admired the fact that I was totally prepared for the climb and the sun was still up! *I actually don't have anything to do…I'm ready to go*, I thought. I shut the door to my room and headed into the streets of the beautiful city.

Free from backpacks and pre-climb responsibilities, I strolled out of the hotel lobby onto Calle Dorrego in search of whatever my stomach and eyes ravened for—just about anything at that point.

The streets of Mendoza had me charmed. I roamed in the shade of stone buildings and broad trees, admiring the city's finely crafted vintage architecture—comfortable, enduring, stately. Established in the early 1560s by Spaniards roving east from Chile, Mendoza is the capitol of the modern Argentine province of the same name—a province that contains many high Andean peaks, including Aconcagua. The city has a subtle colonial air. The original city was destroyed by a powerful earthquake in 1861. Mendoza was reconstructed starting in 1863—from a large scale urban plan, but with much of the spirit of the original settlement.

My attention turned from beautiful buildings to the gnawing urge in my gut for…I thought about all the things my stomach craved…the image of one treat rose above all else: ice cream. I stopped at a small store a few blocks from my hotel that boasted a huge advertisement for vanilla cones. As I talked with the store's proprietors I ate five of their specialties. "My friend works at Plaza de Mulas on Aconcagua, please give this to her," requested a woman who worked behind the counter. She sealed an envelope with her friend's name emblazoned in big pink letters, and handed it to me—as if climbers preparing to attempt Aconcagua walk into her small, out-of-the-way store all the time. I pocketed her mail, taking the happenstance as a sign of good luck, then continued along the city's streets in search of more food.

In a colorful grocery, I found some of the largest, most succulent-looking tomatoes I'd ever seen. I bought five and ate them on the street like drippy apples. I returned to the shop and bought five of their gigantic green bell peppers—and ate them like apples too. The province of Mendoza is one of the most agriculturally blessed places in the world. A poster on the street bragged "*Mendoza: Tierra del Vino*" and listed events for a week-long festival celebrating the region's most renowned ag product: wine.

I capped the day by eating a fabled Argentine steak dinner at the small restaurant in my hotel. Six dollars bought a huge slab of beautifully cooked, incredibly tender, explosively savory steak, a large carafe of local red wine, a deep bowl of salad, and a loaf of freshly baked bread. The perfect cap to my pre-climb preparations.

Chapter Seventeen

RULES OF THE MULES

Look out! Here they come...

Paul and Gary were already waiting on a bench when I arrived for the bus to Puente del Inca. Paul laughed as I wrestled my mountain of equipment from the taxi's back seat. "You taking all that stuff?" he asked. "You'll need a mule all to yourself—maybe two mules!"

"No…I thought the hotel would store some of my gear while I was away. I didn't find out that they wouldn't until about ten minutes ago. I'll have to store it up at Puente del Inca," I said as I helped the bus driver huff the black bag into the luggage compartment. "I sure hope I can store it there."

"I hope so too," laughed Paul.

A handful of passengers filed silently into the bus under the thick quietude of dawn. The morning felt beautifully cool; I slid my window open a few inches and rested my head against the backrest of the seat in front of me. I was opiated by my brief hiatus from thin air—I could breathe easily, I felt clean, my clothes had been washed, and I wasn't starving.

I swayed gently in my seat, drifting in and out of sleep as the sun beamed morning light on the verdant agricultural fields below the eastern foot of the Andes. The road climbed steeply to the town of Uspallata, where we made a brief stop, then continued in its engine-and-gearbox beating rise toward the continent's spine.

We arrived at Puente del Inca, or PDI as I would come to know it, at mid-morning. PDI is actually more of a tourist center than a town, and it is the main staging area for climbers traveling into the Horcones Valley, the passage to the base of the Ruta Normal.

Paul, Gary, and I piled our equipment near the steps of the Hotel Puente del Inca, where Gary would guard our gear while Paul and I set off to find a muleteer. It didn't take long, and we didn't actually do the finding—representatives of three different outfitters accosted us. "Mules! Mules! Need mules?" each repeated to us—actually *at* us. Paul and I looked at each other and shrugged our shoulders. We turned to Gary, who shrugged his shoulders too. We tried to bargain with the muleteers, but they'd have none of it. The price was fixed at $120 (US) for one mule, each way, for any load up to 60 kilograms (132 pounds). Paul turned to me. "How should we choose one?" he asked. I thought about additional services.

"Who has a bunk house or a place to pitch a tent?" I asked, quickly following with "for free?"

"I do. I have camping. Free of charge."

"And storage of gear while we are on the mountain? I have a lot to store," I said, pointing to my things.

The same guy stepped forward again, this time handing me his company's business card: 'Rudy Parra' it read.

"I do, storage, no charge."

"Okay," I said, "you got it. Oh, wait…when can we go up? Tomorrow?"

"Yes, tomorrow, no problem. Whenever you want to leave. I get my truck, wait here," Rudy's employee, Roberto, said. A pickup truck backed up to our equipment a couple of minutes later. After piling in, I heard Gary speak for the first time.

"It looks like things are going pretty smoothly," he said, with what I judged to be an Australian accent.

"Hey, where are you two from, anyway?" I asked.

"I'm from London," Paul said.

"And I'm from Queensland...Queensland, Australia," Gary answered. I knew the basics of their lives by the time we arrived at Rudy's small compound. Paul worked as a solicitor—a type of attorney—and Gary was a helicopter mechanic in the Australian military. Paul was on a yearlong journey in South America, traveling alone by motorcycle, and Gary, also alone, was on a trip of unknown duration and *wherever* destination. The two met while on a ferry from Puerto Natales (gateway to the renowned Torres del Paine National Park) to Puerto Montt, Chile. They spoke about different travel destinations and somehow convinced each other to try to climb Aconcagua. But they had two problems: the first was that neither had any mountaineering equipment; solved fairly easily by roaming around the various sport shops and climbing hangouts in Mendoza. The second problem would require a bit more effort to solve: between the two of them they didn't have even a minute of climbing experience. Not rock climbing, not ice climbing, not mountaineering, not rope work; only a few days of basic camping.

"I'd actually never seen an ice ax until a few days ago," said Gary.

"I read *Annapurna* when I was a kid," said Paul.

"You guys are kidding, right...I mean, neither of you has ever been on a mountain...not even hiking?"

"Been in the jungle, that's 'bout it for me," Gary stated nonchalantly.

"I went hiking around the base of Ben Nevis in Scotland a few years ago when I was at university. We read in the travel guide that climbing Aconcagua is easy, pretty straightforward."

"Hell, I've never even seen snow!" exclaimed Gary proudly. "I mean until this trip...but I only saw it from a distance when I was down in Patagonia. I've never seen it up close; guess I will on this jaunt, right?"

"Yeah..." I said, "I guess you *will*."

"Hey, do you think that this Rudy Parra guy rents those plastic mountaineering boots?" Gary asked.

"What do you mean, you don't have mountaineering boots?"

"No. None of the places in Mendoza had my size. They had Paul's size, but not mine. I just have these." Gary's big feet were clad with thin, worn, non-lugged, leather hiking boots that seemed barely suitable for springtime beach walking.

184

"You're gonna try to climb..." I paused to catch my breath, "the highest mountain in the Andes in *those!?*"

"I think with some modifications they should do the trick. I rented those boot spikes, um, I always forget the name of those things..."

"—crampons," I interrupted.

"Yeah, crampons, but these boots are too noodly for them to stay put. I'll have to figure out some way to make them work."

"What about gaiters," I asked. "Do you have any type of gaiters that will seal well enough around the boot to keep out the snow?"

"I don't have any gaiters, but I did buy some large plastic bags. Those should work. I think I'll just put my boots inside of the plastic bags, tape them down, then strap my crampons to those," Gary said with a determined look.

"Well, let me know if I can help," I said, imagining that Gary would reach base camp, and then realize that he shouldn't continue any higher.

I worked into the afternoon re-sorting food, film, and gear. The first part of my evolving plan was simple: I would carry my camera, tripod, and basic sleeping gear up to Plaza de Mulas—the base camp of the Ruta Normal—while the rest of my gear would share the back of one of Rudy's mules with Paul's and Gary's gear. The trick was to keep the mule's cargo at or under sixty kilograms total.

"How long do you plan to take to climb the peak, Ed?" asked Paul.

"I recently spent three weeks above 14,000 feet; one of those weeks was at about 19,000 feet on Ojos del Salado. I've only been down at lower elevations for a few days, and I feel pretty strong. I think I'm going to shoot for seven to ten days, round trip. But I'll take food for two weeks," I said, confident that my packets of instant rice, spaghetti, tins of meat spread, sardines, and crackers would keep me going.

"We're going to carry two weeks worth of food as well. I hope that will be enough," Paul replied.

"Why don't you take more, to have a bit of a cushion?" I asked.

"We're going to just hike back down if things don't work out. If a bad storm breaks, we'll come back; if we start running out of food, we'll come back," Gary said. "But I think we should do okay. I'm not too worried."

"How are you going to stage your trek into base camp?" Paul asked.

"I'm going to Confluencia Camp tomorrow, then hike the rest of the way to Plaza de Mulas the next day," I answered, "and you?"

"Tomorrow we'll go to Confluencia, spend a night, then take an acclimatization hike to Plaza Francia, the base camp for the south face. We'll spend a night at Plaza Francia to get acclimatized—it's at 4,500 meters altitude—then we'll hike back out to Confluencia, spend another night there, then hike up to Plaza de Mulas. I think we should be fit and strong by then," Paul said.

"So you'll be carrying a lot of equipment, then, huh?" I asked.

"Not nearly as much as it looks like you'll be carrying," Gary answered. We finished sorting our gear, then weightd it: Paul's gear: 16 kilograms; Gary's gear: 18 kilograms; my gear: 25 kilograms.

"59 kilos total, just squeaked by," Paul shouted. After piling our gear into one of Rudy's storage sheds, Paul and I mulled over our maps of the region and Gary went in search of boots.

Approximately 47 kilometers (29 miles) separates Puenta del Inca from Plaza de Mulas—7 kilometers from PDI to the ranger station at Lago Horcones, approximately 10 kilometers from Lago Horcones to Confluencia, and 30 kilometers from Confluencia to Plaza de Mulas. The total elevation gain is about 1,510 meters (4,953 feet) between Puente del Inca (2,720 meters; 8,921 feet) and Plaza de Mulas (4,230 meters; 13,874 feet)—nearly a vertical mile in two days. "Roberto just told me that he'll drive us up to Lago Horcones tomorrow for the start of the hike, that saves us about seven kilometers," said Paul, "and from there it's meant to be a pretty enjoyable four to six hour walk into Confluencia. Should be nice views of Aconcagua."

"What's it like between Confluencia and Plaza de Mulas?" I asked.

"Supposed to be pretty level walking through the Horcones Valley. Not too tough, except I read that the last bit is a stinger, real steep up to base camp."

"I can't wait to find out for myself," I added, as Gary came walking back into Rudy's comfortable little alcove. "Hey, you're empty handed...don't tell me you didn't get boots."

"I didn't. Checked everywhere, all the muleteers, the hotel, I even asked some climbers who'd just gotten off the mountain...no luck with any of them. Guess I'm just going to have to tough it out with these," Gary replied.

"Hey! I've got something for you, Gary," I said as I remembered a package of gear that had been sitting at the very bottom of one of my bags since leaving California. I ran into the storage hut and returned with 15 heat packs. "All you have to do is open the plastic; the air reacts with the chemicals inside the thing, and it stays warm for at least six hours. You can stuff one of these into the front of each sock, that should help you out."

"Yeah...yeah, thanks! Who needs heavy plastic boots when you have these?" he asked—facetiously, I hoped. "What kind of boots do you have there, Ed?"

"Koflach Viva Softs, hardly the warmest or the best, but they're double-plastic boots, and with supergaiters they stay pretty warm," I said.

"Were those boots expensive?"

"No, got 'em used, up in Banff, Canada. With the favorable exchange rate they cost me only 25 dollars," I said.

"$25 US, that's it?"

"I got lucky," I said.

We each paid Rudy 40 dollars for the mule service, pitched our tents in his small courtyard, then set off to explore the sights of PDI. Puente del Inca translates to 'bridge of the Incas,' and as the name implies, the town boasts a bridge, but the span wasn't built by or for the Incas. Rather, Puente del Inca is a natural bridge—a rather large natural bridge: 65 feet high, 70 feet long, and 90 feet wide. Spanning the Río Las Cuevas, the bridge was formed of hardened sulfur that leaked from natural hot springs over thousands of years. The springs continue to bubble hot water, so much so that a series of rooms has been built to house the springs.

"I think I'm going to take a bath in one of those pools," said Gary.

"Me too," Paul chimed in.

"Okay, I'll see you two later. I'm going to get some food." I found an Argentine greasy spoon by the side of the road and devoured three plates of the house specialty: fried steak sandwiches. I topped off the meal with some wine, then watched the sun set and the day tourists drive off.

I walked along an old set of railroad tracks at dusk. The tracks were put in place as part of one of the greatest feats of railroad engineering in history, a line that linked Buenos Aires, Argentina with Valparaiso, Chile. The great 'hump' over this part of the Andes required a monumental effort, including long series of rack-and-pinion ascending/descending devices and a tunnel that reached just a couple of feet shy of two miles in length. The train doesn't run anymore, but it laid the groundwork for the amazing road that lies in its place today.

Chill air swept across the landscape as nighttime fell. I aimed back toward Rudy's to get a jump on sleep; I wanted at least eight hours. I'd need every ounce of energy I could squeeze out of myself if I was going to make a serious attempt on the mountain. I felt physically strong and well acclimatized, but I allowed myself to think no more than one day into the future. Pondering the ascent of Aconcagua, the exertion, the effort, the planning, the inevitable unforeseen problems, and my possible success—or failure, or worse—was too much for me. *One step in front of the other, one step at a time.* I zipped myself into my sleeping bag and dreamt of the soothing blue glow of the nieve penitentes on Ojos del Salado.

Chapter Eighteen
IN HISTORY'S FOOTSTEPS

Climbers trekking across the Upper Horcones Valley

Nobody could have asked for a more beautiful day to begin a climb of Aconcagua. I woke an hour past dawn to a warm, calm, cloudless day in the waning shade of one of Rudy's sheds.

"G'morning," Gary said to me as he unzipped himself from his thin sleeping bag. "Looks like the mountain wants us to climb it!"

"That's the sleeping bag you're going to take up the mountain?" I asked, gawking at the thin, rust-colored, lumpy bedding that seemed even less sufficient than his boots for the job at hand.

"Yeah," Gary replied, puzzled that I would question the integrity of his gear.

"You know…it does get…kind of…*cold*…up there…with the *snow* and all," I said as I rose into the sunlight.

"No problem mate, not a problem at all. I'll tough it out," Gary said, breaking a confident smile.

"Hey, look at that poor mule with all of Ed's stuff!" laughed Paul as he pointed to our four-legged porter sagging under the weight of our gear.

"So you slept in too, huh? And hey, some of that weight is yours!" I answered, "I don't even remember you guys coming in last night; I must have been dead out." I felt stronger than I had in weeks. I must have slept for ten hours.

"We tried to wake you, to see if you wanted to have some wine with us, but we couldn't get you up. Thought you were dead, until you started to snore," Paul said.

"I feel so great, I can't believe how good it feels to have gotten a full night's sleep," I said.

"Man, I never heard anyone sound so happy about shut eye before. Not even in the army," Gary said.

"I haven't had much sleep lately, not consistently," I explained.

Within the hour we had our gear packed and Roberto had us corralled into the back of his truck with two other Rudy Parra clients, Fred and Dave.

"Okay, this is it, there's no turning back now," Paul said as Roberto shut the tailgate. The five of us sat quietly on our packs and stared at the floor as we began the bumpy ride toward the Horcones Ranger Station.

"Are you three together?" asked Fred in a thick English accent.

"No…not really," I began.

"We're sharing a mule for our gear, but Ed over there is a loner, Gary and I are gonna give it a go as a team of two," finished Paul. By the time the 15 minute ride was over the five of us had thoroughly broken the ice. We'd learned that Fred was a retired colonel in the British military, had numerous ascents of peaks around the world under his belt, and was probably in better shape than the rest of us combined. Dave, an outdoor events coordinator from Wales, was in his early forties, was on his first big climbing trip, would be in tow of Fred, and just "wasn't able to get around to training, but figured that he'd make it up somehow during the hike into Plaza de Mulas."

"We'll see about that one!" Fred replied, shaking his head at Dave's lack of discipline.

"Not a problem. I'll just be a little behind you at first...then I'll do the leading up to the summit!" Dave answered with a huff.

"You guys look like you have pretty hefty packs, how much of your stuff is being carried in by mule?" I asked Fred as we unloaded our gear.

"None," Fred answered stiffly. "We just paid Rudy to drive us up here. We're carrying everything ourselves. No mules for us. That's cheatin'!"

"Fred thinks this is the army—that everything has to be painful as hell, all the time," Dave complained.

"Come on, Dave, lift that rucksack! Lift it! Come on! Let's go!" Fred yelled as he swung his stuffed-to-the-gills, olive-drab pack over his shoulder and bounded to the rangers' tent. Dave lit a cigarette, stared at his lopsided, variegated pack, and nearly threw out his back trying to lift it.

"I hope I brought enough cigarettes for this trip!" Dave yelped.

"Let's go. Quit complainin'!" bellowed Fred like a peg-legged ship's captain.

"Hey, look at that mountain!" Gary said as he pointed to the summit of Aconcagua, "it's...it's...so beautiful. So amazing! It looks like no one could ever have been up there. No one could ever go up there. *Are we really gonna climb that?!* Oh my god. It looks like a giant white pyramid, floating in the sky, ready to go up into heaven!" Gary had been so quiet up to this point that I was amazed to see him so animated.

"Wow. That looks really...*high*," said Paul in a feeble voice, "really, really high. I wonder how hard it'll be to breathe up there. *I wonder if I'll be able to breathe up there!* Aconcagua looks like it's on the edge of space!"

Although it's only a few hundred feet higher than Ojos del Salado, Aconcagua seemed loftier to me than its desert cousin, 400 miles to the north. I think this is due to the differences in the landscape. I remember the relatively homogenous visual nature of Ojos—the higher portions of the mountain look similar to the land surrounding its base. The view of Aconcagua from near the Horcones Ranger Station, by contrast, gives a much greater altitudinal perspective, with a lush green meadow in the foreground, jagged peaks in the near distance, and a bright white crown of snow capping the uppermost portions of the giant massif.

Each of us showed our permits to the rangers, signed the official *Parque Provincial Aconcagua* register, and received numbered trash bags that we would be required to turn in on our way out—full of all of our trash—or else face a stiff fine. "Okay, everyone, Dave and I'll see you at Confluencia Camp," Fred announced as he marched off. "Come on, Dave, let's get a move on!"

"Can't we just enjoy the beautiful morning?" Dave whimpered in response as he struggled to chase after Fred.

"We'll enjoy it when we get to camp. Move out!" Fred roared.

"Look at those two, huh?" Gary said. "They're really the odd couple." I shook my head and joked with Paul and Gary for a few minutes, then got on with my final preparations.

"I think it's going to be hot by the afternoon," I said as I scanned the clear blue sky for a hint of a cloud—*nothing...nothing at all...the clearest of clear days.*

"No shade, no clouds, no breeze, bright sun high in the sky...yep, we'll definitely be sweating, definitely be needing sunscreen," remarked Paul as he swirled SPF 45 sunblock over every bit of his exposed skin. I followed suit, then guzzled a half liter of water. I closed my eyes and felt the cool, pure liquid massage the back of my throat. I scanned the Lower Horcones Valley; heat waves danced off the valley floor.

"Hey Paul," I said, "I know there's supposed to be a reliable source of clean water at Confluencia, but let's just check with the rangers to make sure there hasn't been any recent change in that, huh?"

"Yeah, sounds like a good idea. I'll go ask...and I'll ask about water at Plaza de Mulas as well," Paul said as he ducked into the rangers' hut. He returned just seconds later. "No problems, clean water at Confluencia, clean water at Plaza de Mulas, and snow to melt all the way up from there to the summit."

"Alright, then. I'll see you at Confluencia," I said as I buckled my pack's waistbelt and flipped the lens cap off my Nikon. Gary and Paul waved briskly as I struck off on the first leg of my ascent. I quickly set my cadence, forcing myself into a healthy clip, then got lost in a world of thought.

I'd heard so many alluring vagaries about the mountain, but knew so few specifics. I wondered about the mountain's past, from its geologic inception, to its weather, to its glaciers, to its human visitors...the overall history.

Long after I returned home from my climb, I delved into the known facts about Aconcagua. It is a story that both captivates and confuses. Aconcagua is the zenith of a range dominated and defined by volcanoes (with the exception of the southern tail of the mountain chain), but Aconcagua itself is not a volcano. Aconcagua is the highest mountain in the Andes, but it doesn't lie in the highest portion of the range. In fact, it doesn't even lie on the true geomorphic crest of the Andes. Aconcagua was first climbed in 1897 by a Swiss mountain guide—or was the peak first climbed many years earlier by a long-forgotten Inca explorer? And if the Incas climbed the mountain first, how often did they make the ascent? By what route? For what reasons? And did they climb neighboring peaks as well?

No history of Aconcagua would be complete without recounting the story of the geologic development of the long chain of mountains in which it lies— it really wouldn't be complete without telling the geologic story of all of South America, for that matter. Best to begin more than 200 million years in the past when geography was much simpler: all the world's mountains, plains, valleys—everything terrestrial—belonged to one large super-continent sur-rounded by a huge ocean. What scientists would come to call continental crust had accreted into a giant mass of rock that 'floated' on top of more dense (aluminum rich) oceanic crust. Geologists have given this gigantic landmass the evocative name *Pangaea*, and the surrounding ocean the poetic title *Panthalassa* (Pangaea is Greek for 'all earth' and Panthalassa the Greek for 'all sea'). During the Late Triassic Epoch (200 million years ago, to be as exact as geologists can be) Pangaea began to split in two, forming the mega-continents *Laurasia* and *Gondwanaland*. Around 135 million years ago (the Early Creta-ceous Epoch) the planet's inexorable geologic churnings bifurcated Gondwanaland, creating what would become the modern continents of Africa and South America.

The Andes first took shape in the relatively recent Early Paleocene Epoch (about 65 million years ago) as the South American continent moved west-ward from Africa (powered by seafloor spreading—a process by which the seafloor diverges, as if by opposing conveyor belts, along a margin of upwelling magma), forcing the Nazca Plate to dive underneath South America's conti-nental bow in a process called subduction. The Nazca Plate is part of the Greater Pacific Basin, and continues to take the full brunt of this gargantuan tectonic force at the modern rate of up to six inches per year—lightning fast in geologic terms.

As the eastern edge of the Nazca plate was driven into the searing depths of the earth's aesthenosphere and mantle, it melted. Streams of molten pieces of the Nazca Plate forced their way up through fissures in the western margin of South America. Some of these vertical rivers of liquid rock cooled and solidi-fied underneath the land's surface to form massive bulbs of granite called plu-tons (southern Patagonia has some of the most dramatic examples of exposed and glacially-polished granitic plutons in the world). Many others, however, blasted through the surface in repeated violent eruptions, creating huge strato-volcanoes like Chimborazo and Cotopaxi (two famous volcanoes in Ecuador), Tupungato (near Aconcagua), Nevado del Ruíz (in Columbia), Pico Bolívar (highest mountain in Venezuela), and many, many more. Not only were the Andes rising as a result of this upwelling of magma, but the western edge of South America's crust was being squeezed, deformed, and uplifted, creating numerous faults and folds, thrusting the volcanoes ever higher into the sky.

The end result of this tectonic locomotion and collision is a somewhat tri-angular shaped continent with the Andes as its high spine—a 'backbone' lo-cated not in the center of the landmass where a backbone would logically stand, but on the extreme western edge of the continent, where the topogra-phy drops precipitously into the submerged Peru-Chile Trench, a long rictus created as the Nazca Plate dove under the South American Plate. The trench is at its deepest about 50 miles off the coast of Antofagasta, Chile, at 8,055 meters

(26,420 feet), making the total geologic relief of the Andes mountains (from the bottom of the Peru-Chile trench to the summit of Aconcagua, 650 miles to the southeast) 15,014 meters or 49,245.92 feet.

The land east of the Andes evokes the image of a flag, waving in the lee of the geologic currents that spawned the continent's Andean mast. A large swath of Precambrian rock in the northeastern third of South America sits relatively low, south of which a massive plain of flat sediment—weathered and washed down from the Andes—lies like an alluvial sheet spread across millions of square miles of the earth's surface.

While the birth of the Andes can be traced to one basic phenomenon, the subduction of the Nazca plate by the South American plate, this is hardly a homogenous range of peaks—that would be truly amazing for a chain of mountains over 5,000 miles long! Some Andean mountains, like Volcán Osorno, are symmetric cones; others, like the peaks of the Cordillera Blanca of Peru, are jagged and precipitous. Portions of the Andes, like the mountains on the Caribbean coast of Columbia, are carpeted by thick rainforest, contrasting with the high, dry giants of the Puna de Atacama. The reasons for these variations range from the heterogeneous geology of the South American and Nazca plates, to regional climate, to climate change through the ages, to the altitudes of individual mountains.

South America relief map

Most of the peaks of the Andes can be easily classified under several different schemes. Aconcagua, however, defies any simple form of taxonomy. Aconcagua isn't a volcano, but the peak is comprised of remnants of volcanoes past—ancient pyroclastic flows, decks of lava, and other igneous marvels jumbled together and thrown above the rest of the range.

While Aconcagua is the highest mountain in the Andes, the highest average region of the chain is the Ojos del Salado area, far to the north, which is home to a dense cluster of behemoths, including Cerro Pissis, Cerro Bonete, Tres Cruces, Incahuasi, Nevado del Cazadero, Cerro Nacimiento, and Ojos itself. I find it ironic that the highest mountain in South America is a sort of freak of tectonic nature, lying far from where I would expect the continent's apex to sit. The anomaly reminds me of North America's Denali and Asia's Mount Everest.

The little-known Icefields Range, deep in the interior of the St. Elias mountains of Alaska and the Yukon, is much higher, on average, than the Central Alaska Range, where Denali stands. The Icefields Range contains a wider array of peaks that stand over 16,000 and 17,000 feet (including the continent's second highest mountain, Mount Logan (19,545 feet; 5959 meters) and Mount St. Elias (18,025 feet; 5,495 meters)—North America's fourth highest peak) than the Central Alaska Range. Yet Denali, at 20,320 feet (6194 meters) is the highest on the continent—by just a few hundred feet. The second highest mountain in the Central Alaska Range, Mount Foraker, rises to only 17,400 feet (5,305 meters); the third highest, Mount Hunter, sits at just 14,573 feet (4,443 meters)—everything else in this stunning (and often extremely challenging) mountain group rests below 14,000 feet.

Similarly, the Concordia region of Asia, where 8 of the 30 highest peaks in the world sit (including K2, the world's second highest mountain, Hidden Peak, Broad Peak, Gasherbrum II, Gasherbrum IV, Chogolisa, and Masherbrum) is much higher than that which surrounds Mount Everest. I suppose it's silly to regard this arrangement as unfair—as if any region 'deserves' the honor of having its continent's highest point as part of its orographic repertoire. But I find it interesting that the absolute summits of North America, South America, and Asia lie outside of their respective continent's highest average mountain areas.

Even more compelling to me is that Aconcagua doesn't lie on the actual crest of the Andes. My first hint of this came when I noticed Aconcagua's position on a map. The peak sits entirely within Argentina, just a few miles east of the Chile-Argentina border. Many other great peaks of the Chile-Argentina region of the Andes, including Ojos del Salado, Tupungato, Incahuasi, and Llullaillaco, are split down their centers by the international border—a border which is defined along much of its length by the continental watershed divide, or as many geographers call it, the 'crest of the range.' It turns out that my instinct was correct—Aconcagua does lie just east of the crest. In this regard, Aconcagua is something of a hydrologic island.

Geology isn't the only hand that molds the planet's mountains. While the interior forces of the earth thrust the world's peaks into the skies, those skies whittle, carve, grind, grate, cut, scour, chisel, and generally beat those mountains back in the direction from whence they came. Climate's importance in shaping a mountain landscape varies from place to place. In a desert region such as the high Atacama, the land is weathered and eroded much more slowly than in a region that gets pounded with precipitation such as the mountains of the Chilean Lake District or Sierra Nevada de Santa Marta of Columbia. A number of factors dictate where glaciers and rivers form and how extensive these mountain-shaping instruments become. Among the determining influences are altitude, latitude, and regional climate.

Another element—actually a combination of geology and climate—is vegetation growth. Because the mountain sits to the east of the Andean crest and the region's predominant winds blow from the west, Aconcagua sits in a rain shadow, setting a relatively arid stage for the region's climate. Not nearly as dry as Ojos del Salado—there are green meadows sprinkled throughout the Aconcagua region, particularly around Lago Horcones—it is certainly much drier than the dense jungles covering the Andes of northern Columbia that rise directly off of the rain-drenched Caribbean. The restricted flow of moisture from the Pacific also means that Aconcagua's glaciers, while sizeable, don't compare to the monstrous tongues of ice found in the far southern Andes of Patagonia, where the combination of mountains, high latitude, and frequent storm lashings have created some of the most extensive terrestrial ice fields outside of Antarctica and Greenland. While Aconcagua's modern-day glaciers aren't huge, they were once fairly respectable in size—the terminal moraine of the Pleistocene glacier that carved the Horcones Valley still stands near Lago Horcones.

So just who was the first human to see Aconcagua in all of its geologic, climatological, and floral glory? And who was the first to climb the mountain? There are 'definitive' answers to these questions, but there is also a small pile of evidence leading to a big heap of speculation. On January 14, 1897, Mathias Zurbriggen, a famed Swiss mountain guide, became the 'first' person to climb to the summit of Aconcagua. He was part of an expedition led by Edmund FitzGerald, a British explorer who put forth a tremendous amount of organizational and physical effort in his attempts to ascend the peak. FitzGerald actually mounted two expeditions, one in 1896, and another in 1897. His 1896 expedition team sought a path to the base of the mountain via the Río de Vacas, but was rebuffed and decided to make an attempt from the Horcones Valley, marching in from Puente del Inca. Instead of going up to the head of the main Horcones Valley, however, the team veered into the Lower Horcones Valley at the confluence of the main fork and lower fork of the Horcones Rivers (site of Confluencia Camp). Soon they were faced with the daunting task of climbing the immense south face of the peak; the expedition quickly retreated to the rivers' confluence, where they headed up the main Horcones Valley and established a base camp near today's Plaza de Mulas. The expedition made a number of valiant attempts, but failed to approach the summit.

When FitzGerald returned the next year for his second attempt he brought Zurbriggen with him. After five attempts over the course of six weeks, the Swiss guide stood alone on the summit of South America after climbing what would come to be known as the Ruta Normal, along the northwest ridge of the mountain—my intended line of ascent. Almost a month later, on February 13, 1897, Zurbriggen again stood on the summit, this time with two other members of the expedition, Stuart Vines from Britain, and an Italian, Nicola Lanti. Unfortunately, FitzGerald never made it to the summit of Aconcagua—terrible bouts of altitude sickness mired him in the relative lowlands.

Amazingly, Matthias Zurbriggen, accompanied by Stuart Vines, traveled to Tupungato (6,550 meters; 21,490 feet) after the Aconcagua expedition and succeeded in making the first ascent of that peak a few weeks later. FitzGerald later wrote *The Highest Andes: A Record of The First Ascent of Aconcagua and Tupungato*. Published in 1899, this thick volume contains beautiful photographs, lengthy descriptions of the region, and a detailed map. FitzGerald's book remains one of the classics of mountaineering literature.

The FitzGerald expeditions, however, were not the first attempts to climb Aconcagua. In 1883, a German climber named Paul Güssfeldt arrived in Santiago, Chile, and set off toward the Andean crest with a small army of mules and mule drivers. The team made their way toward the peak by way of the Valle Hermoso, Río Volcán, and finally Portezuelo de los Penitentes, where Güssfeldt struck off to the northwest ridge—by himself. Incredibly, he made it to 6,560 meters (21,522 feet) on his first attempt. He tried again, but was unable to regain his previous altitude. He retreated in summit defeat, but succeeded in bringing back information that would prove vital to the successful FitzGerald expedition 14 years hence.

Predating Güssfeldt in travels to the Aconcagua area was a man who was to become renowned for his work a bit to the west of the Andes, Charles Darwin. After docking his vessel, *Beagle*, in Valparaiso, Chile in 1832, Darwin traveled to Puente del Inca with a French physician, Pierre-Joseph Pissis, and General Jose de San Martín, 'the first mountaineer of the Americas,' who earned the title by crossing the Andes to liberate Chile from Spain. Darwin's group made detailed observations of Aconcagua and environs, but made no attempts to climb it.

These intrepid Europeans certainly weren't the first humans to gaze upon the flanks of Aconcagua. The earliest known inhabitants of the area, the tribes of the Araucanos, Aymara, and Wari must have seen Aconcagua, as the peak is visible from much of the Pacific coast around what is today Santiago. Until 50 years after Aconcagua was 'first' climbed, nobody believed that any of the indigenous inhabitants of the area could have scaled the peak. Then, in 1947, an expedition approaching the top of the peak made an extraordinary discovery: the skeleton of a guanaco (a relative of the llama) was found on a ridge just below Aconcagua's summit. All of those European 'firsts' were immediately thrown into doubt.

While historians agree that the Araucanos, Aymara, and Wari didn't pursue mountain travel and exploration, the Inca certainly did. The Incan empire, which ruled luminously along 2,500 miles of the Andes, is well known to have held mountains and mountain rituals (like sacrifices) as integral to

196

their culture. There are many, many examples of Inca presence on a wide array of Andean peaks—not just travel on these mountains, but purposeful ascents of them. The most dramatic example is a mummy that was discovered inside an Incan altar on the very summit of Llullaillaco—a 6,723 meter (22,057 feet) high mountain! (The mummification process was environmental (like the Laguna Verde cow), not humanly facilitated). Other evidence of Inca rituals include an altar standing near 6,000 meters (19,680 feet) on Lincacabur, a volcano that straddles the Chile-Bolivia border, and a mummy found at the 5,200 meter (17,056 foot) level of Cerro Piramidal, a subsidiary peak of Aconcagua.

Was the guanaco being led to the summit of Aconcagua for an Incan ritual? It would have been some extraordinary guanaco to have climbed to that extreme altitude (well over 22,000 feet) by itself, on its own volition! Without a doubt, an Incan—or Incans—led the animal to that breathless point. Did those who lured the hapless guanaco on this death march push just a little higher, reaching the summit? Are the remains of this guanaco evidence of the one and only Incan attempt on the mountain? Or were there many 'expeditions' launched on the summit? Why, if Incans had been to Aconcagua's summit, did they not leave any evidence of their superlative-altitude passage? Perhaps they did, and the elements destroyed all traces of any altars, shrines, or remains of sacrifice left on the very summit (the guanaco, lying farther down the mountain, was somewhat protected from the most vile of the peak's elemental temperaments). Or perhaps treading on the apex of such a high and awe-inspiring mountain would be considered a slight to their deities. But remember! Not only did Incas get to the summits of Lincancabur and Llullaillaco, they left traces of their passage on both. I want to believe that the Incas did reach the summit of Aconcagua. I can't imagine a member of a civilization so devoted to mountains and mountain worship coming so close to the zenith of their realm and not taking the final steps.

In 1532 Francisco Pizarro and his army of 168 men captured and killed the king of the Incas, dooming the Inca society. Thus began a nearly 300 year rule by the Spanish, which ended when General Jose de San Martín led his 'Army of the Andes'—5,300 soldiers, 9,280 mules, and 1,600 horses—into Chile by way of the Paso de la Cumbre. The general succeeded in his assault, but his was a Pyrrhic victory, exacting the lives of half his soldiers, 1,000 horses, and 6,000 mules.

In January of 1899, England's Sir William Martin Conway reached the summit of Aconcagua. Many sources claim that he was the second person to climb South America's highest mountain, but he was really the fourth person, as Zurbriggen returned with Vines and Lanti after he made the first. Including Zurbriggen's two separate ascents, Conway's climb was the fifth ascent overall (by Europeans, anyway). As with Zurbriggen, Conway chose the northwest ridge as his path to the summit. I suppose this is when the Ruta Normal became the *Ruta Normal*. Conway, like FitzGerald, embarked on an authorship adventure subsequent to his summit success; his book, *Aconcagua and Tierra del Fuego*, is much livelier and more entertaining than FitzGerald's *The Highest Andes*.

37 years after Zurbriggen's first success, In March of 1934, Aconcagua saw the first ascent of its slopes by a line other than the Ruta Normal. A Polish expedition which had just made the first ascent of Mercedario, a monstrous peak to the north of Aconcagua, was set on climbing the continent's highest point by a novel route. The Poles marched up the Vacas and Relinchos Valleys to the base of Aconcagua's eastern aspect, and stormed to the summit in three days on what would come to be known as the Polish Glacier.

A route on the Western aspect of the mountain came next. In 1953, after a great amount of planning and many setbacks, Francisco Ibáñez, Frédéric and Doris Marmillod, and Fernando Grajales pioneered a route that traverses the west face of Aconcagua from Plaza de Mulas to the south ridge, on which the route continues to the summit.

With the north, east, and west aspects of Aconcagua tackled, the greatest of the mountain's challenges awaited an attempt: the south face, one of the most immense mountain walls on the planet. The south face of Aconcagua rises 2,500 vertical meters (a little over 8,000 feet) off the Lower Horcones Glacier, and is defined by huge bands of vertical cliffs, hanging glaciers, and frequent avalanches. The south face is long, difficult, and dangerous—and of course, very high. But none of these obstacles kept a team of seven French climbers from attempting this coveted mountaineering first in 1954. Over the course of one month, the group endured wild storms, avalanches, extreme climbing, and incredible stress. Six of them made it to the summit, reaching their goal at night. Many of the summit team were stricken with frostbite, and after being evacuated to Mendoza, endured amputations.

Many more routes and firsts have been established on Aconcagua's various aspects throughout the years by climbers from around the world. Some of these lines were completely pioneered from base to summit; others are variations on previously established routes. And there still remains a lot of untrodden rock, ice, and snow on Aconcagua on which future climbers may test themselves and claim 'first' status.

Pushing myself under the press of the relentless sun that morning overheated me quickly. The hot, dry air slurped me toward dehydration. I continued at a slowed pace, constantly wishing that I was 'already there.' I crossed a sturdy bridge over the thrashy Río Horcones, then slowed my pace even more as I traversed the east side of a steep ravine. Before long I was hiking along a level plain of gravel, passing the occasional outbound climber, and watching lines of mules trot toward and away from the mountain like box cars along a busy railway. I thought I spotted the mule that Paul, Gary, and I had hired, but the horse-riding mule driver prodded the animals along a little too fast for me to tell for sure.

About three hours after starting out I came to a steep descent that ended at a bridge over the Lower Horcones River. "Hey there!" I yelled at the sight of Dave. He was red in the face, panting, and slouched over his pack.

"I hate this rucksack. HATE IT!" he cried. I dropped my pack and sat down next to him, feeling slightly dizzy from the heat.

"You know, Dave...you have the biggest nose I have ever seen in my life," I blurted as he turned his head into the sun.

"I know. I'm from Wales. I guess we have big noses," he said.

"Here, take one of my trekking poles. I can't believe you don't have a set. They're life savers."

"Thanks. Thanks so much. Oh, my back," Dave groaned.

"Come on. Not to be like Fred, or anything, but let's get to camp. I think it's close. Where is Fred, by the way?"

"He won't wait for me. That's our agreement—I didn't train, so he won't wait for me. So be it...yeah, let's get a move on." Dave stood up and we hiked and talked our way through the last 15 minutes to Confluencia. "Just look at that place!" Dave said as he pointed to the camp.

"Not like I imagined...not like I imagined at all," I said.

CHAPTER NINETEEN
HORCONES SHUFFLE

Confluencia menu

Hamburguer, Beers, Fast Food, Breakfast A large sign greeted Dave and me as we crossed a wambly, sagging bridge over the main fork of the Horcones River. The advertisement had been draped over the side of a boxy tent on the outskirts of the Confluencia Camp. We stopped and stared at it—first in disbelief and slight disgust, then in excitement. "A hamburger does sound kind of good, don't you think?" I asked Dave.

Shaking his head, he replied, "Yeah…but, I just didn't expect this…I…guess we're really not that far from Puente del Inca, and those mules get in here fast. So I suppose there's no reason why they can't have beer and burgers here…right?"

"Let's go," I said. A half hour after we'd ducked into the green Quonset-tent, two tiny, skinny, cardboard-like hamburgers arrived on paper plates. "Those are the size of White Castle burgers," I said, remembering the 29 cent marvels from my youth in New York, "how much do you think these cost?"

"I'm sure they're totally expensive—probably something like two dollars for each of these skimpy things," Dave replied. We ordered two Cokes to go with the burgers.

Confluencia Camp

"You've got to be kidding me! Five dollars for each of these little hamburg-ers! FIVE BUCKS EACH!!" I screamed at Dave. "No way…no way at all." I gulped down some soda, then stared at the top of the can, wondering what we'd be charged for the drinks.

"Three dollars! Three dollars for a Coke!" Dave yelled. I waited until the cook/waiter/money-taker looked my way, then I inhaled my burger in one medium-sized bite. Dave did the same, coughing a little as he ungled down the overcooked, miniscule treat. Then we downed the last of our sodas and paid the bill. We grimaced; the attendant grinned. "Hey look," Dave grabbed my attention, "*hot dogs* is crossed out in duct tape. What do you think they would charge for them if they had any?"

"I bet they aren't real hot dogs, more like little Vienna sausages, wrapped in paper-thin bread," I answered.

"There's Fred." Dave pointed to his partner, who was pitching their tent.

"There now, tent staked out, stove set up, food ready, everything's set to go," Fred announced as we set down our packs. "You feeling okay, Dave?" Fred asked, slapping the dust off his hands. Dave fell flat on his butt, then sprawled in a big 'X' on the grass.

"Oh, yeah…I'll be fine," Dave said, yawning.

"Well, this is the easiest part, you know. You better get in shape—quick!"

"You'll be eatin' my dust all the way to the summit!" Dave snickered.

"There's Paul and Gary; I wonder how they're feeling?" Fred asked. I looked up to see them trotting into camp behind a line of mules.

"Hey, Paul," I asked after he had collapsed on the ground near us, "when is our mule going to get here?"

"Probably already came," he said.

"So…where's our stuff?"

"At Plaza de Mulas by now, or close to it."

"You're kidding, right?" I asked, "I thought they'd drop our stuff off at Confluencia, then continue to Plaza de Mulas the next day."

"Nope, they go all the way in one shot," Paul said. I threw my hands up and flopped on my back.

"I have no food—I have to eat those five dollar burgers for dinner!" I said.

"You brought your tent and sleeping bag, right?" Gary asked.

"Sleeping bag, yes; tent, no," I answered.

"Well, I don't think it'll rain tonight…good thing," Fred added.

"Yeah, but I don't have any food. I'll have to eat those burgers…" I said.

"Just money," Dave said, "just money. Look where you are! Who cares about five dollar burgers?" Dave was right. I sat up and looked around. Confluencia Camp lies in a beautiful verdant nook tucked away in the dry Horcones Valley.

Mule train approaches Confluencia Camp

Every small glance brought big views of the wildly diverse surroundings: yellowish cliffs stroked with swirls of twisted strata; brown, ragged cliffs whisked by clouds and wind; and mules…mules everywhere, trotting into and out of the small green hollow that was the backdrop for the swath of tents that defined the camp.

"Come on, Dave. Let's get some rest. We're going to wake up early tomorrow—long before dawn—for our march up to Plaza de Mulas," Fred commanded. The odd couple crawled into their tent; Paul, Gary, and I hiked up the grassy slopes to a comfortable perch above the camp.

"We're barely into the afternoon and Fred wants to sleep!" Gary whispered to me as we hiked away. "That guy's nuts!"

"He'll get to the summit, watch, he'll get there. Besides, it's probably just a nap, they'll wake up later on and make dinner or something. We should probably do the same, except our hike tomorrow is like half what theirs' is with all that gear they're carrying," Paul added. The three of us rested against a large, cool rock and looked down on the goings-on of the camp like a trio of trolls.

"Look at all those trails dug into the sides of the meadow," I said. "They criss-cross so much that the grass looks like a patterned quilt."

"You'd think they'd just get one trail going for both the mules and the people, instead there's like 20 for people, and, well, I guess the mules are smarter when it comes to stuff like this, so they probably have only one or two," Gary commented. "The mules know what they're doing, even with all of that junk strapped onto their backs."

I counted 15 tents in camp in addition to the large mess tents set up by the 'vendors.' "This place looks like it's far from capacity, look at all those unused tent sites down there," I said just as a lone guy came rushing into camp as if he had a plane to catch.

"What's that guy doing?" Gary asked with a perplexed note.

"Finding...tent sites for...*them*," Paul answered, pointing to a long line of tired hikers tripping over themselves into camp. The group bunched up like a compressed accordion when they reached the river crossing.

"Hey, look. They stopped. Tent-finder-runner-guy is going over to help them across..." I said, mimicking a sports commentator.

"Yeah, now he's helping each of them cross the bridge. Wow! They can't get over that bridge on their own? I can't believe that. How the heck are they going to get up the mountain if they can't even do that?" Paul cried.

"Yeah, and look how fat they all are!" blurted Gary.

"I wonder if this is some strange weight loss program...actually, what a great idea," I added. There were about ten people in the group, most of them noticeably overweight. Once across the river, each dropped his L.A.-purse-sized backpack (probably no more than five or six pounds total) and mulled about, rubbing bellies and scratching heads. "These guys are the Anti-Freds," I said.

"They could definitely use some Fredness, for sure," Paul added.

"He's definitely the leader." I pointed to they guy running around. "I think this is one of those guided expeditions that are advertised in the backs of climbing magazines. And he's the guide."

"How do you join those?" Gary asked.

"Well, for most of them, you have a bank account," I said, "with enough in it to cover your plane ride and the however-many-thousands of dollars for the trip itself. Aconcagua is one of the coveted 'seven summits' and this route is supposed to be really easy. Lots of people want to climb it."

"You don't have to pass any physical requirements?" Gary asked.

"You have to have a pulse—somewhere on your body," Paul quipped.

"They're not all like that, but a lot are. Individual guides with regular clients are different, but this is one of those large, organized trips. I can't believe these people are up here," I said.

"That guy's definitely the leader, he's pointing to tent sites...and...it looks like he's assigning people to different places," Gary added.

"He's the leader all right...he's the duke...the commander...the commander of the Anti-Freds," I continued.

"Commander Taco," Gary said.

"Commander Taco? Where'd that come from?" Paul asked.

"I don't know. I just look at those fat people and think of Taco Bell."

"You have Taco Bell in Australia?" I asked.

"We're not just out running around eating lizards and kangaroos, you know. Of course we have Taco Bell!"

The name stuck. For the next few minutes we sat and stared at Commander Taco leaping about as the Anti-Freds wobbled to and fro. I was amazed by how quickly CT had his group's tent sites claimed and tents laid out. It wasn't that he worked with any kind of grace or exceptional efficiency, he just had a lot of energy, like a Chihuahua after eating a pound of ground-up diet pills. Everything seemed to be moving along—almost at the speed of light—for Commander Taco. Then he hit a rock, literally, smack in the middle of a well padded-down tent site. The rock didn't look very large. It couldn't have been jutting above the dirt more than one or two inches, but Commander Taco just had to move it. Paul, Gary, and I watched intently as CT, surrounded by the Anti-Freds, tried to dislodge the annoyance.

"I say that rock is pretty big. I bet ninety-nine percent of it is under the ground," said Gary.

"Hey look, now he's kicking it—hard...this guy has the brains of a taco!" Paul said. Commander Taco walloped the rock with the heel of his right boot, then slammed it with the toe of his left boot—to no avail.

"You know, hundreds of people have probably set tents up on that site, and nobody minded that little rock. What's wrong with this guy?" I asked.

"Hey look, now he's showing his intellectual might...*Man the tool user*," Paul announced. Commander Taco lifted another rock, this one the size of a small television, arched his back, and shuffled his feet to the pesky protrusion. We could see his red face from nearly 50 yards away as he lurched and tossed the tiny boulder into the air. The projectile missed its target by a foot. He stood still for the first time since arriving at camp as he massaged his lumbar vertebrae. Then, after some head scratching and a little spectator input from the Anti-Freds, he picked up still another rock, knelt down next to the problem rock, and proceeded to beat it with a level of ferociousness I didn't know was possible outside of a battlefield. He screamed every vituperation imaginable—and then some—as he feverishly pounded rock against rock like a crazed dog digging a hole to find a bone. By now everyone in camp had dropped what he was doing and stared in disbelief at the excavation project. After about 20 minutes of this, the offending nubbin of rock finally yielded to Commander

Taco—the exposed portion broke off. Paul, Gary, and I cheered like drunken fans at the big game. Commander Taco scowled at us, then went back to work erecting tents.

I felt naked without my stove, fuel, and food. I considered toughing it out…not eating until I reached Plaza de Mulas, but that would be at least 24 hours. *No way*, I thought. *I'll probably pass out.* So I grabbed my wallet and marched into *El restaurante del Confluencia*, as I thought of it. An hour-and-a-half later I walked out 43 dollars poorer, but satiated.

I woke at dawn after a calm, cool night under the stars. The positive aspect of not having much gear is that packing is easy and takes just minutes. I filled my drinking bottle from a tiny stream of crystal-clear water on the north side of camp, then climbed the steep western slope of the small canyon. Once out of the dell, the grade of the slope leveled, granting me a huge vista of straightforward, enjoyable walking. After 15 minutes of hiking, I stopped in my tracks when my eyes fell upon what must be one of Horcones Valley's most treasured works: a peak built of sinuously twisted, delicately layered, yellow, rust, and silver colored rock.

The trail intersects the Horcones River about a mile-and-a-half out of Confluencia. I easily crossed the shallow water by hopping from one exposed rock to another. I wondered how many more river crossings I'd have before reaching Plaza de Mulas—I also wondered if I'd arrive with dry feet.

I soon faced a well-known Horcones Valley landmark, Piedra Grande, which means *big rock* in Spanish—and that's just what this landmark is, a really big rock. Piedra Grande stands alone on the wide, flat valley floor bounded on either side by high, scabrous peaks.

After ten minutes of musing about solitude, I left Piedra Grande and continued toward my day's goal. The sky was quickly turning gray as puffy cumulus crashed into one another. Clouds of a different sort, dust clouds, came hollering down the valley as the wind revved up. I spotted a line of little black dots in the distance. A string of mules charged out of a wall of dust.

Cerro Piramidal, a sub-peak of Aconcagua that lies a couple of miles to the southwest of the main summit, was my dominant landmark as I walked north from Piedra Grande. As its name suggests, Piramidal is shaped like a huge pyramid. Using Cerro Piramidal to gauge my progress, I moved swiftly, across broad alluvial fans, over small boulder fields, even through sections of sand. Soon Piramidal was to my back and my next landmark was a huge peak that seemed to mark the very head of the valley, Cerro Bonete.

Cerro Piramidal

205

The trail petered out shortly after passing Piramidal. From that point I simply walked up the valley, jumping over strand after strand of the braided Horcones River. The river reminded me of waters I'd seen in Alaska, particularly those on the north side of Denali. I had to stop, scan the river's path, then carefully pick just the right strand to jump—at just the right spot. A few times I got myself boxed in by streams too wide to leap over and had to backtrack. I eventually made it through the labyrinthine section of the Horcones, without a drop of water on my shoes.

Geology of the Horcones Valley

I spotted the trail again shortly after putting the river to my back. By now the sky was so well concealed by thick clouds I didn't need sunglasses. *Pretty dark*, I thought. Not only were the clouds dense, they appeared to be sinking in altitude, an almost sure sign that a storm was on its way. I had to move quickly—I didn't have any food, nor did I have my gore-tex jacket. *Bad planning*, I chided myself, over and over. *Move, move, move!*

The trail climbed away from of the valley floor and contoured along the foot of a large bluff—a bluff that ultimately led to the main flanks of Aconcagua itself.

I was finally on the very base of the massif. I dropped into a small ravine—and stood face to face with Dave. "Hey there!" I said.

"Hi." Dave looked as if he'd been run over by a train.

"You okay?" I asked.

"Uh! This hike is killing me! We got up at two o'clock in the morning and started out. By eight o'clock Fred was already miles ahead of me. He's probably in camp by now." I saw that Dave was eating some crackers and cheese. I felt hungry—then I felt faint.

"Hey, you got any more of that food?" I asked.

"Oh, yeah, a whole can of meat spread and some biscuits. Here." Dave handed me a can of meat and a military pack of crackers.

"You sure?" I asked.

"Hey, if you eat all of that, it's just that much less weight I have to carry!" he said as he lit a cigarette.

I devoured the crackers and meat spread. "Come on, Dave, let's get a move on. There's a storm coming. We'll walk together all the way to camp, huh? And here, take one of my trekking poles," I said.

"Look, that must be Plaza de Mulas," Dave said. Tiny blue, red, white, and yellow dots speckled the top of a dark bluff that stood far in the distance.

"Those are the tents of Plaza de Mulas...you think?" I asked. Dave looked at me and shrugged his shoulders.

"I guess. I don't know what else it would be."

"Looks a long way off...and look at those clouds, they're right on top of the camp. It's probably going to be snowing there within the hour," I said. "Let's move as fast as we can, huh?" The landscape surrounding Plaza de Mulas was so devoid of light under the dense blanket of storm clouds that the camp seemed to be hovering in space. I coaxed Dave along for the next hour. He moved not only slowly, but hesitantly. I offered to carry his backpack for him at one point when I saw he was teetering side to side apoplectically, but instead he 'took ten' and rested. We finally made it to an abandoned stone building that marks the site of the lower Plaza de Mulas—then it started snowing.

"We still have to go almost a mile to get to camp. I don't know if I can make it. That hill is supposed to be the hardest part of the day. It's really steep," Dave said. The hill he referred to is known as the *Subida Brava* (tough climb), and it looked to be a muscle-burning, lung-wrenching finale.

Dust storm, Horcones Valley

Mule train, Horcones Valley

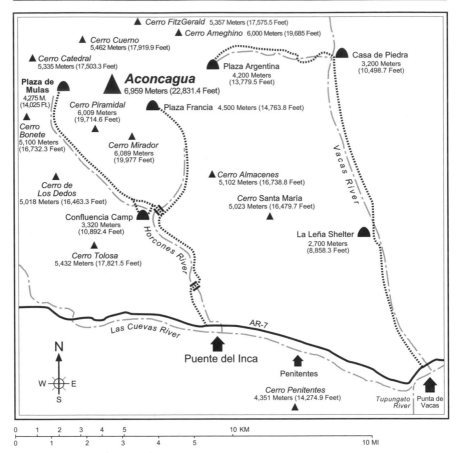

Aconcagua Approach Map

Map details primary approach routes into the various aspects of Aconcagua.

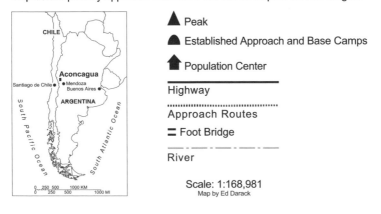

▲ Peak

🅰 Established Approach and Base Camps

⬆ Population Center

Highway

•••••••••••••••••••••••••••••
Approach Routes

⚌ Foot Bridge

River

Scale: 1:168,981
Map by Ed Darack

"Come on, Dave. Let's go! We have to get moving. It's starting to snow hard. Did that trekking pole help you out?" I asked.

"Yeah, it helped a lot. Don't think that I could have made it here without it. Thanks." Dave seemed barely coherent.

"Okay, then take my other one; with two poles you should be able to make it up this thing. Come on!" I urged Dave. He hoisted his pack and leaned on both poles. I started up, ordering him to try to keep close behind me. He did, for about 15 feet, then he stopped in his tracks and hunched over the poles. "Dave! Dave!!" I yelled. "Look at the storm. Pretty soon this place will be covered in snow. Do you need me to carry your pack *and you* up this little hill?" I ran down the steep, loose slope and got behind him, caught my breath, then started pushing him up the slope.

"Okay—okay—okay—I'm going, I'm going!" Dave yelled, then took a slow and shaky step toward his goal. Fortunately, the storm wasn't as bad as I had feared. It dusted us for a while, then lifted, then closed in again and loosed some more snow.

"Hey look at our progress, Dave...we must be almost halfway to camp by now. I'm going to jump ahead, drop my things and come back down for your pack, okay?"

"Sounds good. I'll just wait here," Dave responded in a drunk-like slur.

"Nope, you have to keep moving. You gotta keep moving, okay?" I said as I jumped ahead of him and sprinted up a steep section of the switchbacked trail. "See you in a bit. Keep moving up!" I yelled one last time. "Whoa!" I screamed my lungs empty at the site of a decaying mule carcass, just off the trail. I stood on the steepest section of the hill. "Watch yourself, Dave!" I yelled down. "This section is steep and slippery, enough that even one of those mules couldn't make it." Dave nodded, then continued to noodle his way upslope.

I crested the rise about ten minutes later. Camp appeared to be a good half-mile distant. I felt tired and starved—the last thing I needed was to see that I still had a half a mile to reach my tent and food. But I didn't care, because the clouds around me broke apart, revealing tantalizing bits of Aconcagua's immense west face, freshly sprinkled by a light snowfall. Forgetting about food, water, tents—even Dave—I ripped open my camera pack and propped up my tripod. Within a minute I was shooting as fast as I could advance my film.

"Hey there! Hey there!" came a booming voice. I backed away from my camera and looked up to see a lone figure about 50 yards away. "Ed, is that you?" Fred called.

"Yep, it's me," I hollered back, then ignored Fred and went back to shooting. My tingly fingers fell numb as I adjusted the metal tripod. The day felt colder than I'd anticipated. With a deep ache pulsing from my fingertips, I returned to my viewfinder. I could see that the west face was huge, even though I could glimpse just small portions of it at a time.

"Where's Dave? Did you see him?" Fred yelled as he jogged over to me.

"Yeah, he's down there, I was going to get into camp, drop my pack, then go back to help him…but…uh…I have to take pictures first…he'll be alright."

Fred shook his head, "Thanks, thanks a lot. You don't have to go back for him, I'll run down and make sure he gets up here." I continued shooting, then noticed Dave cresting the bluff. He had made it most of the way on his own. Fred sprinted down and grabbed his pack, then prodded him to tough out the last bit of the hike. I was still shooting when the two of them passed me and headed for their camp, long since set up by Fred. Although I knew that I'd have many more opportunities to shoot the region—likely with far better light—I couldn't wrest myself from my beloved camera.

A half hour later, after most of the day's light had dissipated, I passed the first landmark of the 'new' Plaza de Mulas: an outhouse. The 'old' Plaza de Mulas had been located very close to the crest of the bluff, but it received so much business that clean water could no longer be found there.

Plaza de Mulas was packed with tents, of both climbers and muleteers. The camp looked like a small city of nylon buildings. I tried to count all the fabric structures; I quit at 40, when I noticed that the camp extended well beyond the top of a small rise to the north. Plaza de Mulas was the most heavily populated base camp I'd ever seen, by far.

I strolled into the high *ciudad*, searching for the Rudy Parra tent. I felt the cold, and imagined a tentless night, *very different from the balmy Confluencia*.

Rudy's outfit sat near Exit Three on the Plaza de Mulas Turnpike. A thin woman with braided hair and a bright orange shirt greeted me, then dragged my bag from a back room once I'd identified myself. She must have been up at altitude for a long time. She breathed without effort, even as she tossed the heavy bag my way. I grabbed for it and noticed a full case of Coca-Cola. I gulped my gritty, raspy throat, and in an epiphany realized why some marketer in a place far from Aconcagua coined the term *soft drink*. I had to have one. I didn't care about cost. Even 50 bucks—or pesos—whatever currency they used up there would be worth it to satisfy my need. "Umm…un Coca-Cola…*por favor*," I asked, trying to contain my rapacity. She handed me a can. It felt warm—it was probably colder than any refrigerator I ever knew of, but then the ambient temperature was probably much colder than most industrial freezers. I popped it open—and it exploded all over my face, no doubt due to the altitude and a not-so-gentle mule ride up from PDI. The only choice I had was to drink it in one gulp, testing both my stomach's elasticity and my ability to hold my breath at 14,000 feet. I staggered backward and let out a huge sigh, rolling my eyes as the drink fizzed away the coarseness of my inner mouth and throat. I punctuated my not-too-smooth display with a belch; I couldn't help it. The soda didn't set me back 50 dollars, just three—it was just about the best three dollars I'd ever spent.

I found a small, flat clearing about 75 feet from Rudy's tent, far away from any latrine that I could see (or smell). I hobbled to the pad and dropped my gear. Night was approaching quickly; I guessed that I had less than five minutes to either make camp or start digging for my headlamp. I chose the former. Soon I had my small tent set up and tied down, my stove ready to burn, and my sleeping bag laid out. I'd staked my claim at Plaza de Mulas. Now I could relax.

And relax I did. I rubbed my feet against the dry, soft inner wall of my sleeping bag. The hike hadn't been particularly difficult; the conditions weren't life threatening, but the trek had tired me. I laid back and relished not having a single worry—life was placid and carefree, for at least eight hours or so.

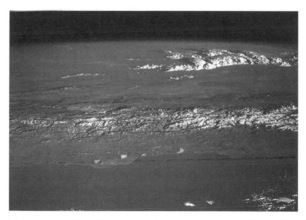

Space view of the Andes that lie between the Aconcagua and Ojos del Salado regions

213

CHAPTER TWENTY

THAT STRANGE PLACE CALLED PLAZA DE MULAS

While a human looks on, a mule ponders existence at Plaza de Mulas

My perceptions during the opening days of the Aconcagua expedition had been ruled almost exclusively by sight and sound. During my first morning at Plaza de Mulas, however, smell dominated my sensory outlook; I awoke to the scent of cigarette smoke. Confused, I unzipped my tent and flung my head into the blinding morning. I tossed on my glasses and stared straight at the source of the smoke—a small, baby blue tent about 15 feet from my tiny cocoon. The door of the blue tent was half-open, revealing the upper portion of a very content, very Nordic looking guy apparently clothed in nothing but a captain's cap; a burning cigarette dangled from his lips. The smoker looked at me and broke a slight smile. I scratched my scalp and yawned. I felt a bit flabbergasted by the scene, but not too much; I wasn't completely awake yet.

I stared at the immense west face of Aconcagua, the foot of which lay only a few hundred yards from me. Big towering washboards of sepia-and-orange-toned-rock stood high, layers upon layers. I skittered my eyes in a maze throughout the wall for a few minutes, concluding that I'd get more excited when the light was right. My gaze returned to the naked-but-for-a-captain's-cap smoking guy as if I was waiting for him to say something profound, something that would kick me out of my sleep-wake limbo.

The 'captain' seemed to be studying the flow of the rising blue smoke in the placid morning air. I stared at the smoke too, wondering if it rose more slowly than smoke would at sea level, or perhaps faster. Then I focused on the wafting patterns themselves, amazed that a place renowned for its extreme winds now had air so tranquil that rising smoke could spin patterns unhindered. "Do you want a cigarette?" the smoker asked in an accent I couldn't place. I stared at him for a few moments, peeved that he shooed away the fractal-like patterns of smoke I'd been studying.

"Yeah. Sure. I'll have a cigarette," I said.

"Hold on. Let me put on my clothes and get you one. Or maybe…you would like…*two?*" the guy said as I slipped my bare feet into my hiking boots.

"I never thought I'd smoke up high. At least not while heading *up* a mountain. I was a smoker for a while, then I quit, then I started again, quit again—over and over. I started again about a month before coming down here, but quit a few weeks before beginning this trip. I figured that it would be bad for high altitude climbing," I said.

"You sound really confused. Like you can't decide whether you want to smoke or not. And no, it isn't true that smoking is bad for high altitude climbing. It's actually good. It's especially good for acclimatization. I smoked at the North Col of Everest—7,800 meters. I have a Russian friend who smoked a cigarette on the summit of Everest—after climbing it without bottled oxygen."

"You're kidding, right? I can't believe that…well, maybe I can, since the guy is Russian," I said.

"No. I'm not kidding. I took 20 cartons of cigarettes with me to Everest, and no bottled oxygen. In America you never hear about the Russian climbers and their techniques. They are good climbers. Really tough."

I stood up and felt a mild head rush. "So you're going to smoke all the way up Aconcagua?" I asked.

"I'll have a cigarette on the summit."

"I think you're crazy. There's no way your lungs can handle it. *No way.*"

"You'll see. If you can make it up there with me, that is." My friend laughed confidently at me, as if summiting was a foregone conclusion for him. "Here, take four. Get smoking. Get acclimatized. You look like you could use some."

"Thanks, I'll take them because I have a craving for one right now. Definitely not for acclimatization, though. I'll probably only have a few," I said as I reached for the cigarettes. "What's your name…and where are you from?"

"I'm Harry, and I'm from Finland. I'm a guide. I'm guiding four other Finns, plus I have two Chilean assistants with me. I'd say that we're having a pretty good time so far. A real party on Aconcagua. Here, let me light one of those for you." Harry reached his arms out of his tent and struck a match. He hovered the flame over the tip of the cigarette as I puffed. I sputtered and coughed as the coarse smoke grated the inside of my lungs. I breathed deeply for a few seconds, then took a long drag. Two seconds later I thought I was floating. The

Harry

sensation came so powerfully that I lost my balance. Harry laughed as I stumbled over small rocks before regaining my footing; I flopped on my rear just outside of his tent. "So what's your name?" Harry asked.

"Ed. I'm Ed. And you're a high altitude dope pedlar. Pushers in inner cities use similar tactics. They give away free 'stuff,' assuring that those recipients will come back for more," I stuttered.

"Except I'm never going to charge you for any cigarettes. You can have all you want. All the way up this mountain and all the way down. I really love smoking up high. Not enough people do it. I'm glad you're smoking. Now I have someone to smoke with."

Harry and I chatted for the better part of an hour that morning. By trade he worked as a stonemason; by entrepreneurial spirit, he pursued his avocation as an international mountain guide. "I don't hate my job back home, but I don't love it either. It's hard. It pays well...but I'd rather do this full time. Problem is, I don't want to be in this part of the Andes, you know, this exact spot. Too crowded, so many people here. Look at all of them. Everyone wants to come here, it's *the highest*, you know. That's what everyone is so obsessed with, the *highest*. Go and see for yourself, go and see how many people are looking around at this beautiful place, I mean *really* looking around, seeing all of it; probably won't find one. Not a single one, I bet. So many people up here just want to go home and say they climbed to the top of South America. Nobody experiences the mountain, or tries to meet other people up here. People here can be really unfriendly, like they are in court and they're afraid of saying the wrong thing."

I smoked another cigarette with Harry; it had far less effect than the first one. "It's never as good as that first drag," said Harry of smoking for the first time at high altitude. After a bit more conversing about Aconcagua and climbing, Harry got up to help his assistants with breakfast and I decided to find Dave and Fred. "It was great to meet you. Come back later and we'll drink some beer, or maybe even some whiskey," Harry said.

"Beer? Whiskey! You brought that stuff up here with you?"

"No, but you can buy it up here."

"Buy it? *Where?*"

"A lot of places. Look around. They bring it with the mules, you can get just about anything up here. Want to call home?" he asked me.

"*What?*" I glared incredulously at Harry.

"Turn around." I spun a 180 and locked my eyes on a sign advertising a satellite phone service that would allow a call anywhere in the world for a ten dollar connection fee plus five bucks a minute. "Want a shower?"

"Not yet," I replied, almost without thinking about the question. *As if there would be a shower up here*, I thought.

"Well look to the west. When you *do* want one you'll know where to go— that's a hotel over there."

I squinted at a wooden building about a quarter of a mile distant that appeared to be the size of a large house.

"You can get a hot shower over there for ten dollars. The trail breaks off down by the ruins at the base of the bluff we're sitting on. They bring tourists in on horseback. There's also a trail from here, if you want to go."

"Do they really have warm water?" I asked.

"Yes. I think they do. People who have been there tell me they do. We're going to go over for a shower in a few days, after we've done a carry to the next camp and are good and smelly."

"How much for a night?" I asked.

"I don't know. Probably a lot. But you never know. They have a phone over there, too. I hear that someone around here even has a way to send e-mail!" Harry walked to his team's mess tent as I grabbed my camera and struck off to find Dave and Fred.

"One last thing, Ed," Harry shouted.

"Yeah?"

"Keep an eye on your things." The wily Finn walked over to me. "I'd keep that tripod of yours inside your tent, along with everything else you have. With all the conveniences of the big city, Plaza de Mulas has a lot of urban problems, too. People come and go like crazy around here, especially with the mule teams; theft is a big problem. Watch yourself."

"Thanks. I will. Do me a favor, Harry, watch my tent while I am out and about. I'll do the same for you guys."

"Thanks, sounds good."

Plaza de Mulas seemed to go on forever. I had no idea of the camp's sprawl until I began hiking around. Paths swerved in and out of tent pads, most of which were occupied. Tents were so tightly packed that I felt a little embarrassed walking among them; I felt like I was constantly invading someone's privacy. Stares and glares shot back and forth. Every now and then I'd get a wave, or even a smile, but welcoming demeanors seemed to be a scarce commodity in Plaza de Mulas.

People raced around the camp, setting up tents, breaking them down, dropping off supplies, and picking up gear to move higher. I never thought I'd describe a place 14,000 feet high in the mountains as 'bustling,' but that's just how Plaza de Mulas appeared that day, bustling. If the tents and sleeping bags were replaced with desks and terminals, base camp might have resembled a Wall Street trading room.

I eventually found the 'city center' and the park rangers. People hollered, music blared, and two-way radios squawked from a large blue tent. I walked closer. A dog watched me from his corner; antenna wires splayed out of the top in every direction; emergency sleds and rescue gear sat piled high. No one took notice of me as I walked up to the entrance. A gaggle of screaming beer-swillers hovered over a well-worn foosball table. "A foosball table," I muttered in disbelief. No one lifted an eyebrow as I walked inside. I noticed a menu hanging from one of the walls, advertising entrees similar to what the 'restaurant' at Confluencia offered. Underneath the menu sat a large selection of wine, beer, and as Harry said, whiskey—all for a premium. This wasn't the official park rangers' tent—that was next door—but the park rangers spent most of their time in the blue bar. The head ranger approached me to ask how I was doing. He even turned down the massive 'super tinny' sound system the group had been blaring. "You are coming up or going down?" he asked.

218

"Up. I think I'm going to do a carry up to a camp tomorrow. I'm not sure which one," I said.

"Well okay, that's good. We are here if you need anything. Have a good time and be safe," he said.

"How long have you been up here?" I asked.

"Too long. Way too long. Two months so far. I have one more month then I get to go back to Mendoza. Back to home. I'm really sick of this place. This has been a bad year. We just had a—" he quit speaking mid sentence.

"—a what?" I asked.

"Nothing. Nothing. Everything is fine up here. The weather, the people, everything. I just miss my family." The ranger scratched his foot around the dirt floor for a couple of seconds before staring intently at me. "Look, we aren't supposed to make this very public. It's bad for tourism and our bosses don't like having it known, but a lot of people have died up there this season. The normal route is easy up the Horcones, and not much more than a hard trek up to Nido de Cóndores, but after that it gets steep in places. There are a lot of spots where you can fall and die. It's not the 'easy walk' a lot of people say. The weather this year has been terrible. Not too many people have made it past Berlin Camp, and there was a storm that blew so hard that it wiped out everyone's tents up at Nido de Cóndores. I'm telling you that it is ugly this year, bad...a lot of deaths this year, over 15—almost all on the normal route. Be careful after the Independencia Hut, the traverse over the Gran Acarreo, and up into the Canaleta, and if the clouds come in, turn around and go back down. We are tired of hauling bodies off this mountain!"

I found Fred and Dave on the southeast corner of Plaza de Mulas. As usual, Fred was busy, this time organizing gear. The duo had built a giant pile of double- and triple-bagged British military rations. "Does the Queen know you took this stuff, Fred?" I asked. Fred didn't laugh. Fred didn't even look at me. Fred just continued his sorting.

"What?" Fred asked. "Oh, hello, Ed. You made it through the first night up here. Good to see you."

"Hey Fred, I have a question for you. I met this guy from Finland and he says that smoking is good for acclimatization. What do you think about that?"

"Well, I have heard a lot of people talk about how smokers acclimatize

Dave

faster when they start going up to altitude. In my experience, they do acclimatize *faster*, but non-smokers acclimatize *better*. The non-smokers always end
up doing better than the smokers. All of this is anecdotal, of course; I don't
think there have ever been any studies done on the subject, but that's my take."

"Us smokers rule the clouds!" Dave interjected.

"Clouds of smoke," Fred shot back. "Oh look, the tape player." Fred pulled a
small Walkman out of his bag. "Now we have music." With a click, 'Total
Eclipse of the Heart' began playing. It continued playing from the two attached speakers, over and over, for the remainder of my visit, about a half hour.
Neither Fred nor Dave made any mention of it. Fred liked the song so much
that he'd filled up both sides of a 60-minute tape with it. "We're heading to
Nido tomorrow to do a carry. When will you be going up?" Dave asked.

"Tomorrow. I feel pretty good, not too much of a headache and I'm breathing well," I said.

"Hey look, a condor!" Fred shot his finger toward the west face. Dave and I
stood silent, trying to spot it. The wall was a huge sweep of highlight and
shadow; I thought that spotting the outline of a 747 would have been next to
impossible, much less a bird—even one of the world's largest. But after a few
minutes of squinting, both Dave and I saw the condor. The bird appeared as a
dark silhouette, fluidly arcing along the pockets of air and twisting eddies that
rolled up and down the west face.

"The air is so thin up there. That bird must be at least at 16,000 feet," I said.
"I wonder how it can maintain its altitude?"

"And keep going up!" Dave shot in.

"The wingspan—up to 12 feet. The Andean condor is huge. *Huge*. A lot of
surface area," Fred answered. "Look, it doesn't even need to flap its wings, it just
slices into air currents invisible to our eyes—invisible to its eyes too; it just
knows where and when to get on and where and when to jump off."

"Must be nice, huh Fred?" Dave asked.

"What's that?" Fred asked.

"Floating around in the clouds like that. Flying."

"Yeah it is. I spent a lot of time in military helicopters. It *is* nice." Dave
looked at me and shook his head as Fred continued, "I remember when I was
on the first ascent of Victoria Peak, thought at the time to be the highest
mountain in Belize. We used Belize as our jungle training ground and thought
that we should climb the highest mountain. Problem wasn't the climb itself,
but the approach: thick jungle, it really buggered us for weeks. Finally we went
up in a helicopter and flew to the base of the mountain and dropped a big
jungle clearing bomb, made a landing zone, and climbed it from there. That
was a neat helicopter ride."

"He really doesn't get it. He's so old-school military, it drives me mad," Dave
said to me under his breath, as 'Total Eclipse of the Heart' repeated.

My stomach beckoned, a good sign that I was reacclimatizing. I found the camp's water supply, a meltwater stream on the north end of Plaza de Mulas, and waited in a long line to fill up with the area's only guaranteed-clean water. I joined Harry and his team and I cooked my lunch, some rice and potatoes. They had a large car-camping style awning set up with five folding chairs in its shade. "We go in style," said Harry, "and now you're living in style with us." While my XGK roared away, Harry introduced me to Juha, Ilkka, Matti, and Kari, all climbing friends of his from Finland, and Pablo and Pamela, his Chilean assistants. Juha, Ilkka, and Matti, were in South America for about a month from Europe; Kari, a diplomat who was second in command to the Finnish ambassador to Peru, lived in Lima.

"I go up to the mountains of Peru a bit, and do some four-wheeling along the coast, but I don't get to go climbing as much as I would like. It's too bad; I'm living in South America, but I don't get to spend enough time in the best part of this continent," Kari said.

"Hey Ed. When you're done with your strange budget food there, why don't we smoke a cigarette, huh?" Harry said, smiling impishly.

"Oh...that food does look...budget," Kari said.

"Maybe. Maybe I'll have a cigarette," I said.

"Oh yes. Yes you will!" Harry shouted.

"Don't listen to him, Ed. He is crazy. Smoking up here like this," said Kari, wiping sweat from his heavily sunscreened forehead.

"You guys should be in some sort of sunscreen ad. I've never seen so much of it in one place in my life," I said.

"Well look at us. We're whiter than snowmen. The sun kills us. We can't go out in it or we turn into tomatoes," Harry said.

"Tomatoes?" I asked, confused.

"Red. Red like tomatoes," Kari explained.

"Hey one of the rangers said something about 15 people dying this year?" I asked.

"We heard 22 so far," Pablo bellowed. "This year is terrible."

"Did you hear about *the Czech?*" Harry asked in a ghoulish tone as he leaned over toward me.

"No," I said with apprehension. "I didn't hear about *the Czech*, do I really want to know?"

"Which part of him do you want to know about, and which part don't you?" Pablo asked.

"What do you mean *which part?*" I asked.

"He froze to death up high," Harry began.

"And they couldn't get him down in a rescue sled because he froze in such a bent-up way," Kari continued.

"So they sawed him up into pieces to fit him on the sled," Harry concluded.

"They sawed him up?!" I cried. "Into how many pieces?"

"I think three," Pablo said. "But that's not the worst of it. After they were finished sawing him up a storm came, and they had to leave him up there, right in plain sight. A bunch of climbers went by his thawing pieces the next day before the rangers could come up and grab him."

"And how do you know this is true? Did any of you see this?" I asked.

"We didn't see it, but the story has been going around for a while. Just happened a few weeks ago. We think it's true," said Harry. "There has definitely been a lot of death on this mountain this year. And it was all unnecessary. "

I looked at my food, then up at Harry, Kari, and the others, shuttering at the thought of the dissected climber. I then shoveled hot-sauced potatoes and rice into my mouth.

"Let's change the subject," I said after a few minutes of gorging.

"No, let's smoke and get ready for high altitude," Harry said as he pulled out a fresh pack.

Space shot of Andes, looking south. Aconcagua lies near the middle of image

Views of west face of Aconcagua

CHAPTER TWENTY-ONE

EAT AT YOUR OWN RISK

Small section of Plaza de Mulas

Ruta Normal ascensionists have several logistical options for moving higher on Aconcagua from Plaza de Mulas. Three established, or should I say, *acknowledged*, camps sit within a day's climb above the plaza. The first (lowest) is Camp Canada, nestled in a rocky perch a few hundred yards off the main route. At 4,900 meters (16,076 feet), it is just a few hours above base camp. The next exit on the highway into the clouds is Camp Alaska, AKA *Cambio de Pendiente* (change of slope). This weather-exposed spot lies at 5,200 meters (17,060 feet), just below Nido de Cóndores. At 5,350 meters (17,552 feet), Nido de Cóndores, known simply as Nido, is the largest of the three. Many teams make a carry directly to Nido from Plaza de Mulas, return to Plaza de Mulas for one or two nights, then reascend to Nido. Others climb to Camp Canada, then move up to Nido. Some go to Camp Alaska and then make their move higher. Obviously, many combinations exist. I began thinking about my climbing itinerary as I relaxed on my first day in base camp.

Once I reached Nido, as my loose plan went, I would rest for as many days as I felt necessary, then move to Berlin Camp. At just under 20,000 feet, Berlin Camp is the launch pad for most Ruta Normalists' summit runs. There is a smaller camp called White Rocks just a hop, skip, and a few huffs above Berlin, and one tiny hut at 21,000 feet (Independencia Hut, the highest mountain refuge in the world), but Berlin would be my final goal before I dropped the bulk of my gear and trained my sights on the summit itself—or so I hoped; I still had a lot of ascending to do.

The late afternoon of my first full day at Plaza de Mulas found me zig-zagging around camp, racing between tents and hopping boulders as I chased light with my camera. The views of the clouds, the colors of the sunlit mountain walls, and the sky above were huge and dramatic. Plaza de Mulas, regardless of my complaints about throngs of people and sometimes smelly latrines, is a box seat to a never-ending play of geology, climate, and light. Physiographically, the camp sits on the edge of a mammoth diving board of glacial debris that juts out over the head of the Horcones Valley. I don't remember looking down-valley very often; it was as if anything below camp was a void, forgotten, or lost. But I looked up frequently, sometimes losing my balance in brief spates of vertigo. The camp's perch made me feel as if I were hovering near the base of the planet's crest, ready to zoom far above the clouds and coast in a dramatic parabolic arc onto the summit crown.

Less than an hour to go before sunset. I jogged back and forth between my camp site and Fred and Dave's. The view from my spot was broad and open, whereas the perspective from Fred and Dave's was boomingly up-close. I shot five rolls from my camp, then raced over to see the more 'inside' view at Fred and Dave's. I shot frames until I got sick of 'Total Eclipse of the Heart,' then returned to the homefront for more wide-angle compositions. I wasn't the only person to be was inspired by the light on the clouds and mountains.

Just about everyone who wasn't tied to a stove or some other chore—or foosball—had his neck craned up to see the region's aesthetic offerings.

The mood around camp that evening was charged with anticipation. Talk of death and hacked-up bodies was muffled by the whisks of nylon being crammed into stuffsacks, the zipping up of backpacks, the hurried pad-pad-pads of people's footsteps as they raced around their tents, and the variety of plans for reaching the summit—in just about every language I couldn't understand. *Buena suerte* was the phrase I heard more than any other. *Buena suerte*, good luck; I began saying it too, to other climbers and then to myself. *The weather...*I tried to keep that great unknown out of my mind as I wound through roll after roll of film, but it was impossible. The cloud formations made for beautiful images of the upper parts of the mountain, but I knew that once I tread those high regions, the same weather could prove to be a deadly enemy.

A quenching rush of satisfaction ran through me as the last of the day's light disappeared. I had seen so much through my viewfinder and exposed so much of it to film that I could have gone home that evening and I would have been more than satisfied with the Aconcagua trip. But...of course I wanted to keep going higher. *Just think what it must be like from Berlin Camp...to have the big Pentax on the solid Gitzo tripod up at nearly 20,000 feet!* In a flash I decided that my plan of action would be to make a carry to Nido, return to base camp, then go back up to Nido and set up camp the following day. I would acclimatize at Nido for as long as necessary before making my move to Berlin. Trying to make solid plans for climbing expeditions, however, is a lot like trying to predict the weather. The further into the future one looks, the less accurate the prediction. Realistically, I count on being able to look just one day ahead—two at the most. The annoying 'unpredictable' always shows up at the party at the worst time, as I was about to learn—once again.

I spent nearly two hours organizing and packing supplies that night. I would take one week's worth of food and fuel, extra clothing, some film, water bottles, and my ice ax and crampons to Nido the next day. When I went up 'for good' I would bring my sleeping bag, tent, stove, and camera. The carry-day load would be easy; the move-up day haul would be much tougher. But I had no way of lightening my move-up day burden. Climb high, sleep low is the rule for summit success, and the heaviest implements needed to stay where I slept.

"You have everything ready for your move to Nido?" I heard Harry ask as I fumbled with the last of my packing.

"I think so. And you? You guys ready?" I responded.

"Yeah. Hours ago. Let's smoke."

"Okay. Give me a cigarette, candy man," I said, getting a laugh from Harry. "Your English is great," I said, "you even pick up on subtle jokes."

"The best movies are American. We watch all sorts of American television and movies, besides, everybody needs to learn English in Europe; it's necessary to get a job. We learn it from a very young age. It's the world language. Spanish helps, but English is so important. Look at you, you speak only a little Spanish and nothing else but English. You get along fine." I was embarrassed to admit my lack of language skills, but Harry was right. I'd like to learn more Spanish, but I got along fine with the paltry amount I spoke—not because anybody understood my Spanish, but because I could understand others' English.

"Tomorrow there will be lots of people moving up to higher camps. Good weather, and everyone wants to make the summit soon, before the season ends and the bad storms hit. The season's supposed to be short this year," Harry said.

"I'll keep moving higher till I run out of film, food, or mountain," I said.

"I can't wait to get out of here," Harry spoke with a tone of anxiety.

"Why?" I asked.

"It's a beautiful mountain, but this camp is too jammed with people."

"Yeah." I finished my cigarette and crawled into my tent.

I almost fell asleep quickly that night. *Almost*...but for the muleteers. They proved to be the loudest group of drunks I'd ever heard, and they just got louder (and drunker, I assume) as the night dragged on. They played two songs from Pink Floyd and a live version of Hotel California, and they played them the same way Fred played 'Total Eclipse of the Heart'—over and over and over again, with no foreseeable end, or should I say, no *forehearable* end. Unlike Fred with his little Walkman add-ons, the Muleteers' speakers rang out power-fully in the night air. I imagined that dental fillings must have been buzzing loose in mouths as far away as Mendoza.

The sonic torture ended at around four in the morning; I could finally concentrate on not concentrating at all. But sleep wouldn't come, at least not in its most coveted, wholesome form. I slipped in and out, but never for long. I had planned to wake up around six and be on my way 15 minutes later. But six o'clock came and went, and so did seven, all the way past eight. I was finally hiking at a little after nine, and groggily at that.

When I finally roused myself, I was surprised to find that everyone else in camp had the fortitude to sleep through what I couldn't, or at least they had the wherewithal to wake up at a respectable hour. Plaza de Mulas was de-serted—but the route above was packed with lines of climbers inching their way higher. The hundred yard walk to the water source served as my cup of coffee. I woke up, filled up, then started making my way up.

The day was warm and clear. The air and the sun seemed to lift me up the mountain. I even jogged in some places. For the first time in my life I met a Bosnian Serb. He was heading back to Plaza de Mulas after succumbing to AMS, a victim of poor planning. The day's first dropout.

A few minutes later I caught up with Kari and Ilkka, who were also feeling the altitude. "Harry is up there, close to Nido I think. We may just be going up a little higher, then we'll turn around," Kari said. "This is a good practice day."

I was also affected by the altitude. I'd had my trekking poles out all morning, but I noticed, shortly after talking with Kari and Ilkka, that I was actually using them, not just dragging them behind me. I passed the cutoff for Camp Canada and gawked at a long staircase of switchbacks disappearing beyond a change of slope that looked exhaustingly far away. I dropped my pack and took out my camera and some water, then tried to drink and take pictures at the same time. The water went down all right, but I doubted that those first pictures would turn out. Quenched, I put my bottle on the ground, locked both hands on my Nikon and scanned the mountainscapes below and beyond. Cerro Cuerno reminded me of a mini-Matterhorn, although the Matterhorn, at 4,478 meters (14,691 feet), is really a mini-Cuerno. It's just that Cuerno (elevation 5,462 meters, 17,920 feet), which means *horn* in Spanish, is so dwarfed by Aconcagua that it seemed *mini*. Mini as it may be, in relative terms, Cuerno whet my appetite for more photo opportunities. I exposed nearly a roll, then began thinking about the evening light possibilities from higher on the peak…with my Pentax. I couldn't wait to get to Nido, armed with the medium format. The southwest face of Cuerno begged to be photographed in crimson light. The thought pushed me onward.

"Traffic jam," I said aloud after a few turns up the switchbacks. I had caught up to the slowest of the climbers heading toward Nido. I passed some folks as they rested, but then I needed a rest too, and a few repassed me. It got to be annoying, all the more so as people became more breathless with each step. Friendly conversation—any conversation—got snuffed out by the thin air. As the pace slowed, the bright openness of the morning got snuffed out too, by a storm that I hadn't seen developing.

I managed to get ahead of three large climbing groups—I even did it politely—then eased my legs into a steady upward beat. I stared at the ground most of the time, a ground that consisted almost entirely of compacted scree and a few large rocks. A few small penitente fields broke the monotony, but the formations were nowhere near as eye grabbing as those of Ojos del Salado. I filed right through them with everybody else.

Two figures caught my eye. I was approaching them quickly, and could see that one had problems. *Dave?* I wondered. It *was* Dave; he stood doubled over wracked with coughing. Fred looked down at him with obvious disapproval.

"Dave! You okay?" I asked after stopping to catch my breath. No answer. I hiked closer, close enough to make eye contact with Fred.

"He's fine. He's just tired," Fred answered. "I think Alaska Camp is just a hundred yards higher. We can drop our stuff there; this weather isn't looking good. I want to head down," Fred continued. I agreed with him; the weather looked to be deteriorating quickly, and I too would stop at Alaska. Both Fred and I offered to take Dave's pack, but he insisted on continuing to carry his own load. I helped Dave to his feet, and gave him one of my trekking poles.

"I'm just out of breath…so out of breath…this is unbelievably hard. I have to fight for every little bit of air!" Dave gasped between shallow, jittery wheezes. Fred disappeared over the top of the rise that marked the base of Alaska Camp. Dave and I ascended in ten-step intervals, pausing between each 'sprint' for a few minutes to catch up on lost respiration.

"Dave, your hypoxia is contagious. I'm having a hard time breathing too." Dave didn't laugh. He actually looked ready to die. His eyes poked a blank stare on a pale face. "Okay," I said. "Let's just make it up there, then we can get down. Get some food and more air." Dave nodded and staggered on.

The final 50 yards took nearly 20 minutes. Dave collapsed—pack and all—next to a tent pad. I barely managed to unhitch myself from my pack before I fell to the ground. Alaska Camp is located at a beautiful spot, with perfect views of Cuerno and the Upper Horcones Glacier. 'Located' is all that can be said about it. It isn't nestled, perched, hidden away, or in any way, shape, or form protected by (or from) anything. It is as open and exposed as a spot can get in the mountains. Only a few tent pads have been scratched into Camp Alaska, and they aren't level.

The storm was approaching quickly. I stuffed my supplies into my mule bag, zipped and lashed it shut, and hid it from the wind and curious passersby with large rocks. The snow that had just begun to fall would soon complete the bag's concealment.

"Let's get out of here," Dave said; the three of us galloped down. Fred, as usual, took the lead, cutting switchbacks in a mad, straight-down run toward base camp. Dave and I took our time, speeding up only when the building storm nudged us to move a little faster, but mostly we strolled leisurely, talking and joking.

I jogged back to my tent just in time for another sunset on the west face. While the storm that had rolled in during my ascent to Alaska Camp still raged high on the mountain, Plaza de Mulas remained in the sunlight. I grabbed my Pentax and headed toward the hotel for a distant shot of the west face.

The hike took longer than I'd expected. Not only was the distance a bit deceiving, but I had to cross a stream that flowed over a bed of ice. Most of the hike between Plaza de Mulas and the hotel traverses the lower portion of the Horcones Glacier, which is almost entirely clothed in dirt, rocks, and a few boulders. Crossing it is tricky.

The temperature plummeted and a gale rolled through as I reached the hotel. I found a rock that gave just enough shelter for my tripodded camera and me. I hardly noticed the strange hotel during the fifteen-odd minutes I spent shooting. I packed my camera away after a few rolls and took a look at the out-of-place structure. The hotel was much smaller than I'd envisioned, and it looked run down. I kept hearing a 'crash' in my mind as if the hotel had been accidentally dropped while being airlifted to a resort.

A man stared at me through a dirty window of the hotel. He seemed lonely, as if a prisoner. I waved to him…and waited for an extended moment for him to wave back. But he just stared; he didn't even nod his head. Just stared.

I returned to my tent a few minutes before darkness fell. I was starved, having only eaten a few bites of bland trail food since morning. I searched through my supplies for an appetizing meal to prepare, wondering which of my dried-up, foil-and-plastic-encased concoctions I would get sick of the slowest…and stumbled across my wallet. *Forget cooking*, I thought. *I'll just go up and buy some burgers!* A flash of genius. A celebration for getting my gear *almost* to my day's goal. I hurried off to the foosball tent.

20 dollars got my gut filled. I smoked another cigarette with Harry as we discussed the day's happenings. He and most of his clients had made it to Nido; they planned to rest for at least one full day at Plaza de Mulas before moving up for good. "And you?" Harry asked.

"Tomorrow. I'll go tomorrow. I feel great. Especially after those hamburgers. I mean, *I really feel great!*"

"Hamburgers! You ate those things?!" Harry looked at me as if I told him I'd just finished sniffing a few tubes of glue.

"Yeah…*what?*"

"Never eat those hamburgers. NEVER! You are crazy!" Harry exclaimed. "Look around here, do you think they are clean with any of the food they cook in those places?" I shook my head as Harry continued. "That stuff heats up like mad on the trek in—on the backs of those mules, out in the sun. Well, I hope you make it through the night! I'll come and check on you in the morning." I thought Harry would punctuate his last sentence with laughter. But he didn't laugh. I did, but not for long.

Penitentes at terminus of Upper Horcones Glacier

South face of Aconcagua

CHAPTER TWENTY-TWO

NIGHTMARE

Storm on Aconcagua

I had a three-hour grace period after eating those burgers before the onset of a gargantuan dose of food poisoning. The ordeal began with a horrible nightmare of a sort that I'd experienced only once before.

I fell asleep easily. A full day and a full stomach, after a night devoid of sleep, shooed me quickly into a heavy slumber. A few hours of bliss, then the strangeness began. The subconscious horror I experienced didn't come on slowly; it arrived like a bomb.

I first had the nightmare when I was seven years old. I'd been sick with the flu. I was put to bed with an intense fever, and never really fell asleep. What I remember is that I was spinning out of control, in slow motion. I floated, but I felt incredible pressure, as if I was buried deep in a huge sand-box. I was spun into a void of nothingness; the sensation was so real that I could feel it in my stomach—a sickly, tickly feeling like dropping too quickly on a roller coaster. I screamed but no sound came out. I reached out for something to hold on to, but found nothing. I couldn't move my feet, my legs, my hands...I couldn't see or hear. I couldn't breathe. But I was alive, if only to experience the horror. Panicked and utterly alone; the nightmare was the embodiment of extraordinary violence, but it was silent, making it all the more frightening.

My Plaza de Mulas nightmare began the same way, only far more intense. I woke up part way through the dream; sweat sopped my entire body. I tried to open my sleeping bag, but my hands shook so much I couldn't grasp the zipper. I could feel my kidneys pounding as if they'd been kicked for hours and were about to hemorrhage.

I rose slowly out of my sleeping bag hoping to unzip my tent for some fresh air. Blue and red splotches flashed in my eyes; I fell to the tent floor and passed out. Coming to, I opened the flap, struggled to my knees and peed. Then I vomited. I nearly fainted again, but slipped into my bag before my energy ran dry.

I slipped unwillingly back into the dream. This time, however, I knew I was dreaming. I felt suspended in heavy, enervating ether.

I woke again some time later, to hallucinations of voices coming at me from an enveloping curtain of gray. I had no concept of time. I couldn't move; the aching was too intense. I continued to sweat like a geyser and shake like the ground before a geyser erupts. My sleeping bag was so soaked that I kept wondering if I'd wet my bed. *This expedition is over, pretty much before it ever really started*, I thought, *damn Plaza de Mulas hamburgers*. I ran down my options—but there was only only one realistic course of action: In the morning I would have to be evacuated to PDI on the back of a mule. Aconcagua would have to wait for another year. Then I had a strange urge to take aspirin. I searched one of my supply bags and found three of the analgesics; I gulped them down and fell asleep.

I woke up an hour past sunrise feeling like nothing had happened. I was fine. I felt strong and ready to go. In fact, I didn't even remember the dream right away. I was outside my tent, enjoying the clear morning before I realized that just a few hours prior I thought I was near death. "Aspirin really is the miracle drug!" Fred told me after I recounted my night. "Really, though, sounds like a bad dose of food poisoning. I've had that a few times, you know that it's food poisoning when your kidneys ache like that. It's awful."

"Never eat those burgers. Russian roulette…with all bullets loaded. I hope you take today as a rest day. Even though you feel well, you should stay down. We are going up to Nido tomorrow. You can hang out with us…smoke cigarettes with me," Harry said after I told him about the experience.

"Sounds good," I said. But hanging around one campsite proved too difficult. I itched to talk with other 'residents' of Plaza de Mulas. I wandered around and met people. The atmosphere seemed friendlier than when I'd first arrived; people acted more relaxed, as if luck was now on their side. Stories of summit success trickled down through the day. Beautiful summit weather prevailed: no clouds, no wind. It was a rare window in an otherwise terrible season. I only hoped that it would last.

I met another American during my day's wanderings. Andrew was also alone, but in terrible shape. He was waiting for a mule to carry him out to PDI. Talking with him, I quickly realized that he didn't belong alone with a lawnmower in his own back yard, much less climbing Aconcagua. He was a middle-aged accountant from Virginia with no climbing experience whatsoever. "My wife thinks I'm a wimp. I thought I'd prove myself to my family, and now I've failed," he whined.

An Argentine woman who had the thankless job of taking care of Andrew rolled her eyes at me.

"This man is so strange," she said when Andrew went into his tent to get some water. "He is just so *strange*. He is so annoying. I *cannot wait* until he leaves. And look at him, he can walk fine. He's making us treat him like a small child. He barely made it to Plaza de Mulas—such an easy hike. He arrived totally unprepared, and then he came down with this 'unknown' sickness. He never went even a bit above camp. He said he hallucinated on his hike in here; he said that the 'river was speaking to him,' or some stupid thing like that. And now he insists that we buy back all of the fuel we sold him to do the climb!"

"Buena suerte," I said to the woman as I scooted away before Andrew reappeared. The 'nurse' scowled and went back to preparing Andrew's lunch.

The system of mule logistics—I began calling it *mulegistics* and *the mulefrastructure*—is surprisingly well-developed on the Ruta Normal. Mule trains arrive and depart continuously during the daylight hours, delivering tons of supplies and hauling out garbage. Not only do the mule companies run the transport services and sell supplies, they also own the restaurants, both in Confluencia and at Plaza de Mulas, as well as provide other services, like the telephone, and one of the more interesting ventures, 'Ecotoilet.' For a small fee, any Plaza de Mulas passer-through can use the Ecotoilet. Just why anyone would want to make a deposit to make a deposit, I don't know—Plaza de Mulas offers a wide range of free latrines throughout the camp, and they're all very colorful.

But the Ecotoilet is no run-of-the-mill Plaza de Mulas latrine. I didn't use it, so I can't vouch for its internal workings, but I did notice that it carries a presence. Comparing any of the regular Plaza de Mulas latrines to the Ecotoilet is akin to comparing a go-cart to an M-1 tank. First of all, the Ecotoilet is big, occupying at least six times the area of a standard latrine. Secondly, the structure is painted olive drab (I suppose to be in concert with the green = ecological semantic). Thirdly, it had two large 'chimneys' protruding from its roof. And last, and probably most (intimidating) was the black tube that led from the main Ecotoilet superstructure to a satellite entity comprised of an old plastic drum, some large gauge copper wire (stripped and open to the world to see and touch), and a good amount of loosely-wrapped duct and electrical tape. Only in Plaza de Mulas.

I spent another hour touring the camp, searching for more oddities, but nothing topped the Ecotoilet. I rejoined Harry, Kari, and the others in the shade of their portable gazebo. The day was hot; heat waves distorted the air in just about every direction. A condor rode high on pockets of rising thermals. "Tomorrow is the day to go up and occupy Nido," Harry announced, to the delight of his team. "This weather can't hold for more than a few days. Tomorrow is definitely going to be it."

I planned to head for Nido the next day, too. The food poisoning was fast becoming a memory. I cared about only two things at that point: getting my Pentax to Berlin Camp, and getting me to the

Muleteer tent in Plaza de Mulas

summit. I laid everything out that afternoon. What I left behind I wouldn't see until I returned—having been to Aconcagua's summit or not. I deposited a plump bag of food, my exposed film, and a few of my Nikon's lenses at Rudy's tent. Everything else would travel on my back the next day.

Paul and Gary showed up late in the afternoon, utterly wasted. Each, however, was as determined as ever to keep going higher—all the way to the summit. Not long after Paul and Gary's arrival, Plaza de Mulas was treated to the grand entrance of Commander Taco and the Anti-Freds. "Wow! They made it this far. I can't believe it," I said to Harry, who stood speechless at the sight.

"Who are these people?" Harry asked.

"Some guided team; their leader is an interesting one."

"They're all so...so..."

"Fat," I interjected.

"Fat. Yeah. Fat. That's the word I was looking for...fat." Commander Taco spared Plaza de Mulas from rock slamming escapades that evening, but he and his troops certainly made their presence known. "There is no way any of them will make it to the summit. No way," Harry said as he lit a cigarette. "Want another?" he asked me, extending a freshly opened pack my way.

"Sure. Why not? I'm not so worried about whether they'll make it to the summit or not, but whether any of them will die trying," I said.

"Just so long as they don't do anything stupid...like eat one of the hamburgers up here!" Harry said, laughing.

"Okay, give me a few more cigarettes. I'll see you up at Nido tomorrow."

I needed only 20 minutes under the bright, warm sun to load my pack for the day's climb to Nido. The load wasn't the heaviest I'd ever carried, but it still weighed around 75 pounds. My cameras occupied the majority of the main compartment, and the tripod, wrapped in my sleeping pad, formed a big 'T' at the top. The sleeping bag was about the only piece of gear that was stuffed where the backpack manufacturer meant it to be stuffed. Most everything else dangled or was in some creative way lashed to the outside of the big green Dana Terraplane.

I took my time preparing breakfast, and watched group after group jump on the path and slowly ascend the route. From a distance the scene resembled a bunch of caterpillars riding a long, high escalator up the side of the mountain. I threw my pack on and joined them.

I finally arrived at Alaska Camp an hour before sunset. As I hunched over my trekking poles and stared at my mule bag, still half-buried under rocks, I decided that Nido could wait another day. I set the Dana on the hard ground and let the afternoon sun warm my face. The evening was as still as a mirror lake. I threw my tent up and ran my stove. While snow melted in my pot I marched around with the Pentax. I was inside the sunset's light, smothered in alpenglow, breathing the mountain's purity. The region hummed with effulgence.

The sun disappeared and my hands began to freeze. I filled my water bottles and cooked dinner; I offered some to a lone Argentine, the only other overnighter at Alaska. He didn't have a stove, or any food, or water—just a tent and a sleeping bag. He said that the friend he was going to meet at Nido the next day had the bulk of the duo's equipment.

The temperature plummeted quickly that night, but I kept my tent door open. I couldn't resist falling asleep under the fading electric blue Andean twilight.

236

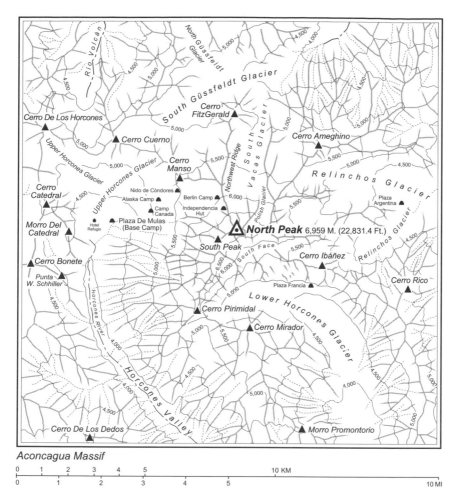

Aconcagua Massif

0 1 2 3 4 5   10 KM

0 1 2 3 4 5   10 MI

Map is centered on the North Peak of Aconcagua, the mountain's highest point. Map shows significant peaks, glaciers, valleys, rivers, intermittent streams, and primary camps of Aconcagua and environs. Map indicates topography by contour lines (500 meter intervals) and simplified ridge lines. Names incorporate both English and Spanish for ease of reader comprehension.

Sources of Information:
IMGA Topographic Sheets: 3369 7-4; 3369 8-3;
3369 13-2; 3369 14-1
American Alpine Club Map of Aconcagua
Observation and Photographs of Author

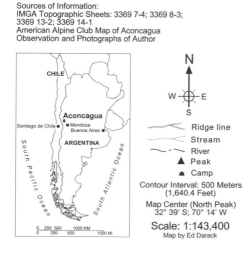

N
W E
S

Ridge line
Stream
River
▲ Peak
▲ Camp

Contour Interval: 500 Meters
(1,640.4 Feet)

Map Center (North Peak)
32° 39' S; 70° 14' W

Scale: 1:143,400
Map by Ed Darack

Mountain Altitudes in Meters (and Feet):
Aconcagua:
North Peak: 6,959 Meters (22,831.4 Feet)
South Peak: 6,930 Meters (22,736.2 Feet)
Cerro Mirador: 6,089 Meters (19,977 Feet)
Cerro Piramidal: 6,009 Meters (19,714.6 Feet)
Cerro Ameghino: 6,000 Meters (19,685 Feet)
Cerro Ibáñez: 5,650 Meters (18,536.7 Feet)
Cerro Manso: 5,557 Meters (18,231.6 Feet)
Cerro Cuerno: 5,462 Meters (17,919.9 Feet)
Cerro De Los Horcones: 5,395 Meters (17,700.1 Feet)
Cerro Rico: 5,380 Meters (17,650.9 Feet)
Cerro Fitzgerald: 5,357 Meters (17,575.5 Feet)
Cerro Catedral: 5,335 Meters (17,503.3 Feet)
Morro del Catedral: 5,330 Meters (17,486.9 Feet)
Cerro Bonete: 5,100 Meters (16,732.3 Feet)
Cerro de Los Dedos: 5,018 Meters (16,463.3 Feet)
Morro Promontorio: 4,561 Meters (14,963.9 Feet)

Camp Altitudes in Meters (and Feet):
Plaza de Mulas: 4,275 Meters (14,025.6 Feet)
Camp Canada: 4,900 Meters (16,076 Feet)
Alaska Camp (Cambio de Pendiente): 5,200 Meters
(17,060.4 Feet)
Nido de Cóndores: 5,350 Meters (17,552.5 Feet)
Berlin Camp: 5,810 Meters (19,061.7 Feet)
Independencia Hut: 6,405 Meters (21,013.8 Feet)
Plaza Argentina: 4,200 Meters (13,779.5 Feet)
Plaza Francia: 4,500 Meters (14,763.8 Feet)

237

Chapter Twenty-Three

REALM OF THE CONDOR

Summit region of Aconcagua from Nido de Cóndores

The morning dawned blustery and cold. Gusts whacked my tent and buffeted my ears. Steely chills swirled through my tent's open door and tousled my hair. I was wide-awake in seconds, and waking quickly at 17,000 feet is an elusive luxury, a rare experience in coherence. I wiped my eyes wide open and watched distant cumulus swoosh into one another. I stretched like an old cat after a long nap, inhaling a huge gush of icy wind, then grabbed my sleeping bag and went about cramming it into my pack.

I chose stuffing my sleeping bag as my first order of business because I wanted to test my acclimatization mettle. Stuffing a synthetic bag into a sleeping bag compartment is by far the best acclimatization litmus test available. It's a chore I loathe, at sea level or at 20,000 feet. I'm sure I would loathe it at 50,000 feet in a custom luxury cabin of a Gulfstream V—given the opportunity. I usually put off the stuffing until everything else is done—once I'm 'warmed up.' Why do I hate it so much? Because, while it's one of the world's most mundane chores, it is also one of the most demanding. It tests dexterity, physical stamina, anaerobic threshold, and the part of the brain that solves jigsaw puzzles—and mostly it tests patience. Note: This isn't the case for down bags. Even the fluffiest down bag fits easily into most sleeping bag compartments. Down bags save time and sanity.

The result of the Camp Alaska stuffing trial? I mashed my bag into my pack in record time and with minimal effort. I passed the test, scoring high enough to feel confident that I was capable of making the summit.

My Argentine campmate was long gone; a group of four climbers descending from Nido were about to take his place—if only long enough for a rest. I finished my packing just as the group arrived. I didn't take much notice of them—I was too busy cinching the last of my gear into place. "Is that you, Ed?" came a voice through the wind. I looked up to see a guy who was completely hidden under a parka, hat, balaclava, mittens, bibs, plastic boots, and glacier glasses. "Ed?" he asked again. I leaned my pack against a rock and stared at the astronautish figure, walking my way.

"Who...*Who are you?*" I asked, wondering if my food poisoning had returned, bringing with it more hallucinogenic dreams. The 'space man' reached his mittened hand out; I shook it, but I was obviously puzzled. The man pulled his glasses and balaclava off. It was Alex Van Steen, a professional mountain guide and a good friend whom I'd last seen on Denali, several years earlier. "Wow! What a way to wake up! I haven't seen you in...like..."

"—Too many years. How are you. I almost didn't recognize you," Alex said.

"I'm doing pretty well. Pretty well, I'd say. It's great to see you! This is really so strange!" I spoke as if I had molasses in my mouth—the cold was bogging down my jaw muscles.

"Not really, lots of people up here," Alex said, laughing as if he'd bumped into friends at 16,000 feet a dozen times before. We spoke for about 15 minutes—the loftiest reunion of my life—and then my friend had to get back to his clients. Alex had just led his group to the summit via the Polish Glacier, and they were anxious to get back to Santiago. We exchanged e-mail addresses. "Did e-mail even exist the last time I saw you?" he asked.

"It wasn't that long ago!" I quipped, stunned by just how much time *had* gone by since I had last seen him. "You look the same as you did the last time I saw you—at 18,000 feet on Denali, headed for the summit at midnight. Did you ever make it?" I asked.

"Yeah, I did." Each of us became quiet. I could see Alex's clients closing in on the end of their patience; the cold seemed to be getting the better of them. "I should get moving, these guys want a hot shower," Alex said, "and so do I."

"Keep in touch…man. Keep in touch," I said, feeling lucky to have met up with Alex, but sad that he had to leave after so short a conversation. Mountain friendships are unique—they develop so quickly and seem to span years, even if they exist only for a few weeks. Alex had been one of my best friends—up high or down low—even though we hung out only a few minutes a day over the course of three weeks while on Denali; he'd boosted my spirits, helping me make the summit. I wanted to sit down and drink a beer with him; find out what he'd been up to since I'd last seen him. But like the last time I saw him, I was headed one way on the mountain and he was headed the other. So we shook hands and said goodbye—once again.

My day's goal, Nido, was only a couple of hundred yards away, directly over an easy, snow-covered slope. I gawked at the trail. *A trail. There really is a trail*

Lone figure on rocks outside Nido de Cóndores; *telephoto view from Camp Alaska*

up here. It really is a walkup. I thought. I loaded my pack and began the day's ascent. *A hard walk, but a walk nonetheless.* Lore has it that dogs have been taken to the summit of Aconcagua and people have run to the top in sneakers, but the most outrageous attempt on the Ruta Normal was launched in January,

Tent remains, Nido de Cóndores

1977, by a Spanish expedition—on motorcycles! One team member claimed to have reached the base of the Canaleta, at an altitude of 6,600 meters (about 21,653 feet), before turning back. I began to wonder if I should have attempted the Polish Glacier, or the Polish Glacier traverse instead of the normal route. Or even made an attempt on the west face. But the big Pentax....

That couple of hundred yards took more than an hour. I probably couldn't have gone much faster on a level sidewalk at sea level with as much gear as I was carrying. I crested a small pass flanked by jagged, vesicular rock, and a short time later stood over a broad, oval patch of dirt and snow: Nido de Cóndores.

Only one tent dabbed the landscape. One standing tent, I should say. I'd expected a mini version of Plaza de Mulas. What I saw was more of a ghost town. I contoured around the northwest lip of the camp and counted six occupied campsites—campsites occupied by the tattered remains of tents and other camping gear. Camps that no one had bothered to clean up after some obviously incredibly destructive storm. Some of the tents were torn cleanly in two; some had less than half of their original fabric remaining. I once covered the scene of a deadly tornado in Jerrold, Texas for a photographic stock agency. I arrived the day after the tornado struck—it had killed 26 people and had marked its passage by tearing blacktop off of roadbeds and tossing cars over a mile through the air. The destruction was complete. Death was palpable. Déjà vu struck me as I took my first steps into Nido that morning. A different part of the world, a completely different type of place, but the two were close siblings in mood. The air at Nido was hauntingly still. No climbers yakked; no stoves roared; no zippers zipped; no mess kits clattered. Only the wasted remains of 'bombproof tents,' sleeping bags, food packaging, and other unrecognizable gear cluttered the area. The scene puzzled me; I shook off a slight headache and focused on staking claim to a good tent site. Later I would set about learning just what had happened to the place.

I found a nice private, level spot on the north end of the camp near a large rock outcrop, the top of which afforded a spectacular view of merging glaciers below Nido and the broad summit of Cerro Mercederio, a huge Andean peak about 50 miles to the north of Aconcagua. I tied my tent down to the largest rocks I could find, then trotted across the flat camp toward a lone guy who was standing still as a statue—looking up toward Aconcagua's main summit. "Hello!" I said, "Hello…" The man didn't turn or look at me until I was practically standing on top of him.

"Hi. Where did you come from?" the man asked, with an American accent.

"Over there. I just set up my tent. I came up from Camp Alaska. Do you know what happened here; I mean with all of these flattened tents and everything?" I asked.

"Huge storm. Absolutely huge storm. I heard 19 people got killed on the mountain."

"When?" I asked.

"A couple of weeks ago. The winds supposedly blew constantly over 120 miles per hour with gusts even more than that. It was the *Viento Blanco*—the White Wind, but it came harder than usual, which is to say, pretty hard." The guy spoke like a robot, softly and without emotion, almost like HAL. He moved slowly too. He seemed shell shocked, but from what, I didn't know.

"Are you alone?" I asked.

"No. Others should be coming down from Berlin right now. I can't wait till they arrive so I can get out of here. I don't like this place. It's a graveyard—literally. All I've been doin' is pukin' and not sleepin'. I'm so altitude sick, and I can't get better. You know what happened to those people when that storm hit? Huh?…There were about twenty tents up here that night. *Twenty*. Of those twenty only about five stood when the mornin' came 'round. Some got shredded so bad that people just jumped out of their sleepin' bags and ran to those rocks there," he pointed toward the high rocks at the west end of camp. "A lot of people froze to death here that night. This place gives me the willies."

"That's awful," I said. *"Awful."*

"You want some leftover food? I got some here," he asked.

"That's okay. I have a bunch. Thanks. But hey, where is everyone? I thought this place would be packed."

"A lot of people already took off for Berlin Camp. Supposedly, this is the best weather the mountain has had all season. Certainly the best since I've been up here. Everybody took off this morning because they want to make a go for the summit tomorrow. There'll be more to take their place, soon enough. Don't you worry, you'll have plenty o'company in a few hours. And hey look, some people coming down now. I hope those are my partners. They went up a few days ago…wonder if they made it to the top. I sure won't be around here to keep you company tonight. I want a warm shower and a steak!"

Not even a continent's highest mountain gets spared from crazy stories, rumors, and exaggeration—especially about death and destruction. I was hearing a lot of 'reports,' passed on from people I didn't really know—who received those reports from people they didn't really know, and possibly couldn't even understand. I took the long way back to my tent to survey the destruction. The scene looked horrible. No one had bothered to clean up any of the destruction. Meltwater and mud had mixed with much of the debris. Many of the campsites resembled giant bowls of nasty, rotting soup. I returned to my tent and cleaned my camera lenses, thinking about the stories I'd heard and what I'd seen of the camp remains. I pondered the veracity of those stories.

The Aconcagua party started revving up again later that afternoon. I'd wondered about Team Harry's whereabouts, thinking that they'd have taken at least one rest day at Nido. They soon arrived back at Nido—from an attempt to make it to Berlin. "We tried to go too fast. Some aren't feeling too well. We'll try again tomorrow," Harry said before rushing off to break camp. "Come over in a little while and smoke with me!" he yelled over his shoulder.

I returned to my tent to find new next-door neighbors. A group of three Americans led by a Chilean guide had just dropped their gear on a level spot adjoining mine. Team Mike, as I would come to know them, wasn't officially led by the expedition's namesake, but Mike was responsible for about ninety-nine percent of their talking. The California trio weren't serious climbers, just three forty-somethings who got together for one large trip each year—anything from long rafting expeditions, to ski mountaineering, to marathons. While they couldn't be classified as 'expert' climbers, they certainly weren't neophytes, either—particularly Mike. "I actually don't need a guide. I mean, I *know* I could make it to the summit on my own," he rattled to me, somewhere between describing his job as an attorney and complaining about his ex-wife.

Team Harry brought good conversation and Team Mike added entertainment; the dour mood that had hung over an almost deserted Nido de Cóndores earlier was replaced by a good measure of relaxation and even laughter—in a now thriving borough of the mountain. By late afternoon the camp was nearly full, and it finally did look like a miniature Plaza de Mulas, sans the mules, telephones, and Ecotoilet. *Almost full…I looked at the people in camp. Quite a hodgepodge,* I thought: Germans, Italians, Poles, Czechs, Argentines, Chileans, and many others. But space remained for a few more. Certainly, I could use an extra dose of entertainment; I'd be hanging around Nido for at least a day, and I needed something to do besides smoke with Harry and wait for good photo opportunities. That extra bit of amusement came when Spike and Company arrived, who'd complete the social aspect of my Aconcagua trip.

Spike and Company was comprised of five adventure seekers who, with one exception, had about as much experience in the mountains as Gary. Guy was an aid worker from Great Britain who lived in the Peruvian jungle, Alan, a French guy who was 'seeking self-employment,' Kirsten, a student from Amsterdam, Andrea, who said he was training to be a mountain guide in his home country of Italy, and of course, Spike, who was from Tokyo and had never seen snow, set up a tent, used a camping stove—or anything else related to mountains or climbing. But Spike 'knows very well the party and its causes.' The group met in a hostel in Mendoza, and somehow, in some drunken haze, decided to climb Aconcagua together.

"We have made it this far...we will climb all the way up this mountain!" proclaimed Andrea, waving his ice ax into the wind in a gesture of defiance of whatever could be thrown against them. Most of the camp at Nido dropped what they were doing and stared, speechless, at the hot-pink-suited Andrea jumping up and down on a rock outside of his tent. Andrea is, without a doubt, one of the world's most instantly likeable people. "Ed! Ed!...Ed!...You are Ed! Everybody...This is Ed!" Andrea introduced me to the rest of the crowd after reeling me in as I wandered back from Team Harry's tent.

The group's tents—rented except for Andrea's—had been set up in a loose circle; all faced inward. Spike poured wine for anyone who wanted to imbibe. "Would you like some?" he asked me.

"No thanks," I answered. "You actually brought wine up this high?"

"Of course we did!" Alan said with an unmistakably French accent.

"We only brought a couple of these Tetra-boxes up. Too expensive," lamented Spike. "The situation is not so bad. I still have many cigarettes."

"You too, huh?" I asked.

"Yes. I have my manufactured cigarettes; Alan and Guy roll their own."

"Oh Ed, you are such an American! I love you!" Andrea jumped toward me with his hands in the air. "I love America so much. I love Los Angeles! And I love New York!" I didn't know what to say. I didn't know what set him off, but Andrea couldn't just say something—he had to dance and sing it in a great emotional outpouring.

"I started smoking again up here," I said. "I don't think it's such a great thing, but it is definitely relaxing."

"But more harder to keep lit the higher up we go," said Spike.

"Yes, I wonder what it'll be like smoking at the summit?" asked Guy.

"Anybody smoking up this high is insane and crazy!" Kirsten said, laughing at Spike. "You are never going to make it to the summit. Never!"

"Yes, yes...the summit is mine. I'll be there, smoking," replied Spike. "I just wish I had more wine to take up there."

Mike talked my ear off that evening as I photographed Aconcagua's pyramidal summit block, the Gran Acarreo (a huge scree slope that sweeps down from the mountain's summit complex), Cerros Cuerno and Mercederio, and distant peaks to the west of Aconcagua. The camp's name translates to 'the condors'

Merging glaciers, as seen from Nido de Cóndores

nest' and with the views I had that evening, I understood why. The camp sits out from the main bulk of Aconcagua.

I didn't exercise much that evening—I never carried my camera more than about 50 yards from my tent. But I still felt tired. No headache, no cough, no dizziness, but I was sluggish enough to know I needed another full day at Nido before I could go up to Berlin. Team Mike's guide, Julio, had a CB radio; after I finished cooking dinner I could hear Julio speaking with the rangers at Plaza de Mulas. I invited myself into their camp to find out what the weather would be like in the upcoming days.

"Bad, my friend. Bad. We have only a few days and then we must abandon our attempt. If we don't make the summit by the next day, then we won't be able to. I think this storm might be as bad as the one that came a few weeks ago,

Afternoon light, distant peaks. Highest peak in distance is Tupungato

Looking north to Cerro Mercedario (top right of photograph)

the one that killed so many people up here." Julio spoke with outright fear. He didn't sound like an experienced guide.

"Who gave you this weather report? The Rangers?" I asked.

"Yes. The Rangers give it to me," Julio said.

"Where do *they* get it?" I asked. Julio responded by shrugging his shoulders; then he noticed his clients staring intently at him.

"Umm...they get the weather from the Argentine authorities. Very reliable sources of information. I think we should just go down, maybe tomorrow." That brought looks of shock from Mike and his partners.

"Wait a minute there...we have to try to see this thing out. We *have* to," implored Mike.

Looking down towards the setting sun

"Well, I don't want to die. Do you?" responded Julio. The intrepid guide disappeared inside his tent. I imagined that he then stuck his head inside his sleeping bag and wished for the mountain and all its tribulations to just 'go away.' Mike and his two partners, Chuck and Robert, scooted over to my camp to discuss their predicament.

"You guys should rest here tomorrow then go up to Berlin," I said. "And then make a summit attempt. That's the best way to go."

"Julio doesn't even have a plan. You know, I don't think he's ever been higher than this camp, and this might be his first time up here!" Mike said. Robert and Chuck stared blankly at the ground.

"You guys okay?" I asked. They both nodded.

"Well, I'm going to be here tomorrow, then go up the next day. And you know what? If I don't feel like going up then, I'll take another rest day after that. You guys should make the calls. Go up when you feel ready. If he doesn't like it, then just take your gear and come with me. Your guide can wait down in Plaza de Mulas," I said

"Hey guys, come here. I have the plan," Julio called. Mike, Chuck, and Robert disappeared into Julio's tent. Mike stood outside my tent five minutes later.

"I can't believe that guy. Just can't believe him!"

"What?" I asked.

"We're making a summit attempt tomorrow. *Tomorrow!*" Mike yelped. "We aren't ready! I have a pounding headache and Chuck and Robert can barely tie their shoelaces, much less climb a vertical mile! We spent one night at Confluencia, two nights at Plaza de Mulas, and now we're here. All this after some 'acclimatization' hike up some small scree pile called El Plomo just outside of Santiago!"

"Well then...don't go. Make him wait for a day or two—"

"Won't work—Chuck and Robert already agreed to it. I think those guys just want out of here. I think they're going to make some half-ass attempt tomorrow, turn around, and use the 'storm' as an excuse to go back to the city. Aaaarrrh! This is so frustrating!"

"Well...sleep on it, then see how you feel in the morning," I said, cherishing my expedition's size and all the decision-making power it afforded me.

"Yeah, I'll try to sleep on it. We'll see if I can sleep at all tonight."

CHAPTER TWENTY-FOUR
PREPARE FOR LIFTOFF

Aconcagua's summit at dusk

S taring at the summit of a huge mountain that I've come a long way to climb—staring at it from close range, where I can see individual details, where I can trace my planned route from where I stand to the very apex of the peak—makes me sick with anxiety. I woke well before dawn on my first morning at Nido, restless about the coming days. A white sheen coated the inside of my tent—frost remnants of my nighttime breaths. I whipped open the tent door and aimed my eyes dead on Aconcagua's summit. The air was so clear that I felt as though my vision would improve by peering through it. *Tomorrow…tomorrow…just one day of rest…all I need is just one day then I can move to high camp—and go for the top,* I repeated to myself, feeling queasy after just seconds of running my eyes across the geometry of the peak's crest. *That's over a mile above me!* If a monster storm really was set to roll in, then my window of opportunity was closing. All variables summed—the amount of food I carried, the storm (if there *was* a storm), and my acclimatization—equaled me having to make a move the next day. My options: either move up to Berlin or forget about it.

Nervousness hadn't been a problem the day before. I'd been able to shut thoughts of motoring higher out of my mind. But now the clock was ticking. I felt strong after a night of rest, strong enough that I believed I could reach Berlin—even with the Pentax. I wanted to return home with spectacular medium-format shots of Aconcagua, and have memories of an unobstructed 360° view from the top of the Americas. I savored those thoughts. I knew that I could make them happen.

I had just stepped outside of my tent when the first member of Team Mike stuck his head into the new day. "Oh boy!" I heard. "It's a beautiful day, but I think we're a little late," said Robert.

"*No* way. *No way* are we going up today. We were supposed to get up at like one in the morning. Julio! Julio!" Mike barked angrily.

"Uh…yeah?"

"What happened to you getting us up at one in the morning?"

"Oh…uh…I think my watch broke. No alarm. Sorry. We can still go. As guide, I say we go. Yes. Get dressed. We go," Julio quipped. The few teams who'd planned to make summit attempts from Nido had departed hours earlier; even the majority of those who would be making the more modest jump to Berlin had already left, including Team Harry.

"We'll never make it. Not even to Berlin!" screamed Mike. "I can't believe we hired you. You just want to go down! This is an excuse for you! You know we won't make it, then you'll just use the supposed storm as an excuse!"

"Come on, Mike—he's right…probably…I mean he's the guide," Chuck said, straining to breathe.

"Okay, Mike. Okay. Look. We try to go up today, and if we don't make it, then we wait and try tomorrow or next day. You are the boss. Fine," said Julio.

"But we should start moving quickly to see if we can make it today. I think we can." One hour later Team Mike embarked on what was sure to be a total waste of energy.

"Good luck," I said to Mike. "But I really think you should rest here a day, then make a move to Berlin, and go for the summit from there. You'd be much better off."

"I agree, but I'm a minority vote here. I'll see you soon." Mike, Chuck, and Robert belonged in their sleeping bags, or maybe on a short stroll to pee. Not on a summit attempt.

The foursome staggered back into camp an hour-and-a-half later. Mike carried Julio's pack; Julio's shirt was covered in vomit. "We wait...go up in two days," Julio said. Mike looked at me and shook his head.

That day I enjoyed some of the most relaxing time I'd ever spent in the mountains. The weather remained clear and windless throughout much of the morning, I wasn't suffering from even a hint of AMS, and the denizens of Nido kept quiet—until 3:00 in the afternoon, when Spike and Company came crawling into the daylight.

I watched (and listened) from afar as Andrea vociferously gathered Spike and Company together and directed the crew in a mealmaking orchestration—complete with clanging pots, dog-like howls, screaming stoves, and rising columns of tobacco smoke. But those puffs produced by cigarettes weren't the only clouds in the area. High cirrus snuck up on the mountain; lower-level cumulus also advanced.

I shot a few frames of the deteriorating conditions surrounding Aconcagua's summit and spotted a lone figure in the lower left corner of the frame. I slapped on my telephoto and scanned the route between Nido and Berlin. Whoever the person was, he or she was descending alone—and moving slowly, taking frequent rests. I checked again 15 minutes later. The figure was close enough that I could resolve color: green and hot pink—Dave's pack. I zipped my camera inside my tent and set off to greet him.

"I'm okay...just fine, now that I'm back down," he said. "Fred insisted that we head for Berlin yesterday and try for the summit today. I gave out a little below White Rocks. God, my lungs felt like they were on fire. They hurt so much, I can't even tell you."

"How's Fred, I take it he kept going?" I asked.

"I'm sure he summited. We had great weather and we got going a couple hours before dawn. I bet he's already back at Berlin. I was wondering if he'd beat me back here—he moves so fast!"

"How old is he?" I asked.

"He's in his sixties. But he sure doesn't act like it. He was passing everybody. Right from the get-go he stormed ahead of me. He just doesn't stop! And me...I'm just buggered."

In the half hour since I'd first spotted Dave, a storm had locked onto the upper reaches of Aconcagua and was quickly descending on us. Team Mike stood quietly outside of their camp when I returned.

"This is not good. Not good. Look at it. It is calm here now, but…it is the calm before the storm. This may be the big one. We may all die," Julio moaned, "I knew we should have just gone down today."

"Hey look! People coming down that huge slope over there!" Chuck pointed his finger at three small specs dropping below the clouds on the Gran Acarreo.

"I hope nobody is stuck up high. I think this might be another bad night. Those people should have come down the normal way, along the ridge. Going down that way is bad. You can get lost, especially in this weather. It is horrible over there," said Julio.

Climbers descending Gran Acarreo

"So you've been on that side of the mountain?" asked Mike.

"Mmmm…no, but…I have friends who have," Julio replied.

"You really think that this is going to be a bad storm?" Robert asked Julio.

"I think so. I really think so."

"I bet you're wrong," I said.

"Who are you to know? I'm a guide for many years. I know this place well!"

"Well…we'll see, won't we," I said, giving Mike a laugh.

The weather rolled through within the hour, lightly dusting Nido de Cóndores with snow and shining a storm of crimson light on the mountains just to the north of camp. "This is atmospheric scattering at its best!" I yelled to Mike, who followed me on the high rocks behind my camp as I ran through film.

"What do you mean by *atmospheric scattering?*" he asked.

"It's what makes sunsets and sunrises red—scatters the shorter, bluish wave-lengths of visible light," I said as I froze my fingers changing rolls. The sun acted as a crimson blowtorch for us that evening—but for less than a minute.

The clouds disappeared as night fell. Nobody died, as Julio had predicted, and everybody in camp—including the group of three who'd descended the Gran Acarreo—enjoyed a clear night and a sliver moon.

Fred arrived just before sunset, having gone from Berlin to the summit and back in five hours; an absolutely amazing feat for anybody, much less a man in his sixties. He'd rested for a while at Berlin, then headed back to Nido. In usual Fred style he acted as if his incredible speed at that altitude was no big deal; he jumped right back into ordering Dave around as 'Total Eclipse of the Heart' tinned away in the background. "Tomorrow we'll be back at PDI, Dave. We have a good walk ahead of us. Let's prepare." It was comforting to know that Aconcagua's summit hadn't changed Fred one bit.

I found Paul and Gary next to my tent when I returned. "What a surprise! Nice to see you two," I said.

"We got up here and didn't know where to go. Gary saw your yellow tent and we figured we'd join you," Paul explained.

"Good. There's enough room for your tent. What's your plan?" I asked.

"There's meant to be a brutal storm coming in a few days. Supposed to pretty much shut this place down. We're going up to Berlin or White Rocks tomorrow. From there, on to the summit the next day."

"That's ambitious," I said. "How do you feel?"

"All right. Both of us have coughs, and we're wiped out from today's climb—it took us longer than we'd anticipated; we didn't do a carry, we just came straight up with all our stuff today," answered Paul with an exhausted slur. Mike walked over and joined the conversation.

"Julio says we're going to stay here tomorrow and rest, see what the weather does, then if it looks like it's going to get bad we'll descend the next day; if not, we'll make a go for the summit."

"From here?" Gary asked.

"Yeah. Our guide says he doesn't want to spend a night any higher than this. Says he doesn't want to get stuck in a storm that high," Mike said, shrugging his shoulders.

"Oh man, the summit's a long way off. I would hate to try to go for it from down here. It's crazy. Too far off, unless you're really strong," said Gary.

"What do you think about that, Mike?" I asked.

"I don't know. I think I'd rather try for it from Berlin. But I really don't feel well enough to go anywhere right now. Probably not tomorrow, either. Maybe Julio has a point. Maybe we could make it from here. I've heard about this storm from others now too, I think it's really going to be big. Maybe you should think about going for the summit from here, Ed," Mike said.

"I'm going up to Berlin tomorrow—storm or no storm. I'll see you all in the morning," I said hastily. "Come and get me if you want any help setting up your camp or if you need anything," I said to Paul and Gary before crawling into my tent.

What Mike had said to me must have had more impact than I realized. I woke up thinking that it really *would* be a better idea to rest another day at Nido. *Quit lying...quit making stupid excuses to be lazy*, I thought. I stood outside my tent just after the sun had risen. *Another gorgeous day*. I stared at my tripod and imagined how great it would feel to have my medium format with me at 19,000 feet. I grabbed my camera and took some morning shots.

I climbed to the rocky perch behind my tent and searched for an image to compose. "Hey there. Look at that camera, huh!" Spike scrambled up to my spot. "You gonna go up to Camp Berlin today?" he asked.

"I think so...yeah, I'm gonna go up."

"Good. So are we. I think the weather is good for it now, but may be bad soon. That's what everybody in camp is saying," Spike remarked as he pulled out a pack of cigarettes. "Want one?" he asked.

"Sure. Give me a few," I said.

"All right! Dat's my man!" said Spike as he handed me five. "I think we gonna be on the top together, that's when we finish off this pack, you know?"

"Sure....sure...come on, let's take our pictures so we can get moving," I said.

When I returned to my camp I found a large olive-drab garbage bag, filled with British military 'assault ration packs' and a note: "Nice knowing you, Ed. Here's some extra food for the storm if you get trapped up here—Fred and Dave." I stuffed the cache into my mule bag.

"So, you're going?" asked Mike.

"Yeah," I answered, "I'm going. I'm just trying to decide at the last minute whether this big camera and tripod are going with me." It was easy to fantasize about bringing the Pentax to high camp, but when it came down to actually hauling it, I began to lose my resolve.

"Leave that thing here. It's huge. Must weigh like 50 pounds, with the tripod and all. You have a regular 35mm camera, right?"

"I do. I don't know if the pictures from Berlin will be worth the pain of carrying the medium format up that high."

"Leave it. That's way too much. You've got to leave it," Mike said.

I'd have been an absolute idiot to try to haul that camera to almost 6,000 meters given the approaching storm and the amount of time I had.

"I'm taking it." I stuffed my pack, rolled the tripod in my sleeping pad, secured my mule bag, and aimed for Berlin. "I hope to see you up there, Mike. Good luck to you, man."

"Same to you. Take a lot of really good pictures. Good luck."

CHAPTER TWENTY-FIVE

WRESTLING GRAVITY

Berlin Camp

I began my ascent to Berlin Camp with a brisk march across the flats of Nido de Cóndores. The weight of my pack was oppressive; the strain on my shoulders made me want to turn around and quit right then and there, but the view of Aconcagua's summit punching into a cobalt dome of crystalline air reeled me closer. Spike and Company, led by the flamboyant Captain Andrea, had broken trail about 15 minutes ahead of me; Paul and Gary struck off shortly after I started. We formed just a small sample of Nido's upwardly mobile that morning. Many others were either already on their way up or preparing to get moving. I soon reached the south end of camp and began huffing toward the crest of the northwest ridge.

As it had on previous days, the sun struck with full force through pellucid air. I soaked my face in sunscreen and snugged my glasses firmly against my forehead. I was happy to be moving along at a healthy, steady clip, even with the overloaded Dana strapped on. I even passed a few people in the early going.

After about an hour of marching I found that the route so many call 'just a walk' traverses a few spots worthy of more respectful terms. I kick-stepped up a short section of hardened snow—the first ascending that wasn't just plain-old hiking—and plopped down for a rest on a level pad of loose volcanic rock.

Andesite.... One of my favorite effects of exertion at high altitude is the strange gallimaufry of thoughts that come streaming through my mind. I began pondering etymology and geology during my brief rest—*andesite,* I thought. The word 'andesite' looks like the word 'Andes' with an 'ite' tacked onto it. I remembered my friend and former university geology professor, Tracy Tingle, reciting the three primary types of volcanic rock: basalt, rhyolite, and andesite. I looked at the rocks at my feet. I grabbed some. One was light tan; another was yellow. I remembered learning that andesite is gray; and that it sits between basalt and rhyolite in its level of viscosity— and that was about all I could recall. I'd never made the connection between *Andes* and *andesite* until that moment. But...which came first? Were the Andes named after a type of rock or was andesite named after a mountain range?

As it turns out, the word 'andesite' followed, and was derived from, the word 'Andes.' Andesite was so called because so much of it is found in the Andes. Not too much has been said or written about the origin of the word *Andes*, however. It most likely has its beginnings in the Aymara word for the color of copper, *anta.*

"Rock! Rock! ROCK!! Look out below!" I looked up—probably the stupidest thing to do—and saw two basketball-sized chunks of Aconcagua rocketing down. I dove to the side as they whistled by me—just feet by me. I crawled to a small, solid outcrop, covered my head, then peeked up. A few more chunks, these the size of baseballs, sailed across my field of view, but I seemed to be safely out of the fall line. "Sorry!" echoed through the air. *Watch where you step!* I screamed in my head. I waved off the mishap and got back on my way.

The route grew steeper above my resting spot, but I continued my ascent at a healthy clip. I caught up with Guy and traveled with him for about a half hour; but two hours into the day I started feeling weak—just as the weather caved in. Soon I was traveling through mist. Navigation? I just kept going up. *Up—up—up—just go up!* I roared in my head. I teased myself no less than ten times with what I was sure was the first sight of Berlin Camp; each time it was a mirage. I finally concluded that I would be heaving on my calves, quads, and lungs in a Sisyphean odyssey forever—only the rolling boulders would be coming at me, not from me.

"OOOOOOOHHHHHHHHHH!" A scream came at me from every direction, slightly muffled by the cloud that was enveloping the mountain. *Andrea?* I wondered. *It sounds like him.* I stared into the nothingness of the whiteout. I swayed around and looked down—up—right—left—for Camp Berlin.

"YYYYYEEEEESSSSS! Come up here everyone! I have arrived! And tomorrow, THE SUMMIT!" It *was* Andrea. He was proclaiming Camp Berlin victory in a way only he could.

"God...I'm so sick of this pack!" I yelled at myself as I wrestled against gravity. Then more of Andrea's battle cries rang through the misty air. I felt a surge of spirit and energy—thanks to Andrea's enthusiasm. I raced up the mountain for a hundred yards and stood face-to-face with two small, wooden huts. I'd arrived at Camp Berlin—with food, fuel, tent, sleeping bag, and the Pentax system. I felt like I had done something that no one had done before: hauled a medium format camera high on the slopes of Aconcagua.

I collapsed against the smaller of the two shelters, an A-frame only slightly larger than a spoiled poodle's doghouse. It was built in 1946 and christened *Refugio Plantamura*, after Nicolás Plantamura, the first Argentine to climb Aconcagua. It's useful for cooking but I wouldn't want to sleep in it. Plantamura's next-door neighbor was built in 1951 and originally named *Refugio Eva Perón*. Now known as the *Refugio Libertad*, it is similar to the Plantamura Hut but with three-foot-high vertical walls at its base. It could be useful as an emergency shelter, but most modern tents are more comfortable.

The heydays of both huts had long since passed. Trash lay everywhere—stuffed in and around both the shelters—and their walls didn't look like they could take even as much punishment as modern ripstop nylon would. It's inaccurate to describe the wood that these structures are built of as 'rotten,' as nothing really rots at 19,000 feet, but the huts are certainly extremely weather-beaten. That they were built at all is a remarkable feat, however. Building a hut at nearly 19,000 feet doesn't compare with the construction of the Sphinx or even the Brooklyn Bridge, but it is a monumental testament to architectural

will power and tenacity. The Berlin Camp huts are some of the highest permanent structures in the world. I really thought I had pulled off a big one by
carrying the Pentax to that altitude. Seeing those huts, however, tempered my
self-complimenting a bit.

I pitched my tent near the two huts, then set off to visit the third Berlin
structure, which lies about 50 yards farther up the mountain. It is the largest,
newest, and the camp's modern namesake. Another A-frame, this one is reinforced with steel and looks as if it could survive a direct hit from an F-5
tornado. It was built by a group of German climbers in memory of a friend
who'd died on the Ruta Normal. Climbing teams covet a chance to sleep in it,
and sometimes fight for the space.

"You made it!" I turned to see Spike, smoking a cigarette. He had just arrived
at camp and looked not so much tired, but mellowed. "Here, smoke with me?"
he handed me a cigarette.

"Why not?…sure," I said as we watched the whiteout dissolve, revealing
Aconcagua's summit, directly overhead. The view of the summit pyramid was
awesome to the point of being frightening.

"Wow! Tomorrow we go there!" said Spike, between drags. "You really have
to try hard to get smoke from cigarettes up here. No air for them to breathe.
You have to bring the air to them by really inhaling hard!" he said. I took a
drag and nodded. I knew that smoking—at any altitude—was stupid. But it did
have a surprising effect; it kept an increasingly nagging cough at bay. "It warms
you from the inside, very good for you," said Spike—and he wasn't kidding.
Still, I doubted that Fred would approve.

While Spike and Company settled into camp, I did what little I could at that
altitude—not a whole lot more than massage my temples, shoot some film, and
drink a few sips of water. Much of the time, however, I simply laid on my back
and listened to myself breathe.

After a few hours of resting at Berlin, I cared about nothing other than the
bare rudiments of survival—shelter, water, food, and the all-important funda-
mental: dryness. *Dryness….* The ground outside was wet and mushy, but the
inside of my tent was bone dry. I looked at my camera and shrugged. Beauty *is*
in the eye of the beholder, and what I regarded as beautiful at that moment, in
that high place, wasn't the mountain vista outside, but my implements of warmth
and survival inside. I just knew that my perfectly-crafted XGK would burn
efficiently and without glitches for hours. My Gore-Tex tent would hold off
all but the worst that the atmosphere could throw at me, and what a comfort
my thick sleeping bag was. I didn't just appreciate my tools…I relished them. I
peeled off my sweat-soaked socks and hung them up to dry. I stuffed the liners
of my boots into the footbox of my sleeping bag. One fresh pair of heavy socks
and one pristine set of liner socks remained in my clean-clothes stash. *My
summit day socks.* I cradled them in my hands. I rubbed them on my cheeks.

I sunk my nose into them. They didn't smell repulsive—as all my other garments had by that time—so they were like spring wildflowers to me. I couldn't wait to slip my feet into those socks and make a go for the summit. True beauty awaited....

My rapture with socks and other banalities didn't last long. Even at 19,000 feet, socks are just socks. Rational thought soon returned. The Pentax, my ultimate lord and master on that climb, beckoned me to satisfy its purpose in this world after my spate of gear coddling. I, and the mountain—and the mountain's weather—obliged. I couldn't wait to see the processed results; but I also couldn't wait to see the views from even higher on Aconcagua.

During one of my trips around camp to find photographic vantage points, I noticed a tent about 30 feet from mine, partially hidden behind some rocks. I approached to see if anybody was home, but it was utterly silent and shut tight—even when I called out a few salutations. I thought its owners must have been on a summit attempt. But I was wrong—they had been sleeping. When they woke and emerged from their shelter, I learned that they were a team of two American ex-military policemen who'd been at Camp Berlin for three days. Their previous occupation gave me a great idea. "Are you guys going to be staying here a while longer?" I asked.

"We're going to try to make the summit...we've been trying...but haven't had luck so far. We'll try again tomorrow and then maybe the next day, but

Northwest ridge of Aconcagua

then we'll be out of food and we'll have to go down," the more vocal of the two replied.

"Well, if you guys are around tomorrow, could you just keep an eye on my tent? I hear there are some problems with theft down in the lower camps. I just want to make sure that someone will be watching."

"Sure...no problem. We'll keep an eye on it for you whenever we're here."

"Thanks, it's just me, so if anyone else goes into my tent, just throw him off the mountain." My summit attempt would be the first time on Aconcagua that I wouldn't have my Pentax within eyesight. Theft should be the last worry at that altitude, but vigilance is prudent due to the popularity of the Ruta Normal.

I returned to the 'mezzanine' of Camp Berlin later that afternoon. The weather was more fickle than ever at that hour, making for dramatic, gorgeous photo-opportunities as well as instilling nervousness in climbers. "I just know the skies will shine on us tomorrow," proclaimed Andrea. "I feel it. We will be making the summit!" But not everyone at Spike and Company was so positive. Guy acted withdrawn, Kirsten was dizzy with AMS, and Alan was faring just slightly better than Kirsten. Even Andrea, who was usually a Ferrari, was now just a Fiat. The only member of Spike and Company who seemed his usual self was Spike.

Where's the other Aconcagua chain smoker…Harry? I wondered.

"Hey Andrea, do you know Harry?" I asked.

"Harry, the Finnish?" he asked.

"Yeah. Harry, the Finn."

"Of course I know Harry!" Andrea stated.

"Where is he and his group?"

"Not here. They move fast. Probably up at the next camp, White Rocks. A bit higher up. Harry is a tough one. You can tell just by looking at him. He is a great guide, a classic mountain guide."

I returned to my tent at sunset to find Paul and Gary struggling into Berlin. They both looked wasted. "Look, here's a good spot for you two. I'll set your tent up and get some water boiling while you guys rest." I acted as if the two were about to die.

"No. We're going to White Rocks," Gary stated with difficulty.

"Yeah. We want to be closer to the summit than this. We have to keep going," added Paul. Then they limped onward.

"Wait! Gary! I have something for you." I reached into my tent and grabbed the last of my hand/foot warmers. "I really didn't think you two would make it this far. I don't know if you're stupid, crazy, or just superhuman, but Gary, *you've got to take care of your feet!* Those boots are too thin for this altitude, much less the summit."

"I have my system worked out. Don't worry about it. Do you have any duct tape?" Gary asked. I looked at him and rolled my eyes.

"Sure…" I grabbed my ski poles, around each of which I had wound a good supply of the wonder-mender. Here, you wind that one up and I'll get this one. You can use all the duct tape I have."

"Thanks. Really. Thanks a lot," Gary slurred. We finished the transfer and the duo resumed their pained slog.

Berlin Camp was silent that evening. I broke the quietude with the roar of my XGK, then tried to force down some almost-cooked spaghetti and a packet of rice with mushrooms. I managed maybe 600 calories, if that. What was I burning each day? Probably over four or five thousand calories—maybe more. *Altitude does such strange things to the body*, I thought. I recalled the Anti-Freds and my comment about a high altitude weight loss program. The higher one travels, the more calories needed to maintain the status quo—and that's just for sitting around. Throw in lugging 75 pounds of gear to nearly 19,000 feet, and the caloric balance sheet tips precipitously into the red. And what happens when the intake falls pathetically short of the outflow? The body wastes away, first burning fat, then muscle. I didn't know what level of marasmus I had suffered by the time I was in Berlin Camp, but I knew that I'd be cinching my belt quite a bit tighter once I returned to Mendoza. I reminded myself of the importance of bringing savory meals, not just cheap, light food. *I'll never bring bland food up into the mountains again,* I resolved as I scraped pasty chunks of rice off the side of my bowl.

I cleaned my pots and packed my stove—and glanced at a phalanx of beautiful thunderclouds hovering to the north of Aconcagua. Their ruffled, fluxional peripheries were a testament to the divine aesthetic hidden deep within nature's chaotic maxim. A crescent moon pricked the darkening sky above a prismatic gradient of sunset fire.

Gnomes of self-doubt lurked in my mind that night. *Go or no go?* I kept asking myself in hypoxic delirium. *Is tomorrow a rest day, or THE day?*

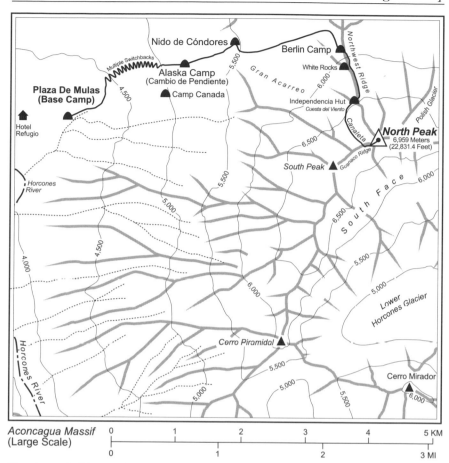

Nido de Cóndores

Berlin Camp

Multiple Switchbacks

Alaska Camp
(Cambio de Pendiente)

**Plaza De Mulas
(Base Camp)**

Camp Canada

White Rocks

Gran Acarreo

Northwest Ridge

Independencia Hut
Cuesta del Viento

Hotel
Refugio

Canaleta

Polish Glacier

North Peak
6,959 Meters
(22,831.4 Feet)

Horcones
River

South Peak

Guanaco Ridge

South Face

Lower
Horcones Glacier

Cerro Piramidal

Horcones River

Cerro Mirador

Aconcagua Massif
(Large Scale)

| 0 | 1 | 2 | 3 | 4 | 5 KM |

| 0 | 1 | 2 | 3 MI |

Map shows significant peaks, valleys, glaciers, rivers, intermittent streams, and primary camps of Aconcagua and environs. Map indicates topography by contour lines (500 meter intervals) and simplified ridge lines. Names incorporate both English and Spanish for ease of comprehension. Map shows author's route (normal route; *ruta normal*).

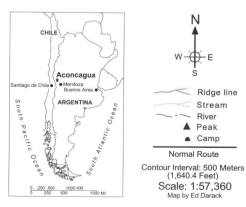

CHILE

Aconcagua

Santiago de Chile ● ● Mendoza
Buenos Aires ●

ARGENTINA

South Pacific Ocean

South Atlantic Ocean

| 0 | 250 | 500 | 1000 KM |
| 0 | 250 | 500 | 1000 MI |

N

W ⊕ E

S

Ridge line

Stream

River

▲ Peak

▲ Camp

Normal Route

Contour Interval: 500 Meters
(1,640.4 Feet)

Scale: 1:57,360
Map by Ed Darack

Mountain Altitudes in Meters (and Feet):
Aconcagua:
North Peak: 6,959 Meters (22,831.4 Feet)
South Peak: 6,930 Meters (22,736.2 Feet)
Cerro Mirador: 6,089 Meters (19,977 Feet)
Cerro Piramidal: 6,009 Meters (19,714.6 Feet)

Camp Altitudes in Meters (and Feet):
Plaza de Mulas: 4,275 Meters (14,025.6 Feet)
Camp Canada: 4,900 Meters (16,076 Feet)
Alaska Camp (Cambio de Pendiente): 5,200 Meters
(17060.4 Feet)
Nido de Cóndores: 5,350 Meters (17,552.5 Feet)
Berlin Camp: 5,810 Meters (19061.7 Feet)
White Rocks: 6,250 Meters (20,505 Feet)
Independencia Hut: 6,405 Meters (21,013.8 Feet)

Sources of Information:
IMGA Topographic Sheets: 3369 7-4;
3369 8-3; 3369 13-2; 3369 14-1
American Alpine Club Map of Aconcagua
Observation and Photographs of Author

261

CHAPTER TWENTY-SIX

¡VÁMONOS A LA CUMBRE!

¡Vámonos a la cumbre!—Let's go to the summit!

ummit Day. I staggered out of a murky dream into semi-lucidity. I tried to formulate a plan of summit attack, but the altitude had my thoughts bogged down like quicksand. I struggled to get moving—get packing—anything that would pump my blood and kickstart my spirits. But I could muster only enough energy to open my eyes. They were thick with lachrymal goo. When I rubbed them, cold air snuck into my sleeping bag and nipped at my fingers and toes. The infamous 'pumping effect' had struck again, where even the slightest movement within a sleeping bag sucks frigid air in and blows warm air out. *My body worked so hard to heat that air,* I lamented.

I laid flat on my back. A shower of ice crystals fell back on my cheeks and nose after each breath. I whisked my hand across a tent wall. Thick frost covered the fabric. The air felt colder than I'd experienced since sleeping at 18,000 feet on Mount Logan in the Canadian subarctic, about -40°. My summit motivation started to tank. *Life inside a sleeping bag is just so much easier than going outside right now…Just sleep a while longer…get going after the sun comes up…no need to go before sunrise,* I thought. But procrastinating on summit day is like showing up late for a final exam—or your wedding. You just don't do it. But I was doing it.

Just as I started falling back into sleep, the crunching of snow squealed through the thin air, followed by a flood of blinding light. I was definitely awake after that. I jumped up as if a big rig were crashing into my camp, then I nearly broke the tent door zipper racing it open: "Hello!" I yelled, my eyes cinching in pain as I stared into a high-power halogen bulb.

"¡Hola!" came the reply. A lone climber stood just feet from me, his headlamp trained directly on my eyes. "¡Vámanos amigo! ¡Vámanos a la Cumbre!" he yelled at me like a drill sergeant.

"¡Un minuto! ¡Un minuto!…uh…uh…what time is…no…¿que hora es?" I asked, trying to wake up and pack at the same time.

"Cuatro," he answered. *Four in the morning.* I flipped on my headlamp, jumped into my bibs, shot my feet into my beloved socks, laced up my boots, strapped my ice ax and crampons onto my pack, grabbed my Nikon and two lenses, stuffed my medical kit in the pack's top pouch, put on my jacket…took a half second to breathe and to check if I had forgotten anything…grabbed my trekking poles—and set off with the soloist, who I suspected was a local from Mendoza, but I didn't know for sure.

I tried to follow close behind him, but by the time I got to the upper Berlin hut he was 50 yards ahead of me and I was out of breath. "Ed! Hello, Ed! Yes! Yes! You are coming up too? Are we all going to be on the summit together? Yes! Yes! We'll beat this big storm coming! We'll beat it!!" sang Andrea at the top of his lungs. I'd arrived at the hut in time to meet Spike and Company.

"What storm?" I asked. "What *storm* is it now?" I repeated sarcastically.

"The big one coming in. Supposed to be here today. We have to move fast!"

"Okay, okay…let's go." I still wasn't completely awake, but Andrea was certainly helping me along. The cold was intense, I could feel it in my bones. My right hip, site of nearly 16 hours of surgery, definitively told me that it was cold—freezing cold. My toes, after only 15 minutes of being outside of my sleeping bag, were already numb. The tip of my nose stung, then went numb as well. The only cure for the cold was to keep moving as fast as possible until the sun emerged. And move we did.

We used headlamps for another 30 minutes, until the predawn glow was bright enough to see by. I fell into my sprint—rest—sprint routine, doing between 35 and 75 steps during each run. At each rest the view loomed larger and more inspiring. The altitude was overpowering; spates of vertigo lashed me a few times. Cerro Mercedario commanded my attention. The mountain's broad summit plateau stood alone above the clouds like an island in a sea of rolling white vapor. After an hour of travel our group was spread out; I was somewhere in the middle of the pack.

The climbing—if it could be called *climbing*—was fun. Nothing scary, but not a hiking trail, either. I donned my crampons a couple of times—mostly to justify carrying them—and relished the sound of my ice ax squealing into the Styrofoam-like snow as I moved higher.

White Rocks—I passed the 20,000 foot level where White Rocks Camp sits. Paul and Gary were just finishing their morning preparations. Team Harry's tents were in place, but the wild Finns were long gone. "They left at like one in the morning!" Paul said.

"How are you feeling?" I asked.

"Okay, I guess. Neither of us slept much last night, and Gary's really cold," Paul replied.

"Oh my…." I gasped as I looked at Gary's high altitude footwear: he'd placed each booted foot into a thin plastic garbage bag, tightened the bags around his ankles with duct tape, and sealed them off at his knees. Then he strapped crampons over his 'supergaiters.'

"This oughtta work," he said confidently. I looked at Paul with wide eyes.

"You guys spent a night at 20,000 feet…all you have for a jacket, Paul, is a Kevlar-reinforced motorcycle jacket…and Gary…those boots…. Did you know that most people would be dead by now?" I asked, getting a small chuckle from Paul. "I didn't think you two would make it past base camp. I really didn't. I guess I'll see you up there…all the way up there."

"On the summit, for sure," Paul added.

I felt a surge of adrenaline rush through my body as the sun seared the horizon with long streams of yellow-white light. I looked up and saw nothing but a long haul ahead. How many thousands of feet, I didn't know, nor did I want to expend the energy calculating. I just knew it would be a very long day. *Am I going to hold out? How long can I hold out? How much longer will I*

264

feel good enough to keep going? And what about the weather? Is today really when the storm will hit? I chased doubts from my mind. *I'm going to make it—I'm going to make it!*

Five minutes after sunrise the whole region exploded in bright light. Soon I was seeing blue. I sprinted up to rest on some rocks and dig out my... "sunglasses! I forgot my sunglasses!" I screamed. I dropped my pack on the rocks and rummaged through every pocket to see if somehow—*some way*—I had brought them. But I remembered *not* grabbing them from my tent's side pocket—I just passed them by. *This is it,* I thought, *there's no way—NO WAY— I'm ever going to be able to keep going without sunglasses.* I sat down and mulled over the possibility of another attempt the next day. *Maybe...maybe not. More likely not, especially if there is any real weather coming.* This had been one of the worst seasons on record for Aconcagua in terms of summit success, and I was basking in what was probably one of the best summit days of the season. Ironically, that good, bright weather is what would keep me from heading higher. Snowblindness comes quickly and is incredibly painful. It can take days to heal, during which time the afflicted person can do nothing, especially a solo climber. I didn't have much time to decide. The sun rose higher and the day got brighter.

So I gave up. Retreat was the only option. And I would have to race back to my tent to keep from being exposed to too much bright, snow-reflected light on the descent. Once safely back at Berlin I could make a decision on whether to continue down to base camp or try again the next day. I definitely didn't have the energy to go down, grab my glasses, then retrace my steps and continue to the summit. And I probably wouldn't have the energy to make another full-on summit bid, even the following day.

I looked up toward the summit. *All this way, all this time...and no summit. At least I can get some more photos, though.* I pulled out my Nikon. Attached to the trusty FE2 body was a 50mm lens. I peered at Mercedario through the viewfinder. *Another gorgeous scene.* I adjusted the aperture and shutter speed, then felt the ring of an attached polarizing filter. *Good,* I thought, *the polarizer is already attached to the lens.* I twisted the dark-glass filter, axing glare from the scene, and made a few shots. *Now it's time for a wide-angle view.* I grabbed my 24mm—and saw that it too had an attached polarizer. *Stupid. Waste of weight, only should have brought along one polarizer...wait...wait a minute...just wait....* I reached into the top pouch of my pack and pulled out my medical kit. In it was a full role of medical tape. I looked at the two polarizers, at the roll of tape, at a spare pack strap, at my Leatherman tool...and then looked up at the summit. *I'll make sunglasses out of polarizing filters and tape!* 15 minutes later I had the world's ugliest pair of sunglasses. They all but completely blocked my peripheral vision, didn't fit well, smelled like tape, fogged up, and didn't stay on my face without constant adjustments…but they worked just well enough so that I could make it to the summit without burning up my retinas. I rolled back on the rocks and laughed. "Let's Go!" I screamed at Guy, who was passing my rest spot. *"¡Vámanos!"*

21,000 feet. The highest permanent structure on earth, Independencia Hut. The only human-made habitats higher than this miniscule A-frame are in orbit.

"You are making it!" Andrea howled into the wind as I dropped my pack next to the small hut. "Look at those sunglasses! They are so huge! Where did you get them?"

"I didn't get them, I made them. I forgot mine back at camp."

"Oh, you are such an American—MAKING THINGS! Look, not much more to go, a little less than 600 meters, and then we are on the summit!" I caught my breath and combed my fingers through my greasy hair. I felt awake, strong, ready to storm up the remainder of the mountain, but I knew that my condition could turn on a dime. I took a 15 minute break with Andrea and Guy, during which time the rest of Spike and Company caught up to us.

"Hey Ed, how 'bout smoking a cigarette with me?" Spike said as he crested the slope below the hut.

"Sure," I said, feeling further powered by the warmth of the sun on my face and the cold, strong wind flopping my hair around. An American team arrived at the hut as Spike and I lit up. They had traversed to the Ruta Normal from the Polish Glacier, and looked haggard.

"You have to try hard—really, especially in this wind. Make it *sooo* difficult to make a cigarette," said Spike after working his lungs for a drag.

"Are those guys smoking cigarettes?" I heard from the Americans. I laughed at myself. It was a truly idiotic scene: standing next to this little doll-house-sized refugio, smoking a cigarette in the howling wind, and wearing medical-tape-polarizer sunglasses—at 21,000 feet. Soon another team arrived from the Polish Glacier traverse, and yet another team came up from behind us on the Ruta Normal.

"Time to go, Andrea," I said, anxious to beat the traffic jam to the summit.

"You lead the way. Go!" The lively Italian shouted. A burst of energy surged through my muscles and spirits. I pushed hard up the icy slope that leads from the Independencia Hut to the Cuesta del Viento. One cramponed boot in front of the other, the steel points pricked the hard, steepening surface. THUD—THUD—THUD came the sound from my lugged soles as my legs and lungs boosted me up the slope. I'd never felt so aware, so confident. My heart slammed inside my chest as hard as my boots hit the icy snow. I couldn't make a mistake. Falling was impossible. *Any* screw-up was impossible. *There's nothing like running up-slope at high altitude,* I thought. With each lunge I gained more focus, more resolve—a lunge of ability, a fleeting sense of immortality. I roared in an arrow-straight line up the slope until lactic acid in my quads burned so badly I thought my legs would melt into the thin air. "Run? You crazy American!

Run! I can't believe you, running!" Andrea yelled. A few more sprints later I was on the most airy spot of the Ruta Normal, El Cuesta del Viento—the windy ridge. I sat in the snow, took off my goggles, and buried my face in my hands. My legs shook from the sprint. I massaged my calves and stretched out my legs. Andrea crested the ridge a few minutes later.

"Look, a big crowd," he said as he pointed at all the climbers inching toward us. "So now we just have to cross here, go up the Canaleta, and then onto the summit." Andrea spoke in an uncharacteristically subdued tone.

"Well then, let's get going!" I yipped.

"I'm waiting for the others, you go," Andrea said as he slumped over his ice ax. "Now the altitude gets to me. Just when it looks like you are playing at the beach, it gets to me—but just a little."

The section that runs between the Cuesta del Viento and the base of the Canaleta is the most exposed slice of the Ruta Normal. It traverses the top of the Gran Acarreo, and on the morning I was there, it was iced-over. There was something of a trail beaten into the traverse, but I wondered if that trail would cause more problems than it would solve by giving me a false sense of safety.

I double-checked my crampons and traded one of my trekking poles for my ice ax. My left hand, the upslope hand, carried the ax. If I slipped, I'd grab the shaft of the ax with my right hand and self-arrest after a slide of just a few feet. That was the plan, a plan I didn't want to test. I gripped both my ice ax and trekking pole a little harder than usual when I stood up and looked straight down the Gran Acarreo to Nido de Cóndores—an unbroken line. I could even see base camp. To my left was the base of the main summit block. Looking up was dizzying; looking down was dizzying, too—so I set my sights dead ahead.

With gusts of wind whipping at my back, I began the traverse. I had the first half of it to myself—then I looked up to see Harry and his team descending. "I smoked one for you up there," he said.

"You made it. Good," I said between heavy breaths.

"We were the first to make it to the summit today. A storm's coming, you better hurry up, keep ahead of the weather." I nodded. "What's with those glasses?" he asked. I quickly explained my jury-rig. "I like them. They're really...*cool.* Do you want a cigarette?"

"No. No way. I just have to keep going. I'll smoke one with you back in base camp, if you're still there." Our meeting was brief. Harry, Kari, and the rest of team stepped aside and let me pass.

When I finished the traverse 20 minutes later, I sat down by a big rock to defog my glasses, then looked up to witness a cloud slamming into the mountain. Instant whiteout. I leaned back and breathed deeply, wishing I'd had that cigarette. The winds died, leaving a thick silence. A few minutes later the quiet was broken by the sounds of trekking poles whisking over snow. Then I heard voices. Spike and Company emerged from the whiteout followed by Paul and Gary. Then my Argentine 'alarm clock' came from above, bounding back toward Plaza de Mulas—"¡Tormenta! ¡Tormenta en una hora!" he cried as he foot-skied by me with a look of terror in his eyes. A few minutes later even more climbers—Americans, Poles, Australians, and others—arrived from below. Individual voices were drowned out by the din of the large and growing herd of climbers gathering to stampede up the last of the mountain.

"Gary…GARY!" I yelled as I watched him collapse in the snow. "Gary!"

"He's okay…I think," Paul said.

"He doesn't look too good. Are his feet holding out?" I asked.

"Who knows. He won't turn back until he has the summit. And neither will I," Paul said quietly. The whiteout lifted slightly, increasing visibility to about 30 yards. Antsy climbers passed me.

"Ed. Let's go. Let's all go together," droned Andrea. "Make the summit." Each of us dropped our packs, taking only our cameras and a few other necessities with us. Guy took the lead, followed by Andrea and Alan. I managed to get Gary to his feet, but Paul held back. Kirsten and Spike headed up, but then so many people crowded by me that I couldn't keep track anymore.

Ten steps—five—two—*take a rest.* I sucked in ten gulps of air for every two or three steps I took. I looked down at my boots, the toe section of my supergaiters were jammed far back, allowing snow to pile in—melt—and turn to ice. I beat some of it out with my ice ax, but I thought that at least a pound remained hidden away in each gaiter. My toes felt wet and cold—when I could feel them at all. I probably should have fixed the problem—by going down, but I chose to ignore it. Forgoing prudent, intelligent behavior is often—although not usually spoken about—a big part of 'going for the summit.'

The whiteout plopped down, lifted, then set back in—conditions opened and closed like an eyelid in a dust storm. I lost my bearings; all I knew to do was to go straight up. "Where are we?" asked Gary. *"Where are we?"*

"Just below the summit, I think." I said. We had been traveling a good 45 minutes since dropping out packs, and while we weren't making great time, we were moving.

"WHHHEEEEEEOOOOWW!!!!" Andrea's unmistakable voice rang through the clouds and ricocheted off the rocks. A heartfelt Italian soliloquy followed.

"Okay, he made it. We're up next," I said to Gary, expecting an immediate response. "Gary? Gary?" I looked over my shoulder and was appalled to see him lying motionless in the snow, his head resting on a rock. I shook him and yelled, "Gary! Wake up!"

"What? Where am I? What's going on?" He spoke as if he'd just downed a gallon of vodka.

"Look you're ASLEEP—we're almost on the summit, but come on, we're in a whiteout, and…" I stared at his boots. Only one boot had a crampon attached; the other he held in his bare, unmittened hand. I grabbed him by his thin jacket and pulled him to his feet. "Come on. Let's move it!" Gary staggered along, tearing off the last of his plastic bags, revealing his thin leather boots, completely soaked with melted snow. "Oh God...."

"What's going on. Are we there yet?" Gary asked.

"Just follow me. Keep going up, and once we reach the crest of this ridge, make sure to turn left. I think there's a pretty steep cliff on the other side."

A few minutes and what seemed a year's worth of exertion later I stood on the crest of Guanaco Ridge. I could hear more people hollering from the summit by now. I lunged upward, gasping for air after each effort. I turned to see how Gary was doing and watched the whiteout curtain break apart for a few seconds, revealing the upper part of the awesome south face of the mountain. *Come on Gary, don't forget what I said about not going too far—turn left...turn left....* I pleaded in my head. He turned left, and crawled toward me like a hurt dog. I grabbed a few shots of the south face then watched the sky fall back on top of us. The summit was close...so close....

"Keep going, Gary...keep going!" I yelled down, feeling a burst of energy. Gary looked up at me like he'd just been run over by a truck and was living his last moments. His eyes were puffy and bloodshot, his lips cracked, his hair greasy and matted. But somehow he managed to smile and raise his thumb.

"Go. Go! I'll see you up there," he said, just loud enough for me to

Guanaco Ridge in storm; just below Aconcagua's summit

hear. So I quit waiting for my friend, turned, and went on.

I knew I'd reached the summit when I saw Guy silhouetted casually against the clouds. I stopped for one final rest, then hopped up the last of the rocks in a hypoxic burst. The whiteout still held strong, but visibility was a good 30 or 40 feet. The summit was much broader and far flatter than I'd imagined. I stumbled over to a small aluminum cross, lavishly adorned with expedition stickers and flags from around the world—the summit marker. Andrea gave me an Andrea-sized hug, then a big kiss on the cheek. None of us said much; Guy didn't speak at all. We simply gazed at the innards of a really high cloud and hobbled back and forth on the summit cobbles of a continent.

"Hey, Andrea, so just where was the Canaleta?" I asked.

"I think that last part before we came to the ridge that comes to here. Starts around where we leave our packs down there. I don't really know, though."

I'd heard much about the 'infamous Canaleta,' a long chute of loose rock that lies just below the summit ridge. I'd feared it; I'd heard that it was the stinger at the tail end of many climbers' attempts of the mountain—a loose talus slope where every three lunges up resulted in at least two slides down.

"I think it's lucky for us that there's snow in there now. We just climbed snow, not rocks. Much better for us. Much more lucky," Andrea concluded.

Ruining my lungs on the summit of the Americas

More than half a dozen teams from both the Polish Glacier and the Ruta Normal made the summit in the 30 minutes that followed my summiting. At one point there were at least 25 people standing on the top of the Americas. Cheers rang out when the clouds parted for about a minute, framing an incredible view of the mountains north of Aconcagua. I smiled when I saw Gary hobble the last feet to the aluminum summit cross. "I can't believe you made it. You're amazing. Truly amazing," I said. Paul followed shortly—and then, to my surprise, Chuck, from Team Mike.

"The rest of the team turned around a little after Independencia," Chuck began, "everybody thinks this is the last chance for summiting this season. A big storm really is coming—or I guess the first of it is here, that's all anybody is talking about down at Nido. There were so many people crowding that traverse that one person fell and had to be rescued. Our guide demanded that we return. Mike was bummed but he went down. I jumped on another guided team—I completely ignored Julio. It's a mess. I can't wait to get back down. No one else is coming up. Tons of people turned around behind us. I just hope we can make it back. I'm not staying here for more than five minutes," Chuck said. I looked at him and nodded.

"I'm getting outta here. Now!" I grabbed my camera pack and walked to the edge of the summit plateau—in time to see Spike's spiked hair spike above the lip of the plateau.

"What you doin', Ed?!"

"Hey! Goin' down. Straight down!"

"Not yet, no way. Come with me to the very top, there we smoke…smoke cigarettes!" I looked at him. I looked at the swirling clouds careening into the mountain. I thought about how nice it would be to be in my warm tent, my warm sleeping bag. I wanted down…but I wanted to hang out with Spike on the summit for a few moments just a little bit more than I wanted anything else at that moment.

"Come on…follow me!" I said, then turned into a gust and headed back to the mountain's zenith. Spike produced two bent—nearly broken—cigarettes.

"Now's the hard part, brutha." Spike dangled his cigarette from his mouth and worked his lighter with both hands. I put my hands around his to try to keep the growing wind from blowing the flame out. Five minutes of frustration passed. "Can't get it…LIT…there it goes!" Spike puffed until I swore his face turned green. I grabbed my cigarette between my chapped, split, blood-and-goo-crusted lips and lit it off his, puffing away like a hopped-up asthmatic. I saw glowing orange embers and took a long drag. I watched Spike smile and roll backwards. I felt a gargantuan headrush. "Let me take your picture, man!" I handed my Nikon to Spike as the wind ripped across the summit. I struck a few stupid poses; the cigarette went out—not enough oxygen to keep it lit.

"Let's go. Let's get outta here. This doesn't feel right. We shouldn't be up here," I said. "I don't think this was such a great idea, Spike…we shouldn't be here." I repeated. I stood up and looked at the people around me. Bright, fluorescent colors flashed around me in slow motion. I felt dizzy, nauseous, almost ready to faint. Smoking really is stupid; smoking at nearly 23,000 feet is beyond moronic.

A team of Americans summited from the Polish Glacier, icicles dangled from their leader's beard. Ropes slithered all around the summit cross like kaleidoscopic snakes. The sounds of coughing, hacking, and cheers rang out. *This is it, this is the mad summit dash. Anyone who really wanted to make it up here had only today to do it,* I thought, *and now it's time to go home.* The wind slammed me off balance. Everyone dropped to his knees and looked up as if bombers had just begun an attack. In the distance beautiful, thick white clouds sped toward us—powderkegs of violent weather, ready to explode once they hit the mountain. Kirsten was the last person to summit. She arrived with a wail, then dropped to her knees—crying.

No one else comes up, and maybe none of us go home. I grabbed my pack and rousted everyone in Spike's group, then Paul and Gary. "DOWN!" I yelled. Winds roared onto the summit and the whiteout clenched in on us ever tighter.

I focused on one goal: getting back to Berlin. I walked to the edge of the Canaleta. My homemade goggles were useless at this point. I took them off and squinted into the white abyss. Visibility dropped to just a few feet. Sometimes I couldn't even see my feet. *One step at a time....* I hopped from one boulder to the next, unaware of any compass direction. Gravity was my sole navigator.

Inside the Canaleta I was protected from the ferocious weather. But like impish messengers of impending doom, small eddies snuck in and slapped my face, reminding me that the Canaleta couldn't protect me for much longer.

The voices of Andrea, Guy, Spike, and others coasted eerily through the dense cloud. I had no way of knowing just where they were—I had no way of knowing exactly where I was. There was no real trail, and it started snowing.

I lost track of time during the first of my descent. I heard nothing but my heavy breathing and the crunch-crunch of my boots in the deepening snow. Visibility seemed to be increasing—a bit, but how could I tell where the white curtain of cloud ended and the white blanket of snow began? White on white!

Suddenly a dark spot appeared, perhaps an outcrop. It wavered in intensity— then disappeared. Snow balled up on my crampons, I brushed it off with my ice ax, but after every three steps I had the equivalent of Frosty's head on each of my feet, so I took the crampons off. The thickness of the cloud was vacillating, and with it, visibility. I ran toward the rocky outcrop—it appeared again— and this time I saw bright colors—our backpacks. I grabbed mine, stashed my camera and crampons, cinched the Dana tightly against my back, took a deep breath, then struck out toward the traverse.

I found the main 'trail' after only a few steps, but it would soon be hidden by new snow. I worried about not having my crampons attached to my boots—I was approaching the icy section...I put it out of my head. *Deal with it when you get there.*

"Help Me! Help Me!" I heard through the wind and mist when I was about 20 yards into the traverse.

"Come on! You can make it!" a more distant voice wailed.

"No! I'm scared. I can't. I can't see anything…I'm going to fall!" The tone of deathly fear rang in the guy's voice.

"Come on! Don't be such a wus! Oh…okay, I'll just come out and hold your hand! One more time that I gotta—HOLD—YOUR—HAND!" I picked up my pace. I feared the trail was being quickly covered by snow. But at least the extreme winds I'd worried about weren't blowing. Less than a minute later I came upon two Americans—one firmly entrenched in the snow, gripping the head of his ice ax, the other standing with his arms crossed, shaking his head.

"Are you guys all right?" I asked.

"Hi there. Yeah, we're fine. My partner here is a little scared," the standing guy said.

"Come on," I said with a good amount of fear in my own voice. "This isn't pretty right now. Not only are there at least 30 climbers heading our way, but a big storm is barreling at us too, I guess it's already here."

"I know. I've been trying to get him going. We've been on this traverse for the last two hours; Matt here is paralyzed with fear. Saw a guy fall on this traverse coming up and he lost it, wanted to turn around. The rest of the team is already back at Nido by now. But we're still up here—coulda' made the summit! Twice!"

"Look, who cares. Can't see anything up there anyway," I said quickly, hoping to inject some expediency into the moment. "I'll lead, Matt here'll go in the middle, and you follow close behind. Okay?" Matt nodded. I jumped ahead and took off—my foot hit a patch of ice and I slipped. I looked down—at a void of white.

"Oh my GOD!" screamed Matt. "He's going to fall and DIE!" I flipped over and dove onto the head of my ice ax, arresting myself after three feet of sliding.

"Come on!" I said, shaking. "Get a grip—let's get out of here." I looked ahead—the cloud allowed me to see about ten yards in front of me—and I did my best impersonation of an olympic powerwalker. "Stay right behind me!" The fall jolted my awareness. I felt more focused than ever. It was the shot I needed. I wouldn't quit until I was back at Berlin. I sped all the way to the Cuesta del Viento, waving at my two new friends to keep close behind. When I looked back, though, they had disappeared in the cloud. I dropped to my knees and listened, but heard nothing except my own breathing and the wind rustling my pack.

"OOOOOOOO!" came Matt's voice. "Look, we're making it." The two of them popped into view. They were well past the difficult section. I stood up and aimed for the Independencia Hut. Some white knuckle moments ensued when I crossed heavily iced sections; I even cussed at myself out loud for not wearing my crampons, but I made it to the dilapidated shack.

I bent over and stared in silence—searching for where I should go next. *I'm lost. I don't know where to go!* I thought. *I don't remember how I got up here! I can't believe I can't remember!* I thought about waiting for Matt and his faithful friend, but they were so far behind me I couldn't see or hear them. I squeezed my eyes shut and struggled for recall. Then it came—drop off to the left. I headed down.

I headed down, all right, straight into the densest part of the whiteout. I found scattered markings of where people had been, but not much. 15 minutes later I stood on the edge of a flat, snow-covered plain. The wind had picked up and the whiteout had lifted a bit—enough for me to see the silhouette of a lone woman climber at the other side of the snowfield. She was standing at the base of some high rocks, and waving at me to follow her. I looked up, hoping to see Matt and his friend—then thought about everyone else behind them. *Would they know how to get down?* I couldn't worry about it. I struck out across the snowfield toward my 'guide.' She disappeared into the rocks when I got within shouting distance. "Hello!...¡Hola!" I yelled. No response. I jogged to the rocks and rested against one of them. The woman was below me, waving me on, so I continued. I followed her for 15 minutes—just long enough for me to descend below the main bulk of the whiteout and find the route myself. "Thank you! *¡Gracias!*" I shouted. I waited to hear something back—nothing; she'd disappeared.

I have no idea how much longer it took me to return to Berlin. I arrived a few hours before sunset. The total roundtrip summit time was something like 12 hours. I jogged up to my tent and dove in—to see if my camera was still there. It was. I turned and faced the huts outside my tent. *I made it. I climbed Aconcagua. Now I'm back*, I thought as I became dizzy with hunger. I grabbed my stove and headed into the larger of the two refugios. "Did you make it?" asked one of the ex-military policemen who'd come to check on me.

"Yeah. I did. Barely. Still a lot of people up there. How 'bout you?" I asked, although I already knew they didn't summit.

"Nope, we got caught in a huge traffic jam just below the Canaleta. One guy fell and we had to rescue him. There was no leadership at all. None of those people should have been up there. It was purely insane. Once we got the guy back to the Independencia Hut the weather was too awful to keep going. So we'll have to save the summit for another day, I guess. It'll still be there."

"It sure will. Now let's just wait and see if everyone behind me makes it back down." I said. The conditions at Berlin were calm—visibility was good enough to see the booming clouds surrounding the mountain. It wasn't so much that we were in the eye of any particular storm, but in the center of a whole bunch of storms that couldn't decide whether to 'attack' the mountain or not. Certainly a storm raged above us on the summit itself—we couldn't even see the summit. I had no idea how violently it was hitting, or if it would descend onto

Berlin, or all the way to base camp, or if it would just disappear. The only thing I did know for sure was that I was starving—both for food and for photographs of the beautiful weather surrounding me. I cooked, ate, and shot until all the food, water, and light were gone—during which time Spike and Company returned and Chuck and his new guide passed by on their way down to Nido. Andrea told me that Paul and Gary managed to limp back to White Rocks, but he wasn't sure about the other teams that had been up there with us.

Climbers trickled into and past Berlin through the night. The storm never did grow worse, but it didn't die off, either. The next morning dawned portentously calm. It was quiet enough to easily light a cigarette without any shelter at all—which Spike did, at least three times before starting down to Nido. It was the great high camp exodus—a lot of people descending, but nobody ascending. That strange storm hovered over the summit throughout the morning. None of us knew what to make of it other than we wanted to be as far from it as possible, as soon as possible.

I reached Nido just as Team Mike was packing up to leave. "I hate Julio. I HATE HIM," Mike said to me. Mike went on to describe all that Julio had done wrong. "And now he's getting on Chuck for making it to the summit! Saying that he was being dangerous!"

Before leaving Nido, I made a quick survey of just who *wasn't* leaving. At first it seemed as if nobody was staying or ascending—just descending. However, a closer look revealed that one team was settled in, and preparing to make a go of it: Commander Taco and the Anti-Freds. Not only were they dug in, but they were setting off to make a carry to Berlin as I was leaving Nido. I looked at them, then I looked up into the sky. Where Aconcagua's summit should have been there was nothing but swirling—and descending—clouds. What would the weather do? I had no idea. It seemed that the peak got hit with a storm every afternoon on its upper slopes, then that storm would die off to nothing by the late evening. What was different about this day was that we woke up to a storm, and it was gaining momentum throughout the morning. But Commander Taco had already proved that he was a very willful guy. I aimed for base camp, wishing the best for the Anti-Freds.

CHAPTER TWENTY-SEVEN

MORE OXYGEN, MORE WINE

Viento Blanco (White Wind) howls over the summit of Aconcagua

Descending a high mountain is a paradoxical experience. A climber's body is exhausted—often starved, sleep deprived, over-exerted, dehydrated, sunburnt, wind-chafed, and sometimes frost damaged, with emotional and mental fatigue in tow. But with mountain descent comes oxygen-level ascent. Each step down brings more energy to the muscles, greater lucidity to the mind, and often heightened spirits.

Though I was definitely exhausted when I arrived at Plaza de Mulas, it was a strange type of fatigue. Individual muscles were sore and limp, but my body—as a whole—felt great, as if energized by some invisible power source that I had no way of throttling up or down. It just pushed me along; I almost felt like I was being carried by it. *Thicker air, more O$_2$ in each breath*, I thought—yes, *I thought*...I was really *thinking* again...formulating complex, abstract, and sometimes intricate ideas. I could ponder concepts greater than 'eat,' 'sleep,' 'urinate,' 'go higher,' and other australopithecine basics. I tested myself by reciting the quadratic equation. I passed. Of course, I had no way of knowing if what I rattled off really was the quadratic equation, but I think I had it right.

I found Harry and his team. After a brief hello I set up my tent and grabbed the gear I had stashed at Rudy's place. My trekking boots were what I craved most. I wrestled off my Koflachs, aired out my smelly, pruny feet, then slid them into the comfortable leather boots. Walking never felt so good—I felt like I could float.

I walked to the north end of camp to fill my water bottles. Spike and Company had just arrived. I congratulated them on their summit success. But their demeanors were anything but jubilant. "Someone stole my tent!" Andrea exploded. I stood dumbfounded. "When I returned to Nido my tent was gone. Someone took it apart and took it away. It was a 400 dollar tent! I am going to go back up to see if someone up there has it...I have to try and find it." Andrea seemed poised on the edge of crying as he tore off toward Nido. I tried to stop him; I wanted to talk some sense into him—to tell him that his efforts would probably bear nothing but more exhaustion and frustration, but Guy intervened.

"Just let him go. He has to see for himself. Meanwhile, let's look around here. But I think it's gone for good. Look at these guys standing around, just staring at us and our gear. Who knows how much stuff has gone out on those mules." Guy, Spike, and I stared at the scattered groups of people—they weren't climbers, nor were they mule drivers, just guys from...Mendoza? None of them smiled, none of them spoke to us. They hovered like vultures, waiting, we thought, to get their hands on our treasured gear. Then Paul and Gary descended—and brought with them more bad news.

"There's a guy up there at Nido wandering around looking for his backpack. Somebody stole his backpack with everything in it!" Paul exclaimed.

"How did he lose his *entire* pack?" asked Guy.

"Who knows? Who can guess? I just want to get back to Mendoza," said Paul as he whumped his pack onto the ground.

"How do you feel, Gary?" I asked.

"Oh…buggered. Buggered." Gary's face was burnt bright red; he looked ten years older than when I'd first met him just two weeks earlier.

"Your toes okay?"

"Yeah, a little numb still, but fine. I need a warm bath."

"Hey Ed…" Spike said with a big grin. "How 'bout a cigarette—a victory cigarette?"

"Yeah, let's light up," I answered.

Back at my camp I made plans with Team Harry to rent space on a mule to carry my supplies and trash back to PDI. 70 bucks would cover it. I handed the cash over to Harry; the two of us then surveyed the upper third of the mountain. "Look at that storm up there," I said. "We made it, though. We got in and then got out at just the right moment. Nobody could be up there right now." Wild clouds spun, emerged, dissolved, contorted—everything imaginable in a mountain tempest. It was beautiful from down low; but couldn't have been anything but monstrously ugly up inside of it. "The winds must be well over a hundred miles an hour near the summit," Harry stated with fear in his voice.

"¡Viento Blanco! ¡Viento Blanco!" repeated an Argentine guide in a nearby camp. I looked to the summit—the Viento Blanco hovered over the mountain's crest. I grabbed my camera and focused on its translucent, ethereal form. What I was seeing, of course, wasn't the wind itself, but the effect of the wind. Once air moves fast

Sliver moon, Venus, and Sirius from Berlin Camp

enough over a mountain, the pressure of the lifted air drops—for the same reason airplane wings make an airplane lift into the air. If the pressure drops enough, then moisture in the air condenses, forming a cloud. I'd seen many lenticular clouds in the mountains of Alaska and the Yukon, and had observed wave clouds a few times leeward of the crest of the Sierra Nevada—formed by mechanisms similar to those that create the Viento Blanco. But the White Wind appeared different from either of the other types. The Viento Blanco didn't have a clearly defined shape, as if the wind that created the cloud blew so hard that nothing distinct could actually materialize. It was more a ghost of a cloud than an actual cloud. Adding further drama to the scene were piles of cumulus—seemingly spawned and then dropped by the White Wind—plowing onto Aconcagua's summit.

The fleeting scene lasted less than a roll of film—being spun through as fast as I could wind the camera's film advance lever. But just because the Viento Blanco itself disappeared didn't mean that the winds aloft were any more hospitable to humans. I counted my blessings that I was back in the relative lowlands of the region. I thought of the monk on the bus—and I thanked him.

"You want sell your crampons? Ice ax? Ski poles?" asked a shady looking guy who had a full entourage of other shady looking characters shadowing him. I looked at my gear—my worn-out boots with torn supergaiters, my crampons…and my trekking poles. They were nothing to me now but dead weight. I made a quick decision—sell all of it except for the ice ax. I was sentimentally attached to my ax.

"I'll sell crampons, poles, and boots, all together." I said.

"How much?" the guy asked.

"200 dollars," I answered.

"No way. 150. No more than 150," the opportunist—who was bound to sell or rent the items for a healthy profit—replied immediately. I added up what I had paid for everything—$150 was a good deal for me.

"Okay. Give me the money," I said as I handed over the gear. The man produced American dollars, scowling at me in the process.

I packed away my trash in the burlap garbage sack I'd been issued by the rangers at the beginning of the trip, then took the food that Fred and Dave left me over to Spike and Company. "Anybody want this stuff?" is a question familiar to anyone who has been on a climbing expedition. In my arms I cradled over 20 bags of British military assault ration packs, spinning around on the balls of my feet to give all those around me a peek at the free stuff. At first I had no takers. Eventually, however, all of it was snatched up.

Andrea returned to Plaza de Mulas just before sunset. He looked defeated. "No tent?" I asked.

"No. No tent. Gone. But wow, what a mess up there right now…"

"What do you mean?" I asked.

"That big guided team, with the really fat people…the guide tried to get them to go to the summit I think, because they are all over the mountain. Two are at Nido, and I saw some up on the Gran Acarreo, but I think others are on the ridge below Berlin Camp."

"What!?" Guy and I interjected in unison.

"Yes. The guide is crazy. One of the people I talked to said that someone might have frostbite, another may have a broken ankle, and the guide has really lost it. He can't keep control of the situation. It is crazy. I wanted to help, but I have no way to do so. I am too tired, and don't have the right clothing or gear—or food—or TENT! Maybe if they need help tomorrow then I will go up. But I don't think so. And this is even more crazy…"

"What?" I asked.

"That guide isn't really supposed to be guiding that team. I don't even know if he is a real guide at all. These two guys I talked to said that their original guide killed himself with a gun two weeks before they were supposed to come here, and this guy just stepped in to take his place. Oh…this place is so strange! So many strange people!"

"Tomorrow we leave early. I'm going to be the first one out of here…" Harry said to me later that evening as we drank wine and smoked cigarettes. "Get up early and walk out with me. We can be back at PDI in five hours if we really move." Harry really wanted to get home. He talked of his family, of his children, even of his job. "When I come back to South America, I think I would like to bring my family…maybe we can see different sides of Aconcagua and other peaks of the Andes together."

Harry and I were the first two in camp to be packed and ready the next morning. I handed my mule bag—stuffed with everything but my camera, a day's worth of food, and some leftover wine—over to Pablo to load onto the mule, then set off. When I passed Rudy's tent my mind flashed to the little store down the street from Hotel Blanco—and I remembered the letter. I stopped dead in my tracks, dug out my wallet, and found the tattered envelope. The name on the letter read 'Ana.' I walked up to the muleteer's tent and found the woman who'd greeted me more than a week earlier. I held the letter out and asked "Ana?" hoping that she might know who Ana was. She did know Ana's whereabouts—she knew quite well; *she* was Ana. She tore open the envelope and smiled as she read the note.

"Thank you. Thank you so much," she said, briefly losing her hard edge. That moment was a good end to my stay at Plaza de Mulas.

I chased after Harry, but his speed and my postal duty put a big gap between us—one that wouldn't be closed until we reached PDI and stopped moving. Instead of racing down the Horcones Valley, I took my time and enjoyed the photographic opportunities. I hiked up to Piedre Grande at noon, watching

Alluvial forms, Horcones Valley

yet another storm head my way. The fleet clouds caused shadows and light beams to dance across the parched walls of the valley. I hid in the wind shadow of Piedre Grande and set up my tripod—and opened up my leftover wine.

The first 'blow-over' rainfall stroked me just as I approached the Confluencia region. Soon I was running from an approaching wall of pouring rain—stopping, of course to take pictures of it—and to drink more wine. I took the shortcut around Confluencia camp, then found myself under a thick blanket of rain clouds. I spent hours passing through the area surrounding Confluencia. I spun through film at a dizzying pace. I didn't want the day to end. I made a ton of images of what I called the 'Swiss Cheese Wall,' then forced myself to move on—it was late afternoon and I still had a lot of walking to do.

The sun reemerged as I traversed the eastern edge of the deep ravine a few miles north of Lago Horcones. Long trains of mules kicked up dust on their journey back to Puente del Inca. No rain had fallen here. I crossed over the wooden bridge and looked back toward the south face. Snow covered the entire wall—the sky surrounding Aconcagua shone stunningly clear. Long streamers of wind-blown snow plumed off both north and south summits. I gulped down the last of my wine, stared in absolute awe for a few moments, then burned through ten rolls of film.

There has been a long-ranging debate about the origins of the word 'Aconcagua.' Some believe that it was derived from the Quechua words 'Ackon' and 'Cahuac,' meaning 'Stone Sentinel,' 'Stone Sentry,' or 'Stone Watchtower.' Others disagree, claiming that the name derives from the Aymaran words 'Acon' and 'Cagua,' meaning 'Snowy Mountain,' or 'White Mountain.' A few attest

South face of Aconcagua

that it is mix of the two—translating to 'White Sentinel.' Looking at Aconcagua—in such tranquil, clear, beautifully comfortable conditions—looking at the fresh coat of pure white snow reflecting that day's austral sunset, I couldn't believe that whoever named Aconcagua could have meant anything but 'White Sentinel.' From my viewpoint, the peak, so obviously high and massive, sat perfectly framed by the Lower Horcones Valley. I didn't want to leave the scene. So I didn't leave it; I waited for it to leave me. The sun set, darkness came, and I felt satisfied that I'd experienced everything I possibly could have experienced of the crown of the Americas.

I hiked back to the ranger hut in total darkness. The rangers laughed at me—the time was ten o'clock at night, I was completely out of food and water—and I was utterly drunk. I signed my name to the register and asked about a shuttle to Puente del Inca. The last one for the day had departed hours earlier. After 15 more minutes of rest and conversation, I dragged myself into the cool night and set off on the final leg of my Aconcagua journey. "¡Buena suerte!" the rangers hollered as I ducked out of their tent.

By this point my knees felt like rubber. My legs were wasted from both ascending and descending. The best slope would have been no slope at all, not up, not down, just straight and level. Each step, no matter how small, caused my legs to bow and wobble. Giving in, lying down, and sleeping on the dirt would have felt so good at that point. But pavement was so close, I could hear passing cars. *Once on the highway everything would be okay…right?*

The road was almost deserted by the time I trudged onto it from the trail. Almost deserted—but for the drivers of speeding cars that acted as if they were playing skeet, and I was the sporting clay and their cars were the shot. I stuck my thumb out a few times, but then…*I wouldn't give me a ride if I was a driver either*, I thought as they whizzed by, high beams flashing and horns blaring.

"The last mile is the longest mile," I chanted to myself for each center-divider dash I put behind me. I staggered down the middle of the road, popping my overworked hips and knee joints and swinging my arms about my shoulders. I constantly readjusted the pack on my aching shoulders—and wished that I'd never sold my trekking poles. I finally resigned myself to simply close my eyes and march forward, peeling open my eyelids every ten or so steps to make sure I wasn't about to plunge into the Río Las Cuevas, which parallels the road. The dim lights of PDI never seemed to grow closer.

I finally arrived at PDI a couple hours after leaving the Horcones ranger station. I estimated that I had been trekking for over 16 hours—16 hours for a trip that should have taken less than half that long. I ran into the first restaurant I found, ordered three steak sandwiches and four sodas—and devoured them in about five minutes. Then I scooted off to find Harry and my gear. Just about everything in the small town was locked up tight. The only sounds came from the occasional passing car. I found nothing and worried that I would have to spend the night on the dirt, without even a sleeping pad. I rested against the door of a small restaurant and pondered my next move.

"Ed!" I heard a muffled voice. I looked through a window in the restaurant door. Spike and Company, Team Harry, and Paul and Gary were packed inside. *I can't believe this*, I thought, *too good to be true*. I swung open the door and was greeted—loudly, very, very loudly—by my entire extended Aconcagua family. Soon I was packing steak, salad, wine, and Pisco into my tired body. "You look...so awful, I can't believe it! You look like...*you are dead!* And why are your lips purple?" asked Kirsten.

"Look, I drank all of that wine and took pictures like mad, all day long. I'm really tired right now...really tired."

"Here, look Ed, more Pisco!" Andrea produced a fresh bottle of what I thought of as 'South American Vodka.' Eight hours later I woke up in a bunkhouse with Team Harry and my gear—clueless as to how I got there. When I'd first arrived in Mendoza, I didn't expect to have the climb end with any emotion other than elation or disappointment—regarding photographs and reaching the summit. But...as usual, I can't predict anything accurately. I was surprised to find a fear of loneliness setting in. I wanted the strange high-altitude party to continue with no end in sight. We shared a few more laughs, memories, and cigarettes. Then we split apart. Paul, Gary, and Spike and Company zoomed back to Mendoza on an early bus while I hung out with the Finns, who were awaiting their ride to Santiago. Harry gave me an itinerary for traveling in Patagonia, and Kari invited me to come visit him in Lima before I flew home. We tried to make sense out of the stories of the season's 'body count' and overall summit success rate. We concluded that those in charge of such statistics in Mendoza most likely want to keep it confusing, so we dropped the subject.

I waved goodbye to Team Harry as they sped off in their hired van, then I awaited my ride, the afternoon Uspallata Express bus to Mendoza. I zoomed into town at dusk, feeling a boost of energy from the descent. After nearly two weeks of storms, worry, doubt, a lot of hiking, a little climbing, and a colony of unknown creatures in my gut, I was back in Hotel Blanco, enjoying the evening—and my timing was perfect: the main festivities of the Mendoza Wine Festival had just begun.

BOOK IV
CERRO PISSIS

Cerro Pissis at sunrise

CHAPTER TWENTY-EIGHT

ULTIMA THULE
OF THE ANDES

Brian Kelly on the Pissis Glacier

Distant, uncharted lands have fascinated explorers and scientists throughout history. While many feared unexplored landscapes, these wildernesses have always captured the imaginations of those wishing to experience not just natural beauty, but stark solitude. One of the first intrepid adventurers was the Greek explorer Pytheas, who in 330 BC made the first recorded crossing of the Arctic Circle (latitude 66° 33' north). During his journey, Pytheas learned of a legendary archipelago called Thule (pronounced 'too-lee'), said to be much to the north of his farthest reach. After Pytheas' journey, word of this mysterious land spread. Soon, Thule became more than just a distant, unknown place; 'Thule' came to embody the ultimate in human exploratory imagination, the *ne plus ultra* of adventure. Poetically, 'Ultima Thule' directly referred to the 'land farthest north,' and metaphorically, to those places so distant, so remote, so hidden, and so redoubtable that humans might never be able to tread these lands.

After attempting Sajama, summiting Aconcagua, and nearly summiting Ojos del Salado, I wanted to push far into the heart of the most desolate section of the high Andes and experience this range in its most unfettered state. Cerro Pissis, standing so high and visited by so few, would provide the challenge—it would be my own Ultima Thule.

The only information I could find on Cerro Pissis came from Bob Villarreal. Bob provided my partner, Brian Kelly, and me with a basic route description and, most importantly, the contact information of Patricio Rios, the sole person who can navigate the maze of high altitude land surrounding Pissis.

We spent three weeks on the Cerro Pissis expedition. Brian and I made the attempt completely unsupported; we had no map of the area; we had no guidebook; we didn't carry a GPS; we didn't have a compass; we didn't even bring a watch. The adventure proved to be an experience neither of us could have imagined. Seeing footprints—my own footprints—on earth that probably has never had human footprints stamped onto it before left an indelible feeling of solitude...absolute amazement. How best to convey this experience? I simply copied down the descriptions I made day-by-day while on Pissis itself. Dorothy Ross—who directed me to look into the 'Ultima Thule' metaphor—and I only lightly edited those original entries.

Moonrise, Bonete, and cumulonimbus from Cerro Pissis base camp

Tres Cruces from Laguna Santa Rosa

Southern summits of Cerro Pissis

Storm over the high desert

Main summit of Cerro Pissis

Looking north from 22,578 feet

Brian Kelly and a big weathered rock

Cerro Pissis massif at sunrise

Sunday, March 5: *Departure*

During the past few weeks Brian and I drafted our trip's basic logistics. We received virtually all of our information from Bob Villarreal, probably the world's leading expert on Cerro Pissis, and a great guy to boot. We considered a number of factors while developing our plans. Foremost: Cerro Pissis is incredibly difficult to access. The mountain is isolated by high, windswept puna; roads of any type are nowhere to be found near Cerro Pissis. The approach requires four-wheeling long distances through difficult, roadless terrain. Although Cerro Pissis lies entirely within Argentina, the most straightforward, logical approach originates in Chile—but entering Argentina from Chile in the border netherlands is illegal. However, we reason (with the help of Bob Villarreal, who has been there many times) that if there are no police around to see us breaking any laws, laws don't matter. And why would any police be hanging around in a high, roadless desert?

We looked into approaching Cerro Pissis legally from Argentina anyway, to satisfy some 'due diligence' need, if nothing else. Here's what we concluded: flying to Argentina is more expensive than flying to Chile, and much more expensive than flying to Peru and taking a bus down to Chile. Nevertheless I checked on the Internet, and discovered an Argentine driver who advertised that he could take people into Cerro Pissis by way of Córdoba. I e-mailed him, but he never responded. So the Argentine option was out. We decided to go with Bob's friend, Patricio Rios. I e-mailed Patricio to introduce myself as a friend of Bob's and let him know that Brian and I would arrive in Copiapó around the eighth of March. I also contacted Kari Poti (from 'Team Harry'); he will meet us at the airport when we arrive in Lima.

Brian and I leave Davis at 4:30 in the morning for SFO; Brian's girlfriend, Maria, drives. My gear: my black mule bag stuffed with Dana pack, North Face tent, North Face sleeping bag, La Sportiva K2 leather boots, clothing, MSR XGK stove and cookset, ice ax, crampons, and basic repair and medicine kit. I also carry my large tripod, my Pentax 67 system with 80 rolls of 120 Velvia, and a Nikon FM 35mm camera with a 50mm lens and 20 rolls of Velvia. Brian carries a similar load, but with much less camera gear. We take off at nine on a Continental Airlines flight bound for Houston, where we connect to a flight to Lima. We arrive at Lima at midnight. Kari meets us; we go to his place in Miraflores. We are greeted by his new wife, Susan, who seems happy to meet us—even though it's one o'clock in the morning. Brian and I walk around town and buy some Lomotil and Flagyl—just in case.

Monday, March 6: *Lima, Again*

Brian and I spend the day planning our overland logistics. Our original plan was to leave on March 6, but Kari finds us a good deal on a better bus that leaves on March 7.

I'd been with Kari during my last visit to this city. We were stuck in bumper-to-bumper traffic when a fight broke out between two drivers ahead of us. Before long driver A began beating driver B with an antenna, then driver B pulled a gun. We were stuck in the fracas by gridlocked traffic. A few days later, while waiting in the airport for my flight back home, I met an American who'd had all of his money stolen at gunpoint, very close to where Kari lives—and Kari lives in the 'Beverly Hills of Lima!'

Tuesday, March 7: *'Suck Bus, Part I'*

We leave Lima on a 'Cruz del Sur' coach bound for Tacna. We were happy when the trip started because it's a very modern bus, quiet, and smooth. We've been trying to sleep, but we're having very little luck. The bus is crammed full of people, it's hot and stuffy, and the people surrounding us cough and hack. By now (16 hours into the ride), Brian and I refer to it as the 'Suck Bus.'

Wednesday, March 8: *The Scent of Desert Rain*

We approach Tacna in the early morning. The bus chugs through a rain-storm in the desert. If electricity has an odor, it must be very similar to what I smell as we swoosh through curtains of rain. I've spent a bit of time in deserts, and I've come to love the smell of rain in dry lands. I've noticed something, though: the drier the desert, the stronger the scent of rain when it falls. The scent here is terrific. It is so powerful. I can see and hear the rain and imagine that I can almost taste and touch it.

We find a taxi in the Tacna bus station. After some haggling and the usual bureaucratic rituals, we're zooming south toward Chile in a 'collectivo' (taxi). At the border we endure a drug search (dogs—new since the last time I was here) and then move on to Chilean customs. We arrive in Arica early in the afternoon. We change money and get tickets for a Semi-Cama bus to Copiapó. Brian and I eat some empanadas; they are delicious—the one I devour doesn't seem to melt in my mouth so much as it makes my mouth melt around it's incredibly satisfying taste—but we fear that they will eventually give both of us stomach problems. We depart on 'Suck Bus, Part II'—the air in the bus is moist, stuffy, and reeks like a donkey's ass; we can't sleep. The entertainment for the night is a collection of proselytizing religious movies (in English with Spanish subtitles) meant to instill fear into all heathens.

Thursday, March 9: *Back in Copiapó*

We arrive at Copiapó around eight in the morning. I find our hotel, 'Resedencia Rodriguez,' where I stayed after my Ojos expedition. We check into a double for 6,000 pesos a night. We do a bit of shopping at 'Ekono,' buying mostly soups, pasta sauce, and fruit. I'm happy to be back in Copiapó. Although I've spent just a few days in this town, I feel at home here.

Friday, March 10: *Alex Reunion With Some Logistics Thrown In*

I set out with Brian to find Alex's compound. We navigate by simply wandering the city. Small sights jog my memory, helping me remember where to turn. We come to a busy street and notice a Mercedes-Benz dealership. Now I know exactly where I am. The dealership is just a little south of the house. We walk briskly up the road. I see Alex from a quarter mile away. He is standing on the side of the street, talking with some friends. I run up to him with a huge grin on my face; I say hello in both Spanish and English. He scowls at me, and returns to his discussion. I'm stunned. I stare at the ground for a few seconds and then look at Alex, perplexed. He tells me he's mad because I didn't write. He ignores Brian and me and continues his conversation.

Finally, his friends leave and Alex invites us into his compound. He quickly returns to the friendly, helpful Alex I remember from a year earlier. He shows us some pictures from a recent trip he and Gloria took to a little-known waterfall north of Ojos del Salado. I tell him about our plans and mention Patricio. Alex is friends with Patricio; he seems to know everyone in Copiapó.

Alex calls Pat; I speak with this high altitude four-by-four legend of the Atacama for the first time. He sounds much younger than I'd imagined. I discover that he's just a year older than I am—I thought that he'd be twice my age! He comes over and we discuss our expedition logistics. He speaks excellent English. Turns out he lived in Los Angeles for a year while studying to be an electronics technician.

Here are our logistical factors: Pissis base camp lies at 16,000 feet; Patricio charges 400 dollars per day; we can only afford to use him for three days; one of those days will be the pull-out day; one day will be for taking us to an acclimatization camp, probably Laguna Santa Rosa; and one day will be for taking us from our acclimatization camp to base camp. Ideally, we would approach base camp in three to four legs, the most prudent regimen for healthy acclimatization. Due to our limited budget, however, we have only two stages to work with. We decide to spend five full days at Laguna Santa Rosa, the elevation of which (supposedly) is around 13,800 feet above sea level. Pat will deposit us at Laguna Santa Rosa on the eleventh, then return to Copiapó. He will drive back up to Laguna Santa Rosa on the sixteenth, pick us up, and take us into Pissis base camp. Pat describes the route from Laguna Santa Rosa: we will continue east on the Paso de San Francisco road, then head south on the Mina Marte road. After a few miles we will turn east, and drive off-road up Valle Ancho. The plan is for Pat to pull us out two weeks later, on March 30.

A problem: because we are attempting to climb Pissis late in the season, ours will practically be a winter ascent. While the mountain is surrounded by the driest of the dry, this part of the Andes can get snow from early fall through winter, sometimes enough that roads remain closed for days—and areas without roads, like the many miles we must travel to get to base camp, are totally impassable until the spring thaw, even for Patricio. So…Pat can get us in, but he may not be able to get us out—we may have to *walk* out. A long, long, *long* way to walk—nearly 50 overland miles to the nearest road, at altitudes over 15,000 feet—and we'll be carrying a ton of gear. We're taking a shortwave radio with us, but it's only capable of receiving. If one of us breaks a leg, or gets sick, we can't call out. Once Patricio drops us off, we're on our own for the next two weeks. He tells us that if more than six inches of snow falls, we should plan to walk out. He will search for us along the Mina Marte road, if he can get in that far.

Another problem: the illegality of entering Argentina without procuring the necessary papers. (Receiving permission from Argentina would require ridiculous amounts of effort, including traveling into Argentina. This process could take weeks, and according to Pat, we probably would not receive permission after all our trouble). Pat acknowledges that entering without a permit is a risk, but he has done it before—and has been chased only once. Bob Villarreal never seemed to think much of the risk, but I'm really concerned about it. Pat says most of the risk is for him, not for Brian and me. He says that every now and then the Argentine Gendarmes (national police) patrol the area on quad runners. If we get stopped, they might confiscate Pat's truck (which he will rent) and our gear. We might get our gear back, but they would keep the truck. We also might end up in jail. However, Pat notes that the Argentines enjoy the company of mountaineers, especially those interested in Argentine peaks. So if we get caught, Brian and I will probably be set free with our gear; but Patricio's fate is another story. The risk of capture is one of the reasons he charges 400 dollars per day.

Other considerations for us: we have no map of the area; we have no map of the mountain itself; we have no guidebook; we have only Bob Villarreal's description—which is excellent, but I wish we had a map, even a crude one; also, we will be taking just one vehicle. We decide, after going over all the possible pitfalls, to get enough food and fuel to last us more than a month.

We buy more supplies later that evening—tons of bacon, ham, steaks (12 pounds), and bread. Steaks! Yes! We also buy two bags of tomatoes, a bag of garlic, a sack of onions, a bag of avocados, three bags of bell peppers, four pounds of hot dogs, four pounds of sausage, ten packs of salami, five packs of prosciutto, two huge bags of oranges, and two bags of potatoes, and droves of loaves of bread. We stock up on even more pasta and rice. We spend a total of 240 dollars on food. When it's all paid for we pack everything tightly into boxes. Brian and I want the very best food for the Pissis attempt, especially for the acclimatization stage.

That evening I start feeling the early stages of a cold. My throat is scratchy and my body aches. Brian has similar symptoms and his stomach is giving him problems. We drink some wine and beer, and then fall asleep.

Saturday, March 11, 2000: *Puna de Atacama Steak House*

Pat picks us up at eleven in the morning in a rented, slightly-used Toyota Hilux. We purchase 130 liters of water (in five-liter jugs) and more bread. The bed of the Hilux overflows with our gear and food; Pat straps everything firmly in place for the bumpy ride. We buy fuel for the Hilux and for our stoves. We fill our Sigg fuel containers (about six liters total) and a large 20-liter plastic tank with gasoline. This should be enough fuel to run our super-efficient MSR XGKs every day (melting snow and cooking) for two months.

We zoom out of Copiapó into the bare desert. I remember the scenes from a year earlier. I feel some familiarity with the landscape. Pat drives fast, but stops whenever Brian and I want to shoot a photograph.

When I met Pat I liked him immediately; and now I trust him completely. He seems confident and obviously knows the region well. He is really the only one who can navigate the off-road section of the route to Pissis. The man who trained Pat was the only other person who could get to Pissis via Chile, but he died a few years ago in a snowstorm near Laguna Negro Francisco.

We arrive at a small wooden shack on the western shore of Laguna Santa Rosa at about three in the afternoon. We unload our gear and pay Patricio for stage one of his work. He charges us only $350 for the first day (he prefers US dollars); we're happily surprised. We'll pay him once more when he delivers us to base camp; he'll get his final installment when we're safely back in Copiapó.

Each of us has a pounding AMS headache within an hour. Before leaving Davis I purchased two large bottles of Excedrin Migraine tablets—basically acetaminophen and aspirin doped with caf-
feine. I bought them
because I thought they
would help with alti-
tude headaches. I take
four and my headache
is gone within 15 min-
utes, my nausea disap-
pears, and I have a

Laguna Santa Rosa luxury chalet

strong appetite—but I'm jittery from the caffeine. Brian takes one and he has similar results. We proclaim that Excedrin Migraine is the high altitude won-der-drug, but the caffeine is strong—each pill wires me up as much as three or four cups of coffee would.

After a half hour of sunset photography, Brian and I get to work cooking. The hut is the perfect size for us. It has two rooms: one for our sleeping bags, and a rudimentary kitchen. Past occupants have left various supplies, including pots and pans, some fuel, sugar, tea, dehydrated potatoes, and a large selection of candles. Our menu for the evening: steak and potatoes, with a tomato, avocado, and bell pepper salad. I fry three big steaks, seasoning them heavily. We devour that first course, and then make bacon, tomato, and avocado sandwiches. This is how to acclimatize.

We're unsure of the hut's altitude. We have been told that it's around 13,800 feet. (We learn later that the true altitude is closer to 12,000 feet).

Sleep is difficult. We write in our journals by candlelight and listen to the BBC on my shortwave radio.

Sunday, March 12: *Pink Flamingos*

Today we learn the location of the hut's bathroom—under (and sometimes on top of) any available rock that surrounds the premises. We watch where we step with eagle eyes and thank the powers-that-be that there isn't any odor.

Our colds worsen. Both Brian and I hack up green and yellow phlegm.

We take short strolls in the vicinity of the hut. A half dozen pink flamingos, their stilt legs stuck in shallow water, watch us as we walk along the salty

Laguna Santa Rosa, storm

shoreline. Tres Cruces, the huge triple-peaked volcano, is our backdrop. We see a nice peak to the north of the hut and make a go for it. A long ridge ascends to its summit from a point about a half-mile from the hut. The slope is gentle at the base, steepening along its path into the

sky. We hike about a third of it, but our heads are pounding too hard to continue farther. We return, cook some more steak and bacon, down some Excedrin, and sleep.

Monday, March 13: *Visitors*

Rest day. We're awakened by two guys in need of fuel. We don't know where they came from, and don't know where they are headed. They claim to be gold miners. We give them a gallon of our gasoline and some water; they thank us and hike out to the main road.

Today we just eat, sleep, and take some pictures. Our colds are bad by now. Brian is having a really rough time. This is a bad place for a cold. It's hard enough down at sea level; being up high makes it many times worse.

Tuesday, March 14: *Obelisk*

We feel like we're acclimatizing, but our colds just keep getting worse. We pack some water, food, and our cameras, and head back up the peak we started two days ago. The wind blows powerfully, but we enjoy being buffeted by the gusts. We happen across a large mound of vicuña droppings, then another—and another after that. Then we spot a vicuña. He watches us as we ascend the ridge. He stays near us, but not too close, maybe a few hundred yards. He (or she? I just assume it's a he) grazes on short, thick, yellow tufts of grass. We keep climbing and soon we are above him, looking down at his woolly back.

The weather turns stormy by early afternoon. The wind pummels the area; clouds brush against mountains. Our pace slows by the time we're two-thirds of the way to the summit. What mountain is this? Does the peak even have a name? I don't know. It's higher than anything in the contiguous US or the Alps (I'm guessing about 16,000 feet), but the mountain probably doesn't have a name, much less a summit marker. It's just a few contour lines on some map. But to us the peak is an awesome ramp into the clouds.

We rest and continue. Three-quarters of the way to the summit we sit down in the shade of a large rock. We gaze to the south and east. The view is so huge and awesome. This is why wide-angle lenses were invented.

We can see Salar de Maricunga, the turquoise waters of Laguna Santa Rosa, snow on Tres Cruces, and far in the distance, a huge—I mean absolutely HUGE mountain. The high, broad peak has a large glacier covering much of its northern flanks. It has to be Cerro Pissis. It just has to be. Nothing else in the area could be that bulky. I tell Brian; he nods in agreement. We stare for about an hour. We didn't think we'd see the mountain for another few days. We take a few pictures, then drop into a canyon to the east of us.

The canyon protects us from the wind. We strip off our jackets and hike in T-shirts. We see vicuña scat, but nothing else—certainly no signs of other people. We hike down a small arroyo in the middle of the canyon. I spot something in the distance. I can just barely see it jutting up from the dry earth. I don't know what it is, but I want to check it out. It's tall and white. Brian sees it too; we speculate on what it might be, but we can't decide how large it is. It could be as small as a wastebasket or as big as a house. Gauging scale in this landscape is impossible.

Hiking to the object takes longer than we expected. We finally can see that it is about

Lonely obelisk

the size of a person and is shaped like an elongated pyramid. Five minutes later we are standing next to it: it is a concrete obelisk with a thick piece of steel pointing out its top. We look for signs of a road, some construction, anything. We search for a metal plaque, a simple inscription, even carved initials. We find nothing. The strange obelisk stands in utter anonymous solitude. Brian and I speculate that it's some sort of mining marker, but it sits on an alluvial fan; most of the area's mines are tunneled into the mountains themselves. We have no idea what this thing is or who put it here. We joke that it is some extraterrestrial's landing marker.

We return to the hut for yet another steak dinner, and talk well into the wee hours about climbing Pissis—and many other subjects.

Wednesday, March 15: *Haunted by Hanta*

The Ides of March. We both awaken feeling awful—not from altitude, but from our stuffy sinuses and sore throats. We eat a huge breakfast and hike the

day away. We find awesome welded tuff flows to the south of the lake. Brian discovers what he thinks are arrowheads. The artifacts in question are carefully chipped bits of obsidian; they look like arrowheads to me, too.

Pat is coming tomorrow. We pack our gear then cook dinner.

I find mouse droppings that night. Then I re-member that Hanta virus is most commonly found in areas just like the place we're in: semi-abandoned, dry, dusty structures. Brian and I wonder if our 'colds' are actually infestations of Hanta virus. I guess we'll know soon enough.

Wind-carved welded tuff

Thursday, March 16: *Insane Terrain*

Pat arrives at 10:30 in the morning. We load the Hilux and speed toward the Mina Marte road. Tres Cruces looks enormous. This mountain is on my wish list for another season. Brian and I talk about possibly attempting it after Pissis.

Pat turns onto the Mina Marte road; I begin to feel nervous. I'm anxious

about entering Argentina illegally; I'm anxious about the altitude gain, and I'm anxious about the weather. Pat tells us that the area received a good cover of snow just a few weeks earlier, and that more snow could fall any day. Now I'm also wor-ried about our strength. Brian's health is in the gutter and I'm faring only slightly better. We both have serious flu-like symptoms.

Brian and me

We pass a small mining outpost. Two people I see at the camp are completely covered in cold weather gear: goggles, thick parkas, bibs, giant boots, and huge mittens. The outfits look like spacesuits. What they are doing makes me laugh: they are hanging sweaters and underwear on a clothesline. We wave; the 'spacemen' stare back at us.

Pat slows the Hilux and searches the side of the road. He mumbles to himself and then stops the truck. He scans the area intently. We roll a few hundred yards farther. "Here!" he says. He turns the wheel sharply and the Hilux flies over the embankment.

We're soon in four-wheel drive, high range. Pat navigates to the top of a pass on which sits a large, rusty marker—we have arrived at Paso de Valle Ancho. We drive past the lonely metal sentinel and become criminals—we've now in Argentina without the requisite stamps on our passports. I come up with a plan in case we do eventually get caught: play dumb and pretend like we thought we were in Chile, or just say that we got lost. *Yeah...that'll work.*

Border marker, Valle Ancho (sur)

Pat stops the Hilux; he grabs his binoculars and scans the horizon for border agents, both on the ground and in the air. I see three VHF radios (one short range and two long range) behind his seat, an oxygen mask, and two tanks, flares, two high-powered spotlights, and an emergency locator beacon. Pat also carries 50 extra liters of fuel, three full-size spare tires, a sleeping bag, shovels, two jacks, and a tire pump in the bed of the Hilux. He gets back into the truck and pulls out a can of onion-flavored Pringles. "Pringles time!" he says. Brian and I hold out our hands and Pat fills them up with stacks of the processed treats. Pat assures us that the coast is clear, then nonchalantly recounts a story of his near-capture by Argentines in this area a few years back.

We race down the other side of the steep pass. Pat maneuvers around some snowfields, then steers us into Valle Ancho. The valley is wide but not very deep. It looks like it goes on forever. Most of Valle Ancho is colored a soothing buff tan, spiked in areas by crimson and even some yellow. It's too bad that we can't spend more time here. I see enough photo opportunities to keep me busy for three or four sunrises and sunsets, at least. Lately I've been interested in simple landscapes; a few simple lines and one or two basic colors. Valle Ancho is perfect for this style.

Patricio Rios, Hilux, Cerro Pissis

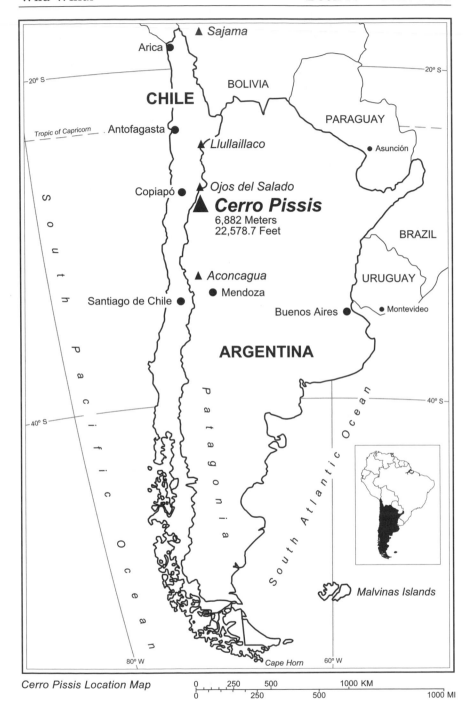

Cerro Pissis Location Map

| 0 | 250 | 500 | | 1000 KM |
| 0 | | 250 | 500 | 1000 MI |

Scale: 1:25,641,026
Azimuthal Equal-Area Projection
Map by Ed Darack

Cerro Pissis Regional Map

Map details Cerro Pissis and environs. Map shows pertinent roads, population centers, huts, and physical features.

▲ Peak

● Population Center

⚹ Hut or Outpost

– – – – – – – – – – –
International Boundary

Panamerican Highway

Secondary Routes

Scale: 1:4,000,000
Azimuthal Equal-Area Projection
Map by Ed Darack

Mountain Altitudes in Meters (and Feet):
Ojos del Salado: 6885 Meters (22,588.6 Feet)
Cerro Pissis: 6,882 Meters (22,578.7 Feet)
Cerro Bonete: 6,759 Meters (22,175.2 Feet)
Tres Cruces: 6749 Meters (22,142.4 Feet)
Cerro Cazadero: 6,658 Meters (21,843.8 Feet)
Cerro Nacimiento: 6,436 Meters (21,115.5 Feet)
Incahuasi: 6,621 Meters (21,722.4 Feet)
Cumbre de Laudo: 6,400 Meters (20,997.4 Feet)
Cerro Veladero: 6,159 Meters (20,206.7 Feet)
Volcán Antofalla: 6,100 Meters (20,013.1 Feet)
Cerro Copiapó: 6,080 Meters (19,947.5 Feet)
Cerro Colorado: 6,080 Meters (19,947.5 Feet)
Nevado San Francisco: 6,020 Meters (19,750.7 Feet)
Cerro Aguas Blancas: 5,760 Meters (18,897.6 Feet)
Cerro Tronquitos 5,740 Meters (18,832 Feet)
Cerro Los Mogotes 5,380 Meters (17,650.9 Feet)
Volcán Lastarria: 5,700 Meters (18,700.8 Feet)
Cerro Azul: 5,070 Meters (16,633.9 Feet)

305

We move quickly; Pat tells us that there was a small, remote gold mining operation for a short time about 40 miles from Cerro Pissis, but that it's now probably shut down. If it's operational again then we might be spotted and the authorities may arrive shortly thereafter. We keep our fingers crossed.

We splash through a couple of streams and get a great view of the northeast aspect of Pissis. The mountain reminds me of a desert version of Mount Logan in Canada's Yukon Territory. What these two mountains have in common is not just that they are high and broad-based, but that their upper sections are girthy as well. They each have a 'shoebox' form.

Pat drives the Hilux across a level plateau scribed with tire tracks. The tracks may be Pat's from years past, or they may be from a gold miner. We see metal stakes near the tracks. Pat says they might be markers for landmines, but he doesn't think this area was ever mined. Still, he doesn't want to do any experimentation; he stays well away from the stakes.

We pass the gold mine. The place looks completely shut down. There are no signs that anyone has been there for years. We speed into a labyrinth of insane terrain. The place is a maze of land—like a sand dune field, but with hidden cliffs. The trick here is to keep moving fast enough so that the tires don't sink into the ground, but not so fast as to take a wrong turn—and there are many opportunities to turn. Pat tells us that he made a bad turn once that resulted in his car flying down a cliff and flipping—luckily his friend was traveling close by in another truck; together they managed to roll Pat's truck onto its wheels so he could drive it back to Copiapó.

I can't understand how Pat is navigating. The small valleys we travel through are steep, narrow, and sinewy; we can't see more than about 50 feet ahead at any one time. Pat is like a homing pigeon.

We emerge from the maze and follow the path of a small stream. I'm surprised to find a stream here and wonder if we really needed to bring so much water. Pat tells us that running water is unpredictable in this area. Better to have our own and not need it than to need it and end up like the Laguna Verde cow.

We reach the base of the monstrous peak. Stepping out of the Hilux we stare up a long ridge. Cerro Pissis is a hidden giant. The solitude and tremendous scale are palpable. I'm excited; I love being here. I crave going higher.

We hop back into the Hilux; Pat puts it into low range; the rig crawls into thinner and thinner air. My ears pop; my breaths quicken; my pulse races. We're gaining a lot of altitude, quickly.

Pat is soon coursing around washing machine-size boulders. The underbelly of the Hilux slams a rock—Pat cringes. I imagine a rear axle tearing away. We slam another rock—then another. Pat stops the truck and tells us that we have two possibilities for a base camp. We can go higher on the ridge, or cross over to the base of Pissis Glacier, a bit to the south. Brian and I decide to stick with the ridge.

The terrain reminds me of pictures that Viking took of the surface of Mars. The rocks are red and vesicular, classically volcanic. We are soon winding our way around boulders too big to drive—or scrape—over. Pat finds a somewhat level spot and stops the Hilux—but doesn't shut it off. He tells us that we are at 16,000 feet. Brian and I jump out of the cab and unload our gear. We're giddy with hypoxia and excitement. We count out four crisp one hundred dollar bills and hand them over to Patricio. Then we remind him to return in 14 days.

We ask him to point out the route to the summit. He shrugs his shoulders— he doesn't know. We ask him which of the many summits is the very highest.

He points to one that is second from the far right, and says that he 'thinks' that's it, but 'isn't sure.' Then we realize that the climbing instructions Bob gave us are for a route that begins at the base of Pissis Glacier, not this ridge. Pat wishes us good luck, then heads back to Copiapó.

We stack our gear against some boulders,

Our tents, our wall, and our food, fuel, and water cache

then go about leveling two tent platforms. We're both coughing like mad and gasping for air. Not only does the wind blow, but it carries fine dust. Our eyes cake up with it; Brian starts sneezing.

In spite of the wind, we manage to get both tents pitched; then we set about building a wall as a windbreak. But we tire quickly and can find motivation for nothing more than lying in our sleeping bags. The wind howls into the evening, then it starts to snow. My worst fears are materializing. I wonder what will happen if it really dumps. I start to think that we won't be able to make a go for the summit. I worry that our health will crash—that we won't even be able to climb above base camp…and Pat won't be able to pick us up. We'll spend the next two weeks slogging out to the Mina Marte road.

This region is one of the most remote and forlorn I have ever visited. I could never have imagined how I feel right now—we are on another planet. We're so cut off from everything. I like it. I open my tent a few hours after sunset and see that the snowstorm has passed; it deposited only a slight dusting. My eyes lock on a huge thunderhead in the distance. It is parked over the lowlands of Argentina. We are nearly as high as the top of its anvil. POW! A bolt of lightning blasts inside of it. The entire sky lights up. We are too far away to hear a thunderclap.

I yell for Brian, who is coughing and hacking up his own storm. He stares silently at the cloud. Another bolt fires; he jumps at the sight, then goes back to his sleeping bag.

The wind never dies throughout the night. It lulls for a bit, teasing us that we'll have some peace, but it always returns, yanking at our tents and whistling over the rocks. I curl up in my sleeping bag, eat some bread and bell peppers, and try to sleep.

Friday, March 17: *Hypoxiville*

I rise at dawn. I have a bad headache and pop some Excedrin. The ground is lightly covered in sparkly snow crystals. I set up my camera; a painful process in the extremely cold air. I keep the camera's cold weather extension cord buried deep inside my pocket.

The rising sun paints the snow-frosted mountainside pink, then yellow, then the day begins and I need sunglasses.

Brian and I cook breakfast—some bacon and potatoes. We discover Christian radio on shortwave from Quito. It's 'The Voice of the Andes,' broadcast in well-enunciated English.

Brian feels terrible. I think he has the flu. He aches, he coughs, and he has a pounding headache. He remains in his tent for much of the day. I don't feel great; but I know that if I had what he does (whatever it is) I would want to go down. Amazing that he keeps his spirits up.

I take a reconnaissance hike later in the day. I see penitente fields, exploded volcanic calderas, distant ash fields, and other Atacaman treats. On a second hike, I watch the weather build around distant mountains—I peruse a mental map of the area, those distant peaks I see are Ojos del Salado, Tres Cruces, Incahuasi, Nevado El Muerto, and some other huge mountains I believe to be Cerros Cazadero and Nacimiento. I look to the south at Cerro Bonete, listed by some sources as higher than Cerro Pissis. There are actually two Bonetes, side-by-side: Bonete Grande and Bonete Chico; confusingly, Chico is the higher of the two.

I travel almost a mile from camp on my third hike. Breathing is difficult and so is balancing in the gusty wind. I'm taken by a fantastic

"Combed" landscape

earth form: the ground in some areas looks slightly furrowed, as if stroked with a giant comb. But the lines aren't straight, they are curved and twisty, and they're barely visible. I speculate that they were caused by freeze-thaw heaving, or may have some relation to solifluction lobes

Bowl of rocks

found in the arctic. I'm not sure. I see this type of formation in a few places, but I don't have the energy to investigate any of them closely.

I find something even more quizzical on my return to camp: a rock with a bowl ground into it; I find loose rocks and some gravel laying in the nadir of the bowl. I initially assume that it was made by a person, but a closer inspection leads me to think of similar rocks I've found near rivers. The 'bowls' I've discovered around rivers were carved by the swirling motion of water digging

Weathered rock.

smaller rocks into the 'bowl' rock. I'm standing at the crest of this gentle ridge. Even if this area could support a river large enough to cause currents that could carve a bowl into a rock, such a waterway wouldn't flow on the crest of a ridge. I'm too hypoxic to study the formation further. I photograph it from a few different angles and return to camp.

At sunset Brian and I photograph wispy clouds over the summit of Pissis. Those clouds then merge with thunderheads over the plains of Argentina.

We stay up late in Brian's tent, listening to the shortwave. We laugh at not having a map, a compass, a GPS, a two-way radio, a guidebook, an altimeter, or even a watch. But we're definitely keeping track of the days in our notebooks—we need to make sure we're back at base camp when Patricio returns.

I don't sleep well; the wind keeps me up and I'm plagued by a headache. I drink some water and the pounding subsides for a while.

Saturday, March 18: *Aeolian potholes*

I awaken to those black crickets I saw on Ojos. They are hopping around, no doubt eating little bits of our waste that we can't even see. Brian still has his cough, but wants to do an exploratory carry. We have no idea where our route goes, but we think that if we go straight up the ridge we'll figure it out.

We pack some supplies: each of us carries about ten pounds of food, a bottle of fuel, and one of Brian's MSR dromedary bags—filled, of course, with some fresh water (fresh out of one of our plastic jugs).

The going is slow. I use any excuse to stop and rest. I discover another 'pothole' and point it out to Brian. I venture that it may be caused by the wind, as this place just couldn't get enough water to make a flowing stream, especially on the top of a ridge. I proclaim that this feature is an 'aeolian pothole.' Brian is skeptical. We continue farther and Brian finds two more. We talk about it further, but can't reach any conclusion.

Brian collecting water

We stare at the Pissis Glacier. It's huge for such a dry area. We even see crevasses. This must be the largest glacier in this part of the Andes. As a matter of fact, I don't know of any other glaciers in this part of the Andes. Summit snowfields, yes, but large, flowing glaciers with crevasses? No. Only on Pissis—I think.

We drop down the southern side of the ridge and hike into a ravine. After a few hundred yards we discover a frozen stream. A little bit farther and we find the stream is running! We have a supply of water. We rest and drink.

We ponder our next course of action—Brian thinks that we should move up a slope to the south of us and course around a small subpeak. I agree. We pass more of the 'combed land.' The surface appears to be comprised of homogenous pebbles with a large rock every now and then, but it is soft, almost like wet sand. We ascend the section and contour around the southern side of the subpeak. It's a slog, and we're winded, but the reward is a great view of the upper section of Pissis Glacier.

We can't go any higher. The wind and cold are too much for us. We drop our supplies at a good campsite, then turn to descend. I see a huge turquoise circle in the distance. A perfectly round lake (at least it looks round from this angle). I believe it to be Laguna Verde (a different Laguna Verde from the one that lies near Paso San Francisco). Brilliant turquoise in this red, brown, and gray landscape. And that it is circular…I don't really know. Too surreal; too beautiful.

We see haze at sunset from base camp. It reminds me of marine haze.

I wonder how haze could be here. I then realize that the sublimation of the Pissis Glacier and evaporation of Laguna Verde puts water vapor in the air. Water vapor is the prime constituent in haze.

The night is clear and cold, but the wind settles down—a little. I take some star-trail shots over Pissis, and then bed down.

Sunday, March 19: *The Yeti and His Gold*

Today we're going to make another carry to our supply dump, which we decide to make our advanced base camp. We fight headaches with Excedrin, cook breakfast, and listen to The Voice of the Andes. We take Brian's other dromedary bag and as much food as we can stuff into our packs.

We move quickly, resting only briefly to fill the dromedary bag at the creek; we're soon at our next camp, adding today's supplies to yesterday's. Building up this camp in such a hostile environment brings a thrill of satisfaction. Real work, visible results; I look up and see the ultimate goal.

We rest, but Brian—even though he is in the throes of what I think is the flu—wants to keep going higher. We aim for a sloping plain that has a long line of penitentes at its center. The wind beats us, stinging our ears with cold. Soon my ears hurt more than my pounding head. We reach the penitentes and gaze up the mountain. We decide that our route should go straight up the east face.

Brian sees something—he thinks it's a falling rock. I stare at the bright landscape. I see a black dot, moving down the mountain. I can see moving legs. I think it's…a…person! But who? I look again, and return to believing that it's a rock—but a rolling rock would be moving much faster, I think. How could another person be up here? We would have seen something, or someone, some tracks, some vehicle—*something!* Brian jokes that it's the Yeti. I joke too, but then I wonder if it really *is* the Yeti. I worry that it will see us. It takes big lunges down the mountain. This thing—or person—or whatever it is—is huge. But we can see only its silhouette. Brian and I face each other, turn, and run. Soon we are back at advance base camp. We search for the Yeti-guy again, but can't find him. We're both sure, however, that we saw *something*.

We wrestle the wind on our descent, finally escaping it when we reach the stream. I take off my jacket and feel the sun's warmth on my back. I stick my head in the water and start slurping. Then I open my eyes and see…gold! Thousands of gold-colored flakes. I jerk my head out of the stream and stare at a small bed of glimmering sparkles. I tell Brian; he comes over and takes a look. I realize that the 'gold' is probably just feldspar (fool's gold). I lose interest in the commodity and go back to drinking the cold mountain water. Shooting photographs, reaching the summit, and just staying alive are so much more important to us than material wealth at this point. Besides, another concern taunts us: what if we take some 'gold' and the Pissis Yeti finds out?

That night we hang out in Brian's tent and listen to CBC (Canadian Broadcasting Company) and laugh at a variety show out of Toronto, and then drool over 'Nova Scotia Cooking Party.' We decide to make tomorrow a rest day.

We freak each other out that night when we hear the sounds of the wind. We think that the Pissis Yeti is coming to get us. Brian swears he hears distant footsteps; I keep hearing pots clanking. I open my tent at least six times, sure that I'll be staring face-to-face with some immense, woolly monster.

Monday, March 20: *Pothole Epiphany*

Average morning, I feel pretty good. It's cold and the wind is howling (of course). I investigate the 'aeolian potholes' again. This time I'm stricken with a new idea: what if this mountain receives more snow than its surroundings—maybe it has its own microclimate, much like Mammoth Mountain in California? That just may be possible, as evidenced by the size of Pissis Glacier. If that's the case, then this ridge gets covered in deep snow each winter. During the spring melt, small creeks would form, which could swirl rocks into larger cobbles and boulders, creating the mysterious potholes. I'm still skeptical. It sounds like a stretch—but something created these holes. I took a closer look at one of them—some hardened sand lay on its bottom. More evidence that they were carved under the influence of water, not wind.

The wind pounds hard by afternoon. I have a difficult time walking. Cooking, even in Brian's vestibule, is next to impossible—vexing eddies smother the priming flame. I cuss aloud in frustration, but still don't want to be anywhere else. Tomorrow we will move our tents to advanced base camp, and sleep there. Hopefully the winds will be less intense up there.

Tuesday, March 21: *Another Day, Another Haul*

I estimate that my pack weighs 80 pounds. I'm carrying food, water, my camera, tripod, sleeping bag, tent, and stove. I make pretty good time as far as the stream. I drink some fresh desert water while waiting there for Brian. He

joins me, and we agree that the stream must be a gift from heaven. After some lounging, we huff it to advanced base camp. Brian's flu is practically killing him. His hacking not only worries me, it scares me. He wants to help me set up camp, but I refuse. He needs to rest. But I'm not feeling so hot myself.

Our site is sheltered from the wind. I begin excavation. I clear two tent pads and level them as best I can. The work takes three hours and leaves me wasted. I barely have enough energy to set up my Pentax when the light starts to get good. I feel like I'm borrowing against future energy reserves. Climbing

Loaded up. BK photo

mountains and photographing them is the hardest work in the world. Nothing else even comes close. Nothing that I've ever done, that is.

The sunset is awesome—Laguna Verde radiates an intense blue; it seems almost radioactive. So much of what exists in the natural world is a superlative of some type. I've said "this is the most beautiful scene in the world" time and again; and I'm sure I'll say it a million times more—and each time I'll be right, for that moment.

I'm not sure of our altitude. I guess that we are maybe 17,000 or 18,000 feet above sea level. We can see the summit—or what we think is the summit, and it is a long way up.

Shortly after sunset I unzip my tent to see the full moon rising above a blanket of clouds. We are looking *down* on the layer of clouds, *and* the moon rising above them. Incredible.

Wednesday, March 22: *Red Hill*

I don't know what we'll be doing today. We discuss our options and decide to embark on a day hike to the top of a sub-peak that lies just beyond our camp. I don't know where Brian gets his energy. He moves slowly, but if I were in his condition, I wouldn't be moving at all. We battle the wind as we ascend a steep ridge and maneuver through small penitente fields to the summit of what we christen 'Red Hill.' There is no summit marker, nor is there any evidence that anyone has even been there before. But this is an insignificant peak—it is barely a peak, really just a small spur off the main bulk of Pissis. The top of Red Hill affords us excellent views. This is our high point on the trip so far. We can see both Pissis Glacier and the glacier on the north side of the mountain.

We really like our new camp; it's

Brian Kelly going strong; Laguna Verde in background

warmer than base camp and less dusty. Cooking is easy in the relatively staid conditions. We eat a good dinner, but Brian and I each explode in spates of coughing throughout the evening.

I see some distant cirrus clouds. Cirrus worry me because they often signal an approaching front. If a front moves in, and it's powerful enough, we may be in serious trouble. I constantly hope that the weather holds out for another eight days. But that hope is ridiculous. *Hoping for eight days of good weather in the mountains...HA—HA—HA.*

Brian and I decide to push higher on the mountain tomorrow. In fact, we want to try for the summit. We're anxious. Climbing Red Hill really makes us want to go all the way to the crown of the massif.

Thursday, March 23: *Hypothermic*

Brian wakes me hours before sunrise, probably at 3:00. By 3:45 (estimate) we are on our way. Brutal cold spears us. We move straight up the slope, through the penitente field, and onto a section of steep, loose rocks. I stop to photograph an incredible sunrise. The wind is fierce. Small, translucent lenticulars are parked far too still for comfort. Through the years I have noted a paradox with lenticular clouds: the faster the wind blows, the more stable these clouds become. I fear what conditions on the summit must be like.

I can expose my bare hands to the icy gale for only about 20 seconds before they go numb. I thaw them by twirling my arms. This is a loathsome process; the pain is similar to having my fingers slammed in a car door.

The clouds above Bonete explode in color—reds and yellows. We continue higher. I work my Nikon furiously. The surrounding rocks glow like molten lava as the blooming daylight washes the mountain with crimson light.

We reach what we think is the summit plateau and hide behind some wind-pummelled rocks. I find ventifacts—gouges in rock made by sand and dust blown at incredible speeds. I rub my hands across them. These are the most deeply incised ventifacts I have ever seen. I stare into the wind with fear.

Brian is dizzy and has ataxia. He tells me that he can't feel his ass or thighs. I fear that he has hypothermia. He doesn't say much, but when he does, he slurs. When he coughs he sounds like his is going to blow a lung out of his mouth. He hacks up a huge glob of green phlegm. I feel myself wheeze, and then I start to cough too. I hurl a wad of phlegm on the rock next to his; mine is green too, and has some blood in it. We don't know what to do—so we high-five, but since we're both wearing mittens, I guess we really just high-twoed each other.

The summit is hidden from view, but we figure that it is far too high for us to reach today. We drop our axes and crampons in a visible spot (so that we don't have to carry them back up on our next trip) then prepare to descend.

The wind is gusting around 80 miles per hour. Brian lays in the sun to try to warm himself, but he just feels colder by the second.

We head down. I move at a decent clip, but Brian falls behind. I make it to the penitente field, then wait for what seems an hour for Brian. He doesn't show…I get up and look for him. He finally appears. He is staggering, moving so slowly it's painful to watch him. I walk up and greet him, then the two of us descend to our tents.

We crawl into our sleeping bags and pass out. I wake intermittently to drink water and eat (meat spread on crackers, hard candy, and an orange). I check on Brian a few hours later. He tells me that he is feeling better. He says that he definitely had hypothermia. He says that he wanted to lie down and go to sleep back at our day's high point. *He'd be dead by now.* He tells me that he couldn't get warm, no matter how hard he tried, which included running in place and swirling his arms. He's never experienced hypothermia before. He can't believe he couldn't warm himself. He's really shaken by it.

Quietude prevails at our camp for most of the day, but every now and then I can hear gusts crashing over the ridge above like huge breakers on a vertical coast. I hear a smashing sound, then swirling, then my tent flaps and jerks around as eddies spawned by the gusts sprint through camp.

"Never let your legs get ahead of your lungs," I caution Brian. He agrees.

We discuss our plan of action. We feel that we should commit to a full-blown siege of the mountain. We want to establish another camp, located where we dropped our ice axes and crampons, and make a summit attempt from there. We will go back to base camp tomorrow, stock up on yet more food, then return here. The day after tomorrow we will move to high camp. Our siege tactic is a little dated, but I like it. The plan reminds me of the climbing expeditions of the fifties that I've read about.

Friday, March 24: *Restock*

Pat will pick us up in a little more than 6 X 24 hours (I'm too tired to do the math). That leaves us just enough time to safely get to the summit and back to base camp. I just hope the weather holds out.

We eat some breakfast, then move quickly to base camp. Brian is feeling better, but I am doing worse. But we ignore our health and just move.

We arrive at base camp to a small colony of black crickets hopping around our food cache. We load up on more ham, potatoes, oranges, onions, crackers, bread, canned meat, rice and spaghetti and head back to advanced base camp.

We return in the afternoon and prepare a huge meal. We think that we have a lot of food, but at the rate we're devouring it, we are unsure how long it will last. The quick trip to base camp has really energized us. Just those few hours at lower altitude make a big difference. I feel ready to move higher.

Tomorrow is a big day; we need to rest well tonight. I shoot a few pictures with my Pentax, then crawl into my sleeping bag. I'll leave the Pentax in my tent while we go higher on the peak. We'll bring only Brian's tent to high camp. It'll be a little cramped, but it will save space and weight. We're now consumed with reaching the summit of Cerro Pissis.

Saturday, March 25: *Cheyne-Stokes*

I'm starting to think of this mountain as home. I feel like we are pioneering a new route, that we are stepping on ground never before trod by humans. We found the creek, we found the route from base camp to advanced base camp, and we found a good spot for high camp. Not once did we discover even a trace of another person's passage.

The morning is cold and still; the silence is intense. My ears ring loudly. I concentrate on packing and dressing. As Brian says, everything up at this altitude is a chore, even pissing.

It's a long slog to high camp. Not too much wind, though. I strike a bee line to our ice axes and crampons. I start kicking out a tent platform; Brian finishes the job after he arrives about twenty minutes later, then we pitch the sturdy shelter. The sun falls behind a ridge; our world gets really cold, really fast. We jump into the tent and fix dinner.

Later, I venture outside to pee. I can't believe the scene before me: an incredibly bright Milky Way is lighting up Pissis Glacier, the mountain's snowfields, and the summit peaks. The night is so clear and cold—and no man-made lights anywhere. I duck back inside the tent, a bit winded, and fall into deep sleep. Brian's tent is incredibly warm—the double wall construction insulates much better than my single wall design.

The body's autonomic nervous system doesn't work so well at high altitude. Tasks as simple as drinking water require concentration, lest you be left gasping for air. You must learn to gulp with your mouth, inhale with your nose, exhale with your mouth, and gulp again.

I wake a few hours later, craving water. I resist the urge to gulp it down, but I can't—it's so refreshing, so good. I drink till I feel my lungs about to implode, then I gasp for air. When I finally settle down I listen to Brian's breaths—and lack of them. Ten to fifteen seconds of absolute silence follows each of his shallow breaths. I start flipping out—thinking that he is about to die, but then I remember that this respiration pattern is called Cheyne-Stokes breathing. This form of respiration is something many people experience at high altitude. It isn't a serious problem.

Sunday, March 26: *Freight Trains*

We awaken to clear skies and modest gusts. The tent wall facing the east is actually warm. We decide to make our summit attempt tomorrow (Monday), as we are still completely wasted by yesterday's ascent.

We are at a good spot, sheltered from the wind, but large gusts manage to crash through later in the day. I try to light the stove in the protection of some rocks, but the wind always finds its way to the jet. So we move the stove inside the vestibule and it ignites without a hitch. I prepare a freeze-dried dinner and eat it with crackers. I'm starting to feel strong again.

The afternoon winds roll down from high on the mountain and smash through our camp. The only warning of the gale is a freight-train-like rumble that sounds about ten seconds before a blast arrives.

I wish we had an altimeter—we are so high. I'm guessing 20,500 feet or something like that. Last night we looked down on strange yellowish haze—Brian thinks it's from sulfur dioxide being emitted by a nearby volcano. I'm not too sure—there is definitely some haze from sublimating snow. I don't know what the yellow was from, though. As high as we are, it is still dusty—enough to make me sneeze at times. The dust is nothing like it was at base camp, though.

Monday, March 27: *Beaten Down*

We start our summit bid by fighting the wind—what else is new? We climb above our camp and face wind gusts up to 70 miles per hour. We huddle behind some large rocks and wait. We finally get anxious and head off into the howl, straight up the slope. My boots are okay for the terrain, but Brian's aren't. Mine flex with no problems; Brian's are double-plastic Koflachs. He slides six inches down for every foot he gains. I run out of energy just a few hundred feet below the col directly below the summit. Brian also conks out.

We head back to high camp, taking in the incredible high altitude scenery along the way. I wonder if I'll ever come here again; it is so far off, so difficult to access. I want to absorb as much of it as possible—enough to have vivid memories for the remainder of my life. I like descending because I'm constantly faced out, allowing me to look at the surrounding terrain.

We sleep for a few hours. Later in the day I venture out of the tent looking for snow to melt. The wind is menacing as hell. I look forward, for the first time on the trip, to getting out of here.

Tomorrow we'll try one more time for the summit. But our food is almost gone and we are both feeling weak. Our spirits can only carry us so far. I now have those loathsome flu-like aches. I hope to keep going for a few more days.

The temperature plummets. I've noticed that nights are now longer than days. We're in the Southern Hemisphere's autumn—and at this altitude, you could say that we're well into the austral winter.

Brian stuns me later in the night by announcing that he won't make another summit attempt. He wants down. I reply that I want to make a go for it, at least to the pass below the summit. I tell him that I don't want to go without him. I was looking forward to climbing this mountain in its entirety *with him*. I want to be on the summit with him. He tells me that today was one of the most frustrating and most difficult days he'd ever spent in the mountains. He doesn't think he has the energy for another attempt. But I finally convince him to at least make some attempt, even if we just go to the pass below the summit.

Tuesday, March 28: *The Big Surprise*

We jump out of the tent at daybreak. We take the last of our food (crackers, mustard, and some candy) and aim for the summit. Our plan is to traverse to Pissis Glacier, climb to the col, then—if we feel strong enough—ascend the summit ridge to the summit itself.

I climb alongside the glacier on volcanic rubble (possibly a moraine) while Brian ascends the ice. I veer to the right near the top of the glacier, as I stair-

step up a small boulder field. I stroll to a ledge peppered with wildly eroded, wind-carved rocks. Many of the rocks look like contorted mushrooms. 30 minutes later, Brian joins me.

I worry that Brian is too overextended to continue, but he insists he is fine and wants to keep climbing. Noth-

Wind-carved rock

ing stops Brian today. He wants to climb along the glacier, around the back of the small peaklet above us, but I think that traversing the front is a better idea.

After 30 more minutes of rest we move up toward the west; I convinced Brian that we should at least take a look at my route.

We have seen absolutely no other signs of human presence so far. Then I spot a plastic coke bottle…and a tent pad…and some dried-up orange peels. I look to the northwest and see the dark rocks of the main summit. It sits far from where I thought it did. We're also way below it. I instantly realize that we're now at the real high camp. This is the big surprise of our trip. I wish that we'd brought a map….

We have no chance of reaching the summit. It's too far away. I want to quit and return to our high camp. This is total defeat. We try to 'make lemonade,' but all we have are old, dried up orange peels.

Altitude does crazy things to emotions. Most of the time thin air pushes me to descend. But I'm suddenly infused with a rush of mania. I want to at least go up to the col above us, and I want Brian to go with me. He agrees; we set off.

We follow a faint trail for about a half hour. Then we look up: huge peaks of Pissis rise all around us. It is like some fairy-tale kingdom. The landscape is dramatically stark: colored brown, black, purple, and red; bright white snow and ice shines in the sun. The sky is black.

The summit—what we think is the summit—looks almost doable, then impossible, then doable—back and forth. Brian says that he'll wait for me—but I insist that he try it too. It doesn't take much convincing to get Brian motivated, even when he's sick as a dog and at nearly 22,000 feet. It's late afternoon, and for the first time on the trip, thick frontal clouds are cruising over Pissis' summit. We should definitely retreat. The view of the summit reminds me of Aconcagua's summit from Berlin Camp—a 12-hour round trip! I repeat to myself that we should head down, but it's now or never. We drop our packs, including all food, water, ice axes, and crampons, grab our cameras and trekking poles, and head for the summit.

The wind, gusty throughout the day, settles down. Is this the calm before the storm? I don't know. We're high, certainly over 21,000 feet. Life is so different up here. I think about my heart and my blood, trying to get oxygen to my muscles. I am confused by the scale of the place. I can't gauge distance. I can only move like a scared animal. I watch the clouds constantly. I imagine that they will turn into a huge cat, and swat at me, killing me instantly. I hear myself mutter something like "nice kitty."

We traverse a snowfield and drop into a broad field of lapilli. I scurry across it—always with an eye on the menacing sky. The ground below my feet is coarse sand. It would be a really great place to kick back and drink beer—if it were four miles lower.

Brian tells me to go ahead of him, he will continue as fast as he can, but if he can't keep climbing, then he'll meet me back at the col. I weave around gnarled red boulders. They are large, solidified lava globs. Soon I'm ascending treacherous sections of scree that rest on smooth patches of rock. Ball bearings on ice. I can almost hear my heart pounding in my chest.

I reach the summit ridge. I can't believe that I've made it this far this quickly. But I've lost track of Brian. I wanted to summit with him, but with the goal so close, I care about nothing but getting to the top. Adrenaline races through my body. I can't even think. I want the summit so badly. I never realized I wanted to make the top this desperately. I'm on autopilot and just keep going. I hope Brian makes it.

The upper section of the summit ridge is the most treacherous part of the climb. I concentrate on every move over the sharp, jagged, and loosely-balanced rocks. I tear the top of my crew-neck polypropylene shirt to keep it from restricting my breathing. I still feel strong, but wonder just how much farther I'll have to go be-

fore I'm on the summit. I look down and see that I'm higher than every other summit of Pissis; I know I'm close. I sit down for a short rest and eat some snow. Ten minutes later, I stand up and walk about 50 steps and see a small cross—I've arrived at the absolute summit of Cerro Pissis.

On the summit of Cerro Pissis

I walk to the small aluminum marker. It's crookedly propped between some rocks. I grab the summit register can, sign my name, and take some shots from the top of the gigantic peak—of myself, of distant peaks and landforms, of clouds, and a 360° panorama. I look through the register and find Bob's name, as well as the names of about ten others. I find an olive-drab canister left by Greg Horne, who took GPS readings and marked them on a register inside the canister. I later find out that Greg, a Canadian climber-photographer-writer, pulled off a superhuman climb of both Pissis and Bonete—then walked out to the Mina Marte road, alone. And he took GPS measurements of both peaks!

I wait 20 or 30 minutes for Brian. I watch the sky grow cloudier. I begin my descent, thinking that Brian must have turned back. 100 vertical feet below the summit I hear a loud whistle to my lower right. It's Brian; I race over and tell him that he has only a hundred vertical feet to go. I sit and wait for him. He reappears about a half hour later.

Brian and I descend together. I nearly fall twice (possible leg breaking falls). We hurry around the large lapilli field and are soon reunited with our packs—and our precious water. We arrive at high camp two hours later. We have only one-and-a-half liters of water remaining—and no food. We had originally planned to go to advanced base camp tonight, but we are too exhausted. The sunset is nothing short of empyreal. The sky is a pastel palette…and the view of Laguna Verde…just too much. The scene is so beautiful, I'm so relieved at having reached the summit, and the endorphins in my body feel so good that I could die right now and I would die completely satisfied that I had lived a full life. I realize that climbing Cerro Pissis is the culmination of my Andean adventuring as well as my Andean dreaming. Today has been the climax, the focal point. I roll over onto my back, rest my head outside the tent, and watch the shadow of the earth rise above Laguna Verde as the planet spins us into the night.

Wednesday, March 29: *The Beautiful Frozen Gold-Laced High Desert Stream*
Today is my birthday; I turn 29.

Nothing unusual this morning, just a straight shot down. We arrive at advanced base camp around mid-morning.

We repack and realize that we have to double-shuttle everything down to base camp. We have too much stuff for one haul. So I carry down my big green Dana with camera, tripod, and sleeping bag. We decide that instead of going all the way down to base camp then back up again, we will divide the shuttling in the middle, emptying out advance base camp to the stream, then shuttling from the stream down to base camp.

Instead of spiraling up the hill, we choose a line straight up its back. I climb continuously without a single rest, all the way to the top. I'm now above advanced base camp; I sprint down to it and wait for Brian. He arrives about 15

Brian Kelly silhouetted against an icefield below the bulk of Cerro Pissis

minutes later. We grab the last of our gear and spiral back down to the stream. We take small 'showers' and drink our fill of the icy water.

Brian gets his regular hiking boots when we reach base camp. Then we return one last time to the beautiful frozen gold-laced high desert stream. We pan for gold for a few minutes, but can't figure out if what we get is feldspar or the real thing. We don't care—even if it's real gold, we'd leave it alone. We have what we came for, and now want to get back down to base camp and rest. We grab the last of our gear and one last view of one of the stream, then descend.

That night I prepare deep-fried potatoes, onions, and garlic from our food cache. We witness low streaks of clouds racing past Pissis' summit at dusk. The region to the north of us appears very hazy. I worry that what looks like haze may actually be falling snow. We fall asleep with the usual intense wind as our backdrop, hoping—no, *praying*—that Patricio arrives safely tomorrow. We ponder all that could go wrong—he is traveling alone, he may get stuck, he may get captured by the Argentines, he may break down and die of exposure...for all we know something happened to him after he dropped us off two weeks ago! I can't think about these things any more! We just climbed Pissis, and now we deserve a rest.

Thursday, March 30: *Praying for Patricio's Return*

The wind is dead quiet for the first time on the expedition. My appetite is coming back with a vengeance. Brian and I make breakfast and break out the shortwave radio. We jury-rig an antenna with my tripod and trekking poles; reception fades as the morning wears on, but our aerial is good enough to pick up The Voice of the Andes again.

We stand around and enjoy what we hope will be our final moments at base camp. After a few hours of waiting, though, we worry that Patricio might not show up. At mid-morning, as Brian and I are deep in conversation, I catch a flash out of the corner of my eye—Patricio (at least we hope it's Patricio, not an Argentine patrol). The truck disappears behind the toe of the long ridge.

It seems like forever before the roof of the Toyota pops into view again. We have everything loaded within five minutes, and head down.

Listening for signs of life outside of Cerro Pissis

The views of Cerro Pissis as we leave seem different from those that I remembered during our approach. We stop for photos at the base of the ridge and find a blooming flower. I shake my head in disbelief. I can peer at the delicate petals of a wildflower, work my eyes up a long ridge of volcanic rock, point out where the hidden gold stream lies, see a huge glacier, glance at the area where we saw the Pissis Yeti, then mentally draw the route to a point that is eclipsed in height (barely) by only two other points in two hemispheres—all in one sweeping glance! And how many people have been here??? Not many…not many at all. The three of us smile at our good fortune of being able to experience this hidden gem of the planet, then jump back into the Hilux.

Goodbye, Cerro Pissis. We'll miss you.

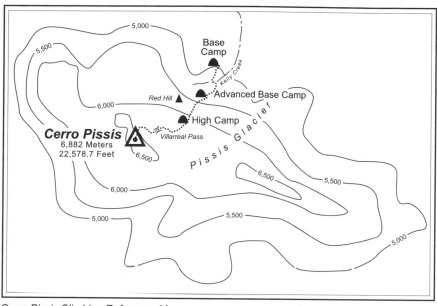

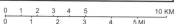

Cerro Pissis Climbing Reference Map

| 0 | 1 | 2 | 3 | 4 | 5 | | | 10 KM |
| 0 | | 1 | 2 | 3 | 4 | 5 MI | |

The base layer for this map was derived from the relevant section of a small scale aeronautical chart of northern Chile / Argentina. The remainder was drawn using author's photographs and personal notes. Three place names were created for this map: *Kelly Creek*, after Brian Kelly; *Red Hill*, for the color of the mountain; and *Villarreal Pass*, named after Bob Villarreal, the world's only expert on this mountain.

▲ Camp

....
Author's Climbing Route

Contour Interval: 500 Meters (1,640.4 Feet)

Important Notes:
Map for general reference; not for navigation.
Altitudes are only estimates.
Altitudes below 5,000 not shown.
Camp locations are approximations.
Cerro Pissis is also known as *Monte Pissis* and, less commonly, *Nevado Pissis.*
Kelly Creek flows only during days warm enough to melt the snow / ice that feeds it. Flow is very slight.

Scale: 1:226,000
Map by Ed Darack

BOOK V
LLULLAILLACO

Looking towards the summit of Llullaillaco

CHAPTER TWENTY-NINE

LANDMINE MOUNTAINEERING

Another way to say 'keep out'

Afer summiting Cerro Pissis, Brian and I decided to travel north and attempt Llullaillaco. This mountain, pronounced "YOU-YAI-YA-KOH," is home to the highest archaeological site in the world. Incan artifacts, mummies, and an altar were found on the 6,723 meter (22,057 foot) summit. This mountain also has the dubious distinction of being one of the most heavily landmined areas in South America—and no one ever made detailed maps of these mines.

The Llullaillaco adventure was short but noteworthy. We made as hardy an attempt as possible, given our drained, post-Pissis conditions. What struck me most powerfully about Llullaillaco were the stunning views of and from that mountain. Llullaillaco can be seen in its entirety from close range; I could pick out individual plants in a swath of color, see how that color blended with a greater hummock of volcanic earth, and view that hummock under the huge flanks of the entire volcano.

As with Book IV, I have simply transcribed the notes from my diary, lightly edited from their original format.

Friday, March 31: *Contacting Bob*

Not much but eating and sleeping this morning. Started smoking again but quit later in the day. We both feel incredibly drained from Pissis. We tell each other that we don't want to even think about another climbing expedition, but we talk about nothing except the highest peaks of the Andes and how great it felt to descend Pissis after having seen the mountain's summit.

We feel a little confused, being thrust back into society—and an unfamiliar society at that—after the weeks on Pissis. We deal with it by eating hot dogs and ice cream.

I bought a big tetrapack box of white wine and started drinking. Brian and I talk about which mountain to attempt next. We consider two: Tupungato and Llullaillaco. Tupungato is just south of Aconcagua and would require a long bus journey. Llullaillaco is farther to the north and would place us conveniently closer to Lima. We e-mail Bob Villarreal and ask his advice. We receive a reply almost immediately. He says that Tupungato has an easier approach than Llullaillaco, but that we are in the Andes during the wrong season to attempt Tupungato. The approach to Llullaillaco isn't as difficult, expensive, or as involved as Pissis, but it is still very challenging. He tells us that Llullaillaco is extremely dangerous as the peak is surrounded by landmine fields. We'll have to rent a Hilux in Calama, or San Pedro de Atacama, or Antofagasta. Because Antofagasta is the largest of these cities, we think it will have the best rates. Renting a vehicle is our only option, because the peak is so remote—no bus lines service anyplace in the vicinity of Llullaillaco and hitchhiking is nearly impossible as so few people travel to Llullaillaco. We go back to our resedencia and drink some more wine. That night we eat a ton of food.

Saturday, April 1: *Planning on Being Squeezed*

We spend most of the day resting, eating, and talking with the workers at the resedencia. Brian and I go to dinner and discuss Llullaillaco. Our one limiting factor is money. We have very little, and will have to find an excellent rate on a Hilux to be able to make an attempt.

Sunday, April 2: *Research*

Brian and I research Llullaillaco at the Copiapó SERNATUR office. We don't learn much, but the few photographs we find whet our appetites to go to Llullaillaco ourselves. We learn of a recent discovery at the mountain's summit of an Incan altar containing the mummified remains of a woman and an infant. The mummification was due not to chemical imbalming, but to the cold, incredibly dry air—I remembered the cow and horse at Laguna Verde on my trip to Ojos del Salado. At 6,723 meters the Llullaillaco find is the highest archaeological site in the world.

Lelia tells us that we should go to Antofagasta, as the CONAF office in that city has more information.

Monday, April 3: *Goodbye to Copiapó*

We visit Alex and Gloria Richards to say goodbye. We buy two bus tickets for April 4, and then pack our gear. We eat another gigantic dinner, and then get drunk. We feel somewhat well-rested; ready for the next challenge.

Tuesday, April 4: *Short Tour on the 'Turbus'*

Leave on bus ('Turbus') for Antofagasta. Big detour to coastal town of Taltal. We arrive at Antofagasta at 8:30 in the evening. Taxi driver takes us to a residencia that costs $20 per night but has a bathroom and a television. We get some food and drinks and settle in. The room is on the third floor, requires climbing very steep stairs, and the woman who owns it demands that we pay for two days in advance. She seems nice at first but is actually a strange one whom we soon begin to dislike. She gets in our faces all the time and is always nosing around. We keep remembering how the taxi driver said 'dos gringos' to her when he first brought us to the resedencial. Anyway, the TV is nice.

Wednesday, April 5: *Landmines—And No Maps*

Our goal for the day is to visit the Antofagasta CONAF office, where we should find the most recent travel and climbing information about Llullaillaco. We search the city for an entire morning, but can't find the office. We finally discover that it's just one block down the street from our resedencia. The rangers tell us that landmines pepper the landscape surrounding Llullaillaco, and no accurate maps of these landmines exist. They tell us that we must rent a 4X4, preferable a Hilux, and take a CONAF ranger with us.

Llullaillaco Location Map

Scale: 1:25,641,026
Azimuthal Equal-Area Projection
Map by Ed Darack

We search the city for a vehicle rental office with good rates on 4X4s. Everything we find is too expensive for us. Finally, we come across 'Econorent,' an outfit that charges only $560 per week for a new Hilux. We tentatively decide to rent it, but figure we should look further. We eat three different dinners at three different restaurants that night.

Thursday, April 6: *Pounding Pavement*

More haggling with rental agencies, and more planning at CONAF with Eduardo, an English-speaking ranger. We find another rental agency with similar rates to those of Econorent, but decide against them, as they seem too fly-by-nightish. We return to Econorent and reserve a Hilux for a week, beginning on the eighth, then pack our bags and prepare to leave.

Friday, April 7: *Confirmed*

We reconfirm the Hilux reservation, assess money situation (I am running out), and visit Eduardo at CONAF one last time. He speaks with rangers at San Pedro de Atacama on a VHF radio, making sure they know we're coming. A ranger will be expecting us. He will accompany us to Llullaillaco to guide us through the landmine fields. We won't be required to pay the ranger, nor will we even have to provide food for him. He will simply guide us into base camp. Eduardo tells us that someone has recently been killed in the Llullaillaco region by a landmine, and that death and dismemberment by landmine is somewhat common in northern Chile, although not usually reported.

Antofagasta strikes me as dreary. The city is always either cloaked in low fog or it is scorching hot. A lot of money goes through here, as evidenced by all the big stores selling TVs, VCRs, cameras, etc. People don't seem friendly; it is much different than Copiapó. The only friendly people are in the CONAF office. The rest of the people here seem interested in getting our money, nothing more—like the woman who owns the resedencia in which we're staying.

Saturday, April 8: *Romancing the Hilux*

We wake up early, get all of our bags together, and then head to the grocery store. We buy bread, mustard, vegetables, and some meat, and then drop the groceries off in our room. We change money at the casa de cambio, and walk to Econorent. 45 minutes of paperwork later, we are throwing our bags into the brand new Hilux. Brian drives. Antofagasta sits on a narrow strip between steep, high, barren mountains, and the cold ocean. Looking east from town, the mountains appear impenetrable. We have a crude map of the city, and seek the fastest, easiest way out of town. We wind up in the slums, far from the city exit. After 15 minutes of white-knuckle driving around the dirt roads of the slums, we find our escape route and shoot into the open desert. Brian and I feel liberated by being in our own vehicle. We pet the steering wheel and the

Llullaillaco Regional Map

| 0 | | | | | 100 | 150 | 200 | 250 KM |
| 0 | | 50 | | | 100 | | | 150 MI |

Map details Llullaillaco and environs. Map shows pertinent roads, population centers, huts, and physical features.

▲ Peak

● Population Center

⚶ Hut or Outpost

– – – – – – – International Boundary

Panamerican Highway

Secondary Routes

Scale: 1:4,000,000
Azimuthal Equal-Area Projection
Map by Ed Darack

Mountain Altitudes in Meters (and Feet):

Llullaillaco: 6,723 Meters (22,057.1 Feet)

Cerro Pular: 6,225 Meters (20,423.2 Feet)

Volcán Antofalla: 6,100 Meters (20,013.1 Feet)

Volcán Socampa: 6,051 Meters (19,852.4 Feet)

Licancábur: 5,916 Meters (19,409.4 Feet)

Volcán Putana: 5,890 Meters (19,324.1 Feet)

Volcán Puntas Negras: 5,852 Meters (19,199.5 Feet)

Cerro Aguas Blancas: 5,760 Meters (18,897.6 Feet)

Nevado de Poquisi: 5,745 Meters (18,848.4 Feet)

Volcán Lastarria: 5,700 Meters (18,700.8 Feet)

Volcán Lascar: 5,154 Meters (16,909.4 Feet)

dashboard. We gaze at the open desert. We revel in being able to pull off to the side of the road to pee whenever we want. We recline in the big seats and turn up the stereo. We love the Toyota Hilux.

Our first destination is the town of Calama. Brian speeds us through the Atacama on Chilean route 25. We get great views of huge mining equipment and a distant glance of the world's largest open pit mine, the Chuquicamata Copper Mine.

We reach Calama about two hours after leaving Antofagasta and top off the truck's fuel tank, then I take the wheel. Next destination: San Pedro de Atacama, the town just outside of the Valle de la Luna, a place I had visited five years earlier after attempting Sajama.

Valle de la Luna appears as I remember it: a photographer's paradise of color and texture. I can't wait till sunset really pulls the landscape to life.

We skirt the edge of the Valle de la Luna and roll into San Pedro. I compare the shops, the streets, the sights, and the sounds (or lack thereof) of the small village to those of my memories. Nothing is changed except for the addition of an Internet café. We drive slowly through the narrow dirt roads and find a shady place to park. We buy some vegetables and beer, then head for the heart of the Valle de la Luna.

We arrive at what, five years ago, I labeled 'Sunset Vista'—a long sand dune that connects two high promontories in the middle of the region's most amaz- ing geology. No less than a dozen tour guides base out of San Pedro, and each one has a group of tourists plodding up the dune this evening.

Brian and I reach the top of the western point after 15 minutes of sand jogging (the eastern point, about a quarter of a mile distant, affords great views also). About 100 tourists—American, German, Israeli, Italian, British, French, and others—stand at the crest of the crumbly rock outcrop waiting for the day's finale. The shot I want is a sunset vista of the twin Licancabur volcanoes with the wild geology of the Valle de la Luna in the foreground. The moment comes, shutters click, and then all the tourists leave. Within a half hour Brian and I have the entire place to ourselves. We casually hike down to the Hilux in the dark. After a few beers we decide to explore the desert. I jump in the driver's seat and Brian opens another beer. I pop on the high beams and we tear off. We head west and motor over a small pass and wind down a steep grade. We come to an intersection: turn right and go out to the main road (the way we came in); turn left and go where we have never been. I ask Brian what he thinks. He replies by shrugging his shoulders and burping, then cracks open another can of beer. I crank the wheel to the left and we rumble off. The road quickly deteriorates. We bump along for few minutes before arriving at a low fence adorned by a big red sign. Beer in hand, I exit the Hilux and read the message painted on the red plywood board. It warns of a landmine field in the vicinity. I smile and pick up a rock, finish my beer, then hurl the stone over the fence with all my might—and run back to the Hilux. THUD! The rock plows into the desert floor. I dive toward the car, expecting a big explosion. Nothing happens. I stagger to my feet. I scratch my head and try to recall the stupidest acts I have ever committed. I decide that throwing rocks into a landmine field tops the list. I jump back into the Hilux and down another beer to celebrate a new personal record. We return to the base of the sand dune and toss out our sleeping bags.

Sunday, April 9: *Pass a Sulfuric Acid Lake and Drive Through a Minefield*
We wake up with the sun after an invigorating night of cool, dry air. Brian drives us back to the landmine field—we want to see it in the daylight. After a quick glance we head into San Pedro. We search for the CONAF office, and find it on the outskirts of town. Once there, we are told that our guide is in the Toconao CONAF station, about 20 miles away. We drive to the small village of Toconao, then find the CONAF station—right under Volcán Lascar, which is erupting a steady stream of smoke and ash into the sky. Our guide's name is Marco. He is a young guy who, by the looks of his legs and barrel chest, has spent a lot of time traveling the Andes. He tells us that we will probably need two Jerry cans in addition to our main fuel tank, as well as a large barrel for water—like Ojos and Pissis, travelers cannot count on any reliable sources of potable water on Llullaillaco. Marco fills the water tank, and Brian and I return to San Pedro to purchase extra fuel.

After a feast of vegetable soup, which Marco had prepared while we were gone, the three of us pile into the Hilux and head for Llullaillaco. Marco guides. I drive. Brian jokes. We course through tremendous salt flats, motor by huge mining operations, traverse massive alluvial fans, and bump over broad plains of sun-baked desert. This is the Atacama I wanted to see: empty, huge, cool and dry. We come upon Mina Escondita, a gigantic open-pit copper mine that sends its ore to Antofagasta by way of a 12-foot diameter by 75-mile long slurry pipe. Marco tells us that breaking down the ore is facilitated by a huge lake—of sulfuric acid! Brian remarks how much the Mafia would love to have a convenient sulfuric acid lake to dump bodies into. I shake my head and laugh, and drive by the strange sight.

We continue along a well-paved road that parallels two sets of high-tension power lines. Marco tells us that the lines were installed specifically for the mine,

Volcán Lascar erupting

as was a generating facility in nearby Argentina. We turn again, passing a building in the middle of nowhere. Marco tells us that it is a pump, slurping water from an aquifer that took nature millennia to stock and which is projected to be depleted within a few years. The pump is just one of many in the area that were built to supply the mine. The mine…the mine…the mine. And it's not even owned by Chileans; like many mining operations in this country it is the property of a Canadian company.

We pass another lonely water pump and turn onto a decrepit, potholed road. After a few miles Marco instructs me to turn again—but I don't see any road.

I stop the car. Marco continues to point briskly to the left. So I drive onto the edge of a broad, roadless plain. We stare at a distant snowcapped volcano: Llullaillaco. Marco grins and motions for me to move on; I step on the gas.

Marco seems happy that we are approaching Llullaillaco and produces a fresh bottle of Pisco. I take three healthy gulps and step on the gas even harder. We're going close to 120 kilometers an hour—about 70 miles per hour—through an area known to be littered with landmines. But Marco knows where they are—I hope.

Cactus; Llullaillaco in distance

A little faster and I realize that the overloaded Hilux has reached its threshold of stability. I feel the rig swaying side-to-side. I slow down a bit, but I want out of the minefield as soon as possible. Marco continues to feed me directions and

Llullaillaco

Pisco. We're high; I can feel the altitude—it adds kick to the booze; I'm soon drunk. Drunk, speeding through a landmine field—way, way, way out in the middle of nowhere. Marco guides me in Spanish. I could never tell the difference between derecho and derecha (respectively go straight and go right in Spanish), so I have to constantly ask Brian—who by now is also drunk—what Marco is saying. Marco barks commands and Brian translates, and I try to keep the truck moving without blowing us up.

Our view of Llullaillaco grows huge. It is such a beautiful mountain, such a magnificent volcano. Llullaillaco dominates its surrounding landscape much as Sajama does, but Llullaillaco seems even larger than its northerly kin. We reach a crude dirt road. I ask if we are through the minefield. Marco nods his head and hands me the Pisco. I breathe a sigh of relief, Brian slaps my shoulder and the three of us laugh hysterically. I jump out of the Hilux and pee like a water cannon. I think I could have filled a gallon jug.

I drive slower now that we are on a road. Marco explains that the landmines were placed in 1978 by Pinochet, who feared the Argentines would invade Chile by sending troops and tanks through this area. The farther along we travel, the crazier that invasion hypothesis seems. Even more insane is that the Chileans never made any detailed maps of the landmines, only vague, general descriptions, leaving a lot of guesswork for today's travelers.

We stop at a natural overlook to take pictures. I walk away from the Hilux; Marco screams at me to come back to the car. Llullaillaco is so beautiful that I forgot about the landmines. The road is the only safe place in many areas around the mountain.

Llullaillaco is Chile's most recent addition to their national park system. Called Llullaillaco National Park, it is the least visited of the country's official tourist sites. I ask Marco how many people come here each year. He replies that between three and six visit. I ask if he means between 300 and 600 or 3,000 and 6,000. His reply shocks me: "no, between THREE and SIX. No hundred, no thousand. Just between three and six persons."

30 minutes later we arrive at a CONAF hut on the floor of a shallow canyon. The accommodation has a kitchen and a bunk room, and can comfortably sleep six to ten people. We deposit some of our gear then set off to see Llullaillaco at dusk.

We drive out of the canyon on a road that skirts the western base of the mountain. Marco tells us that anything on the mountain side of the road is safe; anything on the 'outside' of the road may have landmines. But with all the landmine

Brian, Marco, and me

talk, I am surprised to see countless vicuña tracks. Then, just as the last of the day's light is fading, a small herd of vicuñas bounds in front of our truck, kicking up dust that seems charged with the sunset light. The animals race into the distance and disappear with the sun. We drive a bit farther and search for a route to the mountain's summit. Marco gives vague directions—he has been to Llullaillaco many times, but has never seen its highest point. Brian and I go back and forth about our ascent options. Llullaillaco is supposed to be one of the easiest peaks in the world to climb, but we have no information about any of its climbing routes. We had intended to get that information from Marco, but he says that we should just "go up it." Dusk turns to night and we return to the hut.

Monday, April 10: *Lock the Hubs and Go*

I want to see Llullaillaco's summit. I want to see the Incan altar that is the highest archaeological site in the world. I want to see this mysterious part of the mysterious Atacama Desert from 6,723 meters. I jump out of my sleeping bag and shake off my hangover. Brian gets Marco to draw us a map of where he thinks our route should be. He notes the numerous landmine zones in the area, and draws a large black lava flow that marks the location of a good base camp. We ask Marco if he wants to join us, but he chooses to remain in the hut.

We leave around eight in the morning. I drive; Brian navigates. We pass last evening's turn-around point and eye a low pass. I can't get over Llullaillaco's forms. I imagine that it was hand-carved by some gentle, lonely giant roaming this forgotten corner of the planet. Consumed with beauty in such an austere place, he would have scooped up a handful of earth and made a crude cone. He would have then carefully formed the flowing arcs and hummocks that define much of the mountain's topogra-

Llullaillaco

phy, and scribed the feature of the volcano I find most fascinating: a long ditch on the north side of the peak that bears remarkable resemblance to a playground slide. This ditch, a solidified lava flow, flabbergasts me by the geometric continuity along its length. It is one of the most perplexing mountain forms I've ever seen, and it's huge!

We crest the pass and descend onto a broad plain of volcanic sand; the plain is the size of ten football fields. Basic colors and clean, simple lines define the area's aesthetic. The light sand and flat topography makes me think of the beach. I keep forgetting where we are—and how high we are.

The road runs close to the base of the volcano. We can see every feature of the western aspect of Llullaillaco; nothing is hidden. The mountain is so straightforward. I'm so excited that I want to park the Hilux and walk up the volcano. But I'm sure that distances are wildly deceiving.

Lastarria and lenticular clouds

We spot the lava flow. It is a monstrous tongue of dark rock. It looks as if Llullaillaco just oozed it out a few days ago. The road goes directly under the terminus of the flow. Brian wants to make a beeline for it and set up base camp. I agree, but put the Hilux in four wheel drive anyway. Brian asks what I'm doing; I don't say anything.

We keep looking upslope, trying to find the route to the summit. We paid a lot for the four-wheel drive but haven't needed to use it once. Four wheel drive was invented for a reason, and that reason was not driving over what we'd been driving over so far. I jerk the wheel to the left and floor the pedal. Brian yells at me to get back on the road. I laugh and drive straight up the mountain.

We're in low range in no time. The terrain is so steep and rocky that I never shift out of first gear. The engine sings happily as the Hilux crawls up the steepening grade. According to Marco's map we're at nearly 16,000 feet. Brian keeps trying to coerce me to head toward the lava flow. To placate him I veer that way, but only a little.

The rocks we drive over are too sharp for comfort. I grit my teeth every time the Hilux lurches, and the Hilux lurches a lot. There are places so steep that the motor nearly stalls, even in first gear in low range.

After about 40 minutes of ascent, the grade increases from pretty-much-impossible to absolutely impossible. We begin grazing large boulders; and the ground underneath our tires is dangerously rough. In a few places I fear we'll bottom out. Soon I start wishing I'd stayed on the road—now a long way below us. Brian points to an area that is somewhat level; I turn and head there.

We creep over the terrain for 15 more minutes before we come to a spot level enough for a camp.

We toss aside rocks to make a level platform for the Hilux, then set up our camp. At first I think that we are at nearly 20,000 feet. Actually, we're probably between 17,500 and 18,000 feet. We're light-headed in the thin air.

It is bizarre having this brand new, shiny green Toyota truck sitting in our high altitude base camp with us. We have an Andean tailgate party later that afternoon, drinking beer and listening to music from radio stations in Arica, nearly 400 miles away.

To the south sits Lastarria, its cone powdered with yellow sulfur. I've never seen so much sulfur in one spot. The mountain is many miles away, and yet I can still see all of that sulfur.

Below Lastarria lies a beautiful turquoise lake. Ringed by white alkali, it reminds me of Laguna Santa Rosa near Ojos del Salado. Clouds which had obscured much of Llullaillaco's summit throughout the afternoon disappear at

Lava flow and distant volcanoes

sunset. We still do not know how we are going to get to the summit. We'll just have to make it up as we go along.

In the sunset light, I site strange lines on the mountain. One line goes straight up the mountain a few hundred yards from our camp, where the slope gets steeper. Another switchbacks.

The tracks are barely visible. I decide they are trails left by the Incas. Excited, I get Brian. He can't see the lines at first, but after some looking he locates them. We talk about the altar and the mummies on the summit. We wonder if we'll find any other ruins up there.

We have unbelievable nighttime views from our perch. The air is super clear; we can see lights from town far away. Every now and then we see a lone light moving slowly through the void of night, far in the distance. A car?

The night is dead quiet. I am writing in my journal using my headlamp. I just went outside to pee and jumped at the sight of the Hilux. You just don't expect to see something like that so high up. Being able to see those distant lights makes us feel like we're permanently detached from the world.

Tuesday, April 11: *Wander*

Brian and I decide to make today a rest day. We both have slight headaches. Neither of us slept well last night. We'll make a go for the summit tomorrow.

We love listening to the radio during the day. We get FM stations from hundreds of miles away. Once we thought we were getting a station from

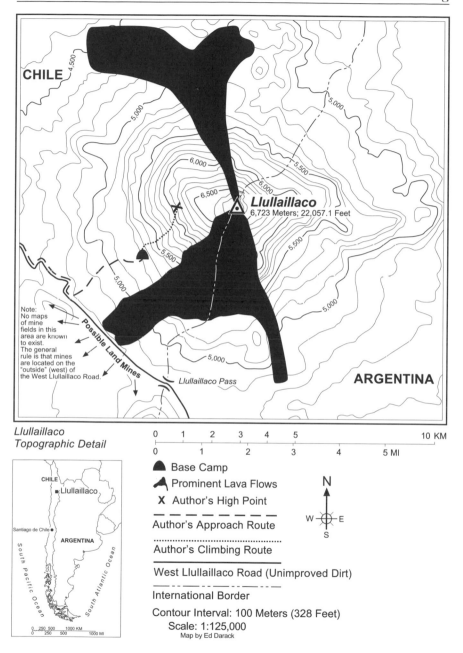

CHILE

5,000

4,500

5,000

6,000

5,500

6,500

6,000

6,000

Llullaillaco
6,723 Meters; 22,057.1 Feet

5,500

5,500

5,000

5,000

5,000

Note:
No maps
of mine
fields in this
area are known
to exist.
The general
rule is that mines
are located on the
"outside" (west) of
the West Llullaillaco Road.

Possible Land Mines

Llullaillaco Pass

ARGENTINA

Llullaillaco
Topographic Detail

CHILE
Llullaillaco

Santiago de Chile

ARGENTINA

South Pacific Ocean

South Atlantic Ocean

0   250   500   1000 KM
0   250   500   1000 MI

0   1   2   3   4   5   10 KM
0   1   2   3   4   5 MI

🔺 Base Camp

🔻 Prominent Lava Flows

X Author's High Point

— — — — — — —
Author's Approach Route

·······························
Author's Climbing Route

——————————
West Llullaillaco Road (Unimproved Dirt)

— ·· — ·· — ·· —
International Border

Contour Interval: 100 Meters (328 Feet)
Scale: 1:125,000
Map by Ed Darack

N
W ⊕ E
S

341

Santiago, but it faded out before we could tell for sure. We have to decipher advertisements and news announcements to discern the stations' locations.

A puffy cloud appeared over Llullaillaco's summit around 11:00 in the morning. By one in the afternoon the entire summit was shrouded. The weather did

the same thing yesterday. Brian said that we should get moving early tomorrow to make the summit; we wouldn't want to get stuck in a whiteout.

The clouds break at sunset. A line of perfectly-shaped lenticulars are hovering over one of the mountain's ridges. The clouds look like a fleet of flying sau-

Lenticulars

cers coming in to land. Brian and I joke that the mountain is a 'power point' where aliens are coming to revive ancient Incan mummies.

The 'sunset lines' appear again—at sunset. It is so strange that they are invisible during all other hours of the day. I figure that they are only apparent when low-angled light hits them, accentuating their shallow details.

Wednesday, April 12: *Chasing Incas*

We begin our summit attempt late. We simply fell prey to lassitude, and couldn't force ourselves out of our sleeping bags. If we are at 17,500 feet then we have almost a mile of vertical travel before we arrive at our destination. I try

not to think that our summit bid is doomed from the start, but that thought persistently creeps into my otherwise optimistic outlook. Brian and I are fine with the altitude, but we are still exhausted from our weeks on Pissis, and we face the all-but-impossible task of reaching the summit (by a route we don't even know) and descending low enough to be out of the clouds within about six hours.

We aim for the 'big boulder,' which lies directly upslope from our camp. What we anticipate will take 10 minutes actually takes 45. We rest at the base of the huge volcanic rock (it is about 40 feet high by 20 feet thick) and eat a can of sliced pineapple. I see a small cave at the base of the boulder.

'Big boulder'

I crawl inside hoping to discover Incan artifacts—but I find nothing but some small rocks and sand.

I estimate that we're near the spot where the 'sunset lines' lie. I scour the area for them, obsessed with finding some evidence of past Incan passage. I'm dumbfounded—both Brian and I saw the lines—they are here, somewhere! But I can't find them, anywhere. Brian eventually convinces me to get back to business. I shoot some photographs, hoping that I might discover the lines on my processed film when I return to Davis. (I never find them).

15 minutes later Brian hunches over his trekking poles. He looks up and tells me that he's been having awful stomach pains and is too tired to keep going. I don't want to continue without him, and know that I have almost no chance of making the summit that day anyway. I still want to climb higher, though. I stash everything but my trekking poles and camera, and hurry upslope. I yell to Brian that I'll be back to the Hilux within two hours.

I cross a small snowfield then arrive at a plateau. I contour around the plateau and get a view of the summit—it looks to be two miles away! I guesstimate that I'm close to 20,000 feet. Big storm clouds are swiftly approaching. I am as high as they are, and soon I'll be inside them. I turn and look down at the ridges and peaklets of Llullaillaco below me. I see a small plateau that I imagine would be perfect for Incan sacrifice. I even think that I can see piles of rocks arranged in a pattern. I wonder if there is a ruin there—I'm sure that there is a ruin. I race down and find nothing. I sit in the sun and look at the expansive Atacama below me.

I never get tired of being in the Andes. I love it up here. Every mountain is different, and each one is a superlative in its own ways.

I search for the Hilux—it is barely a dot. I wonder how Brian is doing. I gaze one last time to the summit of Llullaillaco, then head down.

When I return, Brian and I decide not to make another summit attempt. We are both too exhausted. We still have two full days before we have to turn in the Hilux—we relish the opportunity to see out-of-the-way corners of the Atacama.

We pack up our tents and crawl the Hilux back to the road. A few hours later we pick up Marco and drive back to Toconao. Later that night we're back in San Pedro de Atacama, eating a dinner of chicken and rice at a small restaurant.

Thursday, April 13 and following days: *Where to now?*
I stopped taking notes after April 12. We explored the mountains around the Bolivian border, visited the Taito Geysers, and drove to a town called Tocopilla north of Antofagasta. The next day we took a bus to Arica, got drunk, and wound up lying on the vomit-and-blood stained floor of a Chilean prison cell....

Till next time...

INDEX

(P) = References a photograph.

ACKNOWLEDGEMENTS

Thank you Dorothy, for the tireless effort editing, researching, and helping make this book; Ellen Liebowitz; Brian Kelly; Bill Burmester; Bill Winternitz, M.D., Steve Olson, M.D., and Richard Barry, M.D. for keeping my skeleton together; my mother Judy; Uncle Arthur and Aunt Jean; Ed Ross; Mark Vogel; Elliot Welch, Tracy Tingle, Matt Connors; Jill and John;

 Stacy, the Cranes and the little papillon dogs; Bill, Cate, and Anne at Murray and Young CPAs (**tax geniuses** www.april15.com); Alex Van Steen for continuing to appear in high places and being a great writer; Ruth Ann Van Steen; Bob Koch and AlpenBooks; Mike

Alex Richards and Brian Kelly at the Copiapó bus station

Lowrie Trucking: Mike, Jeff, Dave, Steve the Money Man, Dennis, Mike night dispatcher, Gilley, Butch, and my cadre of MLT tomato trucking brethren; Lucas, Rob, Arnau, and Jon at Omsoft; Adam Darack; Maria Soto; Alex and Gloria Richards; Bob Villarreal for all

Truck 90, the financier

of your research; Lelia at Copiapó SERNATUR; Eduardo at CONAF; Marco from Toconao CONAF; Patricio Rios, four-by-four God of the Atacama; MS Word, Pagemaker, Macromedia Freehand, Photoshop (the programs used to make this book); Kari 'death cheater' Poti; Harry; Black Cat; Girl Cat; Bill Schaeffer; Bill Ross; Rudy Parra; Hotel Blanco; Hosteria Rodriguez; Econorent; Ekono; the entire city of Copiapó; Turbus; the unnamed monk on the bus; Pablo and Eduardo; the Carabineros at Paso de San Francisco; Jerry and

Patricio Rios

Pavalina; Patrick and Silke; Jaromir; Steve Galbreath and the staff at 'The Printer;' the Maricunga Carabineros; Uspallata Express; Scott, Kristen, Ale, and Andy Titterington; The Avid Reader; The Next Chapter; Bogey's Books; Pat and crew at "Cali Color" (the best E-6 lab in the world); Toyota Hilux; NASA (for all of those

free images from the Space Shuttle); Damon Nelson; Conrad Bahre; Nogel Allan; Todd McHenry; Casey Norton; Dana packs, Pentax Cameras; Gitzo Tri- pods; Fuji Film; Nikon.

Jerry & Pavalina

Hilux

INFORMATION RESOURCES

Print Resources

Biggar, John, The Andes: A Guide for Climbers. Scotland: Big R Publishing (Andes). 1999.

FitzGerald, E.A.The Highest Andes:A Record of the First Ascent of Aconcagua and Tupungato in Argentina, and the surrounding Valley. London, England: Charles Scribner's Sons. 1899.

Healy, Kevin. South America, Southern (map). Vancouver, BC, Canada: ITMB. 1999.

Secor, R.J. Aconcagua: A Climbing Guide. Seattle, Washington: The Mountaineers. 1999.

Personal Resources

Alex Van Steen   www.MountainMountain.com; 360-832-3066; (vansteen@seanet.com)

Bob Villarreal (r1villa@pacbell.net)

Web Resources

http://www.campbellsci.com/centers/alpine-a.html

http://www.haramosh.clara.net/Bolivia.htm

http://www.angeleschapter.org/sps/archives/sps00074.htm

http://www.climber.org/TripReports/1998/ojos.html

http://www.aidsinfonyc.org/pwahg/info/tini.html

http://www.ngdc.noaa.gov/seg/topo/globegal.shtml

http://www2.ing.puc.cl/~cseebach/Climbing/norte/ojos.del.salado/

http://www.bielefeldt.de/acone.htm

http://www.haramosh.clara.net/aconcagua.htm

http://www.adventuredynamics.co.za/news/Achistory.htm

http://home.pacifier.com/~intersec/tkutscha/acon_itinerary.html

http://www.infoplease.com/ce6/world/A0856608.html

http://www.thinair.btinternet.co.uk/aconcagua/confluencia.htm

http://aconcagua.hypermart.net/trivu/handbook.html

http://www.sharesim.co.uk/ecmc/aconcagua/aconcagua.html

http://mikes.railhistory.railfan.net/r022.html

http://www.infoplease.com/ce6/world/A0861195.html

http://www.cybernet1.com/aconcagua/itinerary.htm

http://www.aconcagua.com/ax/ax002.html

AUTHOR INFORMATION

Ed Darack is a photographer, author, and cartographer based out of northern California. He began pursuing photography and writing during his undergraduate work at the University of California at Davis. He received a bachelor of science degree in physical geography in 1993 and has since continued his creative work full time. He has published a large line of note cards, posters, and his first book, *6194 Denali Solo* through his company, Ed Darack Photography/Publishing. A few years later, he joined Bill Burmester

Author on the summit of Aconcagua.

and Scott Titterington with their company, Poudre Canyon Press, based out of Fort Collins, Colorado. Poudre Canyon Press published Ed's second book, *Wind • Water • Sun: A Solo Kayak Journey Along Baja California's Desert Coastline.*

Ed's photographs are represented by a number of stock agencies worldwide. His articles, photographs, and maps have appeared in various media forms, including books, album covers, magazine articles, television, newspapers, calendars, and more. His credits include *Climbing,*
Rock and Ice, Time Life Books, *Newsday, The Sunday Times* (London), *Alaska Geographic, Weatherwise, Sea Kayaker, Paddler, The American Alpine Journal, The San Francisco Chronicle-Examiner, Nature Photographer, Outdoor and Nature Photographer,* and many others. He has lectured to a wide array of distinguished organizations, including the Explorers' Club, the Adventurers' Club, and the New York Academy of Sciences, among others. Find out more about Ed Darack's work at **www.darack.com**.

Dorothy W. Ross has been a writer and editor for 40 years, contributing to books, scientific and trade journals, newspapers, magazines, electronic, and broadcast media. She worked with Ed Darack on his second book, *Wind • Water • Sun,* and several of his other projects. Dorothy's own travels have taken her throughout the Americas, Europe, and southern Africa.

Alex Van Steen is an internationally acclaimed mountain guide and author. Alex has led ascents up mountains around the globe, including Aconcagua, Denali (West Buttress, Traverse, and West Rib), Mount Kilimanjaro, Cho Oyu, Huayna Potosi, Cotopaxi, Chimborazo, Cayambe, Mount Rainier (280 climbs with 170 successful ascents via 13 routes/variations), Shishapangma, Paldor, Everest North Ridge (to 28,000 feet). Alex published the definitive climbers guide to Mount Rainier, *Climbing Mount Rainier, The Essential Guide* (Alpenbooks), with Fred Beckey in 1999. Alex started Alex Van Steen Expeditions LLC in 1997, and continues to lead clients to the summits of the world's great mountains. For more information, go to **www.MountainMountain.com**.

ORDERING INFORMATION

You can order Ed Darack's other titles, including *6194 Denali Solo* and *Wind • Water • Sun: A Solo Kayak Journey Along Baja California's Desert Coastline*, at book stores and outdoor-oriented shops around the globe. Consult www.Darack.com for more information.

www.Darack.com
www.HighestAndes.com

Wind • Water • Sun: A Solo Kayak Journey Along Baja California's Desert Coastline
ISBN: 1-881663-08-6
$29.95

6194: Denali Solo
ISBN: 1-884980-80-5
$12.00

Ed Darack's images featured in *Wild Winds* are available as photographic prints in a wide range of sizes. His maps are also offered for sale. For information on maps and limited and unlimited edition photographic prints, contact Ed Darack Photography or visit **HighestAndes.com**.

www.Darack.com
Ed Darack Photography
Post Office Box 2091
Davis, CA, 95617-2091
United States of America
Ed@Darack.com